NUNAGA

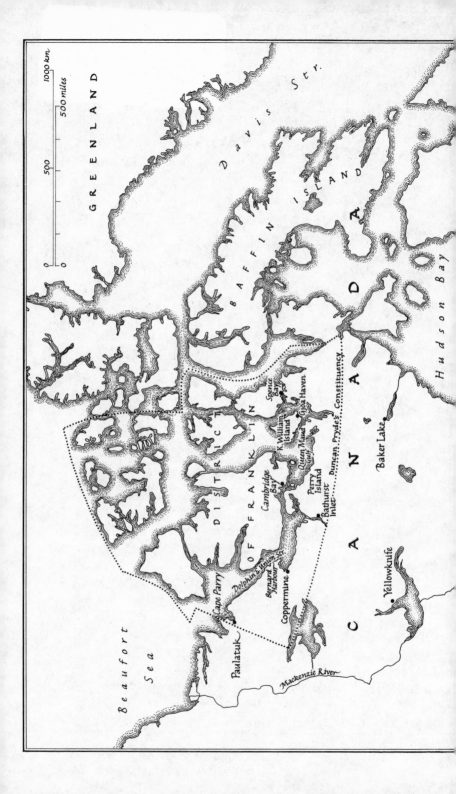

NUNAGA

DUNCAN PRYDE
Ten years among the Eskimos

ELAND BOOKS, LONDON
&
HIPPOCRENE BOOKS INC., NEW YORK

Published by
ELAND BOOKS
53 Eland Road, London SW11 5JX
&
HIPPOCRENE BOOKS, INC.,
171 Madison Avenue, New York, NY 10016

First published in Great Britain 1972 by MacGibbon & Kee Ltd.
© 1971 Duncan Pryde

First issued in this paperback edition 1985

British Library Cataloguing in Publication Data

Pryde, Duncan
    Nunanga: ten years among the Eskimos.
    1. Eskimos—Canada—Social life and customs
    I. Title
    971.064'2   E99.E7

    ISBN 0–907871–21–6

Printed and bound in Great Britain
by Redwood Burn Ltd., Trowbridge, Wiltshire

Map © Reginald Piggott
Cover illustration © Tony Ansell
Cover design © Patrick Frean

For Gina

❈ Contents

✳ *Illustrations*

Nunaga:

My Land, My Country

I

❋ North Toward the Winter Wind

Twenty minutes north of the mouth of the River of Strangers, and past the bleak settlement the whiteman calls Churchill, the plane passed over the last few stunted trees, and we entered the Barren Grounds. Below us swept a filigree of wind-scudded lakes and naked land, so intermeshed that it was difficult to know whether we were crossing a vast lake clotted with innumerable islands or a vast land clotted with innumerable lakes. On that autumn afternoon a haze lay over the land, even in the sunlight. Except for a narrow ruff of cloud around the horizon the sky was clear and blue.

The plane pitched and tossed in the wind. Inside it was cool but not too uncomfortable now that the engine heat was warming up the cockpit. I took off my moccasin rubbers and flexed my toes, grateful for the stream of warm air that flowed around my feet. The pilot raised his eyes from the map spread out on his lap and glanced at me.

'Cold?'

'Not too bad now,' I answered, raising my voice against the noisy engine.

He grinned. 'The old Anson takes a while to warm up. They're not built for comfort... But if you think this is cold just wait until winter comes.'

The radio crackled and the pilot reached forward to adjust a knob, then began speaking into the microphone. The steady thunder of the engine drowned his voice and I turned my attention to the land.

Below lay the Barren Grounds—the interior of the Arctic continent north of the tree line. Even in late summer this region looked bleak and utterly desolate, a blotchy brown flatland devoid of life, a vast panorama of emptiness, so bleak and so desolate that it possessed its own unique beauty. It was a rugged country where blizzards battered the land in winter and mosquitos held undisputed sway in summer.

In 1958 it was almost trackless as far as the whiteman knew. Its native inhabitants were nomadic Eskimos, barely out of the Stone Age.

A few whitemen had penetrated the interior—explorers, traders, missionaries carrying their faith to a pagan people, members of the Royal Canadian Mounted Police and a scattered handful of trappers. In recent years the Canadian government had belatedly discovered the Arctic and a trickle of government personnel followed the pioneers.

Another crackle from the radio distracted my attention from the Barrens. The plane had warmed up considerably. I loosened the safety belt and unzipped my parka.

The pilot leaned forward again and switched off the set. He pushed the earphones back off his head, running his fingers through his straight fair hair.

'That was Baker Lake,' he commented. 'They're reporting unlimited visibility but the wind is gusting to thirty-five. This headwind is holding us up some but we should be there about four o'clock... If you are with the Bay I guess you'll be staying with old Sandy Lunan, the manager there. He's been in charge of the trading post at Baker for the last century or so. He's a pretty good old head... May take a bit of getting used to. They say he runs everything by the clock.'

I shifted in my seat and peered ahead, wondering about this man Lunan and how we would get on with each other. Three years trading for the Hudson's Bay Company had accustomed me to working with different managers and a variety of idiosyncrasies, for it was standard practice for the young men of the fur trade to be transferred frequently. An apprentice, in fact, rarely stayed more than six or seven months at one trading post before being moved to another. This was sound policy as it gave an apprentice the opportunity to gain broad experience in all phases of the operation. One manager might be skilled in the grading and purchase of pelts—the backbone of Company operations in the North; another acknowledged for his adept handling of the native people; yet another noted for his accurate accounts, and so on through the spectrum of the specialized needs of the fur trade. The skills and knowledge of each individual manager were expected to pass to the apprentice, so that when he was promoted to the charge of his own post he would have the background necessary for the competent operation of a business far removed from the control of a central office. Realistically, too, the Company recognized that too much time with the same person in an isolated trading post often led to a clash of personalities.

I mused on as we flew toward Baker Lake. The wind buffeted the plane, but I hardly noticed it as my mind went back over the three years I had spent in the bush. Three good, fruitful, learning years. Three years since I had first noticed the advertisement in the *Sunday Post* back in Scotland in 1955.

'Fur traders wanted for the far north,' the headline of the advertisement had read, '…single, ambitious, self-reliant young men wanted…far north of Canada…must be prepared to live in isolation…willing to learn native language…fur trade… salary: $135.00 per month.'

I remembered walking down Sauchiehall Street in Glasgow to attend the interview. I had never heard of the Hudson's Bay Company before that interview, and my only knowledge of fur traders had been a vague notion, based on motion pictures, that they lived in ramshackle log cabins close by a palisaded fort which was constantly attacked by marauding Indians. But fact or fiction, this was attraction enough for an eighteen-year-old.

Having been brought up in orphanages in various parts of Scotland, I had entered the merchant navy at the age of fifteen. Three years later, after an accident to my left eye, I had been forced to resign. I had been working in a Singer sewing machine factory, thoroughly fed up, when I saw the Hudson's Bay advertisement. My first three years with the Company had been spent fur trading with the Cree and Ojibway Indians in northern Manitoba and Ontario—a life I found too soft and civilized for my liking. I actually resigned from the Company. After a summer of commercial fishing at Lake St Joe, near Pickle Lake, I had rejoined the Company on condition that I be transferred to the Arctic.

The pilot's voice again broke into my thoughts. 'That's

Sugarloaf Hill,' he said, pointing out a distinctive flat-topped hill ahead of us. 'You can see the settlement from there. We should be down in about five minutes.'

The flatlands farther back had given way to low, rolling country. Gentle hills and broad valleys punctuated by ponds and small lakes now passed beneath the plane. Apart from the lack of trees, we could almost have been flying over the Lowlands of Scotland. This variation in topography surprised me. The pictures I had seen of the Arctic had usually shown fur-clad figures with dogteams in the midst of a flat expanse of ice and snow, the horizon a perfectly straight line in the background. It was clear already that my preconceived notions about the Arctic were no more reliable than had been my preconceived ideas about the Indians in the bush country.

A light rain began to fall as we passed Sugarloaf, and within moments water on the cockpit window obscured the view. The sky was suddenly grey; the plane rolled and shuddered in gusts of wind. We passed over the angry waters of Baker Lake.

The lake was in a turmoil. Everywhere to the east, as far as I could see out of the side window, ponderous rollers heaved across the surface of the lake and smashed along the windward shoreline. Close inshore the water was a muddy brown, but out in the open the seas were a sullen grey-black broken only by whitecaps and long streamers of spume. Several islands and reefs, almost smothered in foam, winked through the rain, then vanished behind us. The utter gloom and starkness of the scene took my breath away.

The plane came upon the settlement so suddenly that I was caught by surprise. We shot across it at a height of three hundred feet, and I just had time for one confused glimpse of a long low-slung building before the plane banked to the left. Craning past the pilot, I could see the settlement in its entirety —a score of houses sprawled along the edge of the lake, and a muddy road glistening in the rain. Above the houses, on the slope of a hill, a string of tents flapped in the wind and rain. Outside them, little clusters of people waved as we swept overhead. Eskimos!

Farther on we passed a neat compound of buildings painted in the familiar white and red colours of the Hudson's Bay Company. We began our descent.

Two and a half hours later it was still stormy, but I didn't care. Supper was over. The sound of dishes being washed came from the kitchen to mingle with the patter of rain and the creaking of the house. The very violence of the storm outside seemed to make the living room all the more warm and comfortable.

Relaxed after a heavy meal of caribou stew, I stretched luxuriously, arching my body against the back of the chesterfield, but careful not to make too much noise. To my right Sandy Lunan dozed quietly in an armchair, his feet up on a cushion. He was probably pushing sixty, but he carried his years well. Even in his sleep he appeared well conditioned. I had expected a more rugged-looking individual, one whose face would reflect years of opposing the elements, but no lines were etched in the face of this man. He had an unwrinkled face, almost babyish in its smoothness. He even lacked the telltale crowsfeet around the eyes that were so common a feature of the old-timers in the bush, and his wispy moustache served only to accentuate the essential youthfulness of his appearance. When we met beside the plane he had been wearing a parka and a leather helmet, but now he was dressed in a Harris tweed jacket and grey slacks and looked more like a well-to-do country squire than a veteran Arctic fur trader. The country squire effect was heightened by the tawny dog which lay at his feet, snuffling in a dream.

As I watched him the clock chimed seven. Sandy stirred and opened his eyes. He sat up and rubbed his hands over his face. 'Hello there... Does a man good to have a wee sleep after supper, you know.' He cocked his head, listening to the wind for a moment. 'Let's hope it's not like this at shiptime next week.'

'When the supply ship brings all the freight for the post?'

'That's right,' he answered. 'It's due at Chesterfield Inlet the day after tomorrow, so it should be here some time next week. That's why all the Eskimos are in the settlement. They always come in for shiptime, but they don't hang around long after the ship leaves. They'll make their fall trade and take off for the land and their traps, and we won't see most of them again until Christmas.'

He got up, stretched and walked over to the heater. 'Some of them will be back in after freeze-up to trade their deerskins—especially if they have a good fall hunt. We should get quite a few skins this year if the caribou stay put. We're right in the middle of caribou country here. That's why the Eskimos in this area are called the Caribou Eskimos. Caribou! That's all the Eskimos ever think about. It's their only food—straight meat. No vegetables at all except maybe a can or two of dried onions from the store... Every lake is packed with trout and whitefish, but the Eskimos won't eat them unless they're on the verge of starvation, and don't think we haven't had plenty of that around here!'

I was incredulous. 'But why, if there's lots of caribou and fish? Can't they set nets?'

'Sure,' Sandy replied. 'But by the time they're all out of other grub, the ice is eight feet thick on the lakes and it's almost impossible to set a net without a jigger. We had a jigger in here once and showed the Eskimos how to use it to string a net under the ice, but no one ever bothered to make one. Why bother fishing when there are caribou—that's their philosophy. Some years the caribou migration swings out around Baker Lake and the Eskimos have a tough winter. The caribou aren't gone—they're just not within hunting range. If a herd passes within twenty miles of a camp and the Eskimo isn't out hunting, then the caribou might as well have passed a million miles away for all the good they're going to do him. The only people who do any real fishing are those who live in the settlement. Naigo, our post servant, works a net all summer and fall and gets enough fish to keep him in dogfood most of the year. That way he can save the caribou meat for his family instead of using it all up on his dogs. A good-sized team of dogs will go through a caribou every two days, and then the Eskimos wonder why they run out of meat!'

Sandy Lunan had a basic honesty and straightforwardness that I found appealing; even more important to a newcomer like myself, he went out of his way to make me feel at home. Some traders work well with their subordinates and a true partnership evolves so that their day to day dealings with each other become pleasant and companionable. Others, especially the older ones who have become set in their ways, are more difficult to get along with, and sometimes the relationship between the two men degenerates to the point where life becomes a misery for both of them. Over a period of months the slightest fault or smallest quirk can become magnified out of all proportion.

Sandy Lunan was clearly a man of fixed habits, but he had the warm personality and openness that promotes a convivial atmosphere. I rather doubted that we would have any major clashes during the time we would spend together on the Baker Lake trading post.

When the Eskimos came in next morning, Sandy was checking through the official mail in an alcove of the living room that he used as an office, and I was reading on the chesterfield. We heard the murmur of voices in the porch first; then the front door opened and a babble of noise came down the hallway.

Sandy pushed back his chair and stood up. He took off his reading glasses and rubbed his eyes, then looked across the room at me. He smiled and said, 'Well, I suppose we should go out and show you off to the people. There's no trading today, so I guess they just came in to meet you. They'll do that every time I get a new clerk.'

We went down the hallway and into the native room. It was almost overflowing with people. Women and children sat flat-legged on the floor, crowded against the people around them. One woman was nursing a baby at her breast. The men were packed on the bench alongside the table; others perched on the table itself, while the rest stood against the wall. Everyone was talking and laughing. A smell of unwashed bodies hung in the air.

Sandy looked at them for a moment, smiling, then shouted something in a gruff but good-natured voice. The hubbub stopped, and beaming faces turned towards us. Sandy said something else, speaking in guttural syllables that I could not understand, then pointed his thumb at me. The people all stared in my direction and laughed, then one old woman rose laboriously to her feet and answered Sandy in the same guttural tongue. I stood there with an idiotic grin of incomprehension on my face. She stopped speaking, and more laughter went around the room.

Sandy smiled broadly. He put his arm across my shoulders and explained, 'I told them we come from the same country, and the only difference between you and me is that you are a lot younger and maybe a bit better tempered.' He added: 'Then the old woman said that you didn't look too bad tempered but you did look too skinny and maybe she should adopt you so that you could be fattened up a bit!'

Still laughing and giggling, the Eskimos surged forward to shake my hand, and Sandy and I were almost engulfed in the crush of people.

The Eskimo handshake is quite different from the white-man's, and there was considerable fumbling before I caught on to the difference. My hand was lightly clasped by each Eskimo, then raised almost to eye level before being released. No firm grip to denote masculine strength. No pumping of each other's hand. And the ceremony was not confined to adults. After a mother or father had shaken hands with me, each child in the family shook hands with me too.

Sandy told me the name of each person as we shook hands, but the unfamiliar sounds and syllables were too difficult for me to remember, and my stumbling attempts to pronounce them gave the Eskimos something more to laugh about. I felt then that my decision to transfer to the Arctic division of the Company had been a good one.

The noise and laughter continued while we had a mug-up. Akomalik, the woman who had served us dinner the night before, brought in the kettles of tea and boxes of hardtack at Sandy's request. Afterwards Sandy and I went outside and sat on an upturned canoe on the beach in front of the house. A few mosquitos foraged around our heads, and we put up our parka hoods to ward off the more persistent of them. The sun was warm on our faces and the breeze mild. A few hundred yards offshore the Company canoe bobbed in the swell as two Eskimos filled the water barrel.

Sandy pointed toward them: 'They're very helpful that way. In all the years I've been here, I've never known them to refuse help to anyone. If one family runs out of grub while another has some, then the well-off family always chips in to help them out. Survival by mutual aid, definitely. They will share just about everything except what they get from trapping. That's the only exception I know. They rarely eat alone unless they are out on the land, far away from other people, and they have about a dozen mug-ups a day—everyone is invited. Actually, that leads to problems when we issue relief. A family receives a ration of grub when they are hard up, then they invite the whole neighbourhood in for a mug-up, and before you can turn around they're flat out of grub again. They would rather offer it to others than have themselves thought stingy.'

The interior of the store was cool and the light poor. As Sandy switched on an additional light, I threw back my parka hood to get a better look at the place where I would spend most of my working time at the Baker Lake post.

It was a typical furtrade store of the Hudson's Bay Company —very similar to those I had served at in the bush country, and not much different from any small general store in the South. The room was only about twenty feet square but it held a wide variety of trade goods on shelves around three of the walls and in an alcove on the far side. A long wooden counter extended along two walls, separated from the shelves by a space of two or three feet. Pots and pans hanging from hooks in the ceiling gave a cluttered effect to the otherwise neat layout of the store.

The lack of a heater of any kind caught my attention and I commented on the fact to Sandy, wondering what it would be like to trade with the Eskimos at sixty below zero.

'Don't let it worry you,' Sandy replied with a broad smile. 'You'll soon get used to it. We'll toughen you up and make an Arctic man of you. Look!' He gestured around the shelves. 'Flour, sugar, tea, ammunition, traps, all basic stuff. Eskimo stuff, trade goods. We're not set up to handle whites here. This is a trading post, not a supermarket. And what's the point of heating the store when the Eskimos only come in to trade two or three times a year? Think how much it would cost to keep this place heated day in day out throughout the year!'

'Still, in the winter...'

'Oh, it's not that bad. You'll only be in here for a couple of hours at a stretch, and you can always stand on deer-skins to keep your feet warm. Nothing much you can do about your hands, though. If you keep your mitts on you can't write, and if you take them off your hands get cold. The only time you really freeze in here is when we take stock or when the Eskimos come for the Christmas trade. You'll be in here for about ten days or so then, until all the fur is traded off. Is it bitter! What you do is trade for an hour or so until your hands are too numb to write, then you come back to the house to thaw out and have a mug-up. That gives the counterslip book time to thaw out, too. The carbon freezes up pretty quickly in the cold...'

In the months to come Sandy was to prove every bit the 'character' I had been warned to expect, and his slavish addiction to habit and conformity to schedule without deviation was to cause me much amusement.

Sunday night at the post was like watching an old movie run over and over. Invariably Akomalik served the roast at the stroke of six. After supper Sandy would pat his belly a time or two to show how full and satisfied he was; then he would rise and go to his favourite easy chair. Within about five minutes he was snoring, head back, mouth open. His little dog Tippy always settled down at his master's side by the chair, and when Sandy snored so did Tippy.

At precisely five minutes to seven Sandy would awake, stretch his arms a bit, tug an old turnip watch out of his vest pocket and glance at it. He would then reach down to the stack of newspapers that had accumulated unread. He kept them piled up so that the oldest was on top, on the assumption that some day he might read right through the enormous stack from top to bottom. He would adjust his glasses and settle down to an evening of reading.

Yet every Sunday, on the dot of seven, there would come a rap at the door. Sandy would take his glasses off and squint nearsightedly over at me and say, 'What was that noise, Duncan lad? Is that someone at the door?'

And I would say, as though cued, 'Yes, that was someone at the door.'

Sandy, with his glasses in one hand and the newspaper in the other, would go to the front door, open it and peer out. There would invariably be Canon Jimmy James, the Anglican missionary.

'Well, hello, Mr James, hello! How are you?'

And Mr James would reply, 'Well, good evening, Mr Lunan. I just happened to be passing by, and I thought I'd drop in for a moment.'

'Yes, yes, come in, do come in.'

Sandy Lunan and Jimmy James had known each other for close on thirty years. Everyone else in the entire settlement called Mr Lunan Sandy and Mr James Jimmy, but between the two old cronies it was always Mr James and Mr Lunan— two gentlemen of the old school.

Sandy always dressed for Sunday in his very best tweeds.

He looked like a sportsman, one of the highland lairds, always neatly turned out with a carefully knotted tie. Jimmy dressed, too, for these calls, in his blacks and round collar. They didn't have much to do with each other during the week, and Sandy never once went to church as far as I knew. He denounced the Roman Catholics vehemently and he didn't have much respect for the Anglican church.

The two men would sit there in the fusty old living room with its Victorian furnishings and talk on a world of topics. They talked about changes they saw coming about. I never heard them argue once, and I used to think it was because Canon James, who was a single man like Sandy, enjoyed coming over now and then to bum a meal. Akomalik was a pretty good cook.

At about five minutes to ten Mr James would become nervous. He was a tall, North of England man, with skinny, bony fingers; he would start rubbing his hands together, his fingers twining and untwining. He knew how dominated Sandy was by the old chime clock on the mantel. He knew that Sandy, come blizzard or caribou stampede, always went to bed dead on ten o'clock. So at about one minute to ten Jimmy would rise to his feet.

Sandy might be speaking, and he would interrupt himself to insist, 'Oh, no, no, sit down Mr James, don't leave yet.'

Jimmy would say, 'Oh no, really Mr Lunan, I must get back to the church. I've a bit of writing to do,' or some such excuse. 'I must get back to the mission.' He would be looking at the old clock and waiting for it to chime, knowing that if he didn't get out by ten o'clock he'd be thrown out!

I was plunged into my apprenticeship duties at Baker Lake almost at once. A radio message from the trading post at Chesterfield Inlet, two hundred miles to the east, advised us that the annual supply ship would reach the post well ahead of schedule. We worked day and night in preparation for its arrival.

Sandy spent the days in his office. Hunched over his desk, spectacles dangling on the end of his nose, he worked on the numerous invoices and bills of lading that had come in on the plane. One warehouse at the back of the store was crammed to the ceiling with caribou skins bought during the year; we had to sort these out and bundle them for shipment to the coastal posts. One of the prime functions of the Baker Lake post was to buy caribou skins locally and export them to posts where they were badly needed. The Eskimos on the coast had little access to the major herds of caribou that passed by the Baker Lake area on migration and consequently they were always short of skins to make clothing and to use for bedding. Without caribouskin clothing, many of the coastal Eskimos would refuse to trap during the bitterly cold months of winter and would end up on relief. Caribou clothing was the only type warm enough to allow them to spend days and nights out on the land.

Our first task was to sort the hundreds of hides according to grade; winter skins were those taken during the winter months when the hair on the hide was longest; summer skins were those taken during the warm days of summer when the hide was paper thin and of little use except for underclothing; clothing skins were the most valuable, being taken in the fall when the hair was lengthening, but not yet too heavy or bulky to be used for winter clothing.

An Eskimo called Naigo was the general factotum around the post. He kept the mess supplied with fish and caribou meat, handled the dogs in winter, and generally acted as a handyman to assist with any chores that might need doing. He was a middle-aged man with a bony, cavernous face that made him look as if he had barely survived one of the starvations that Sandy had mentioned. When he smiled, which was often, he displayed a set of very bad teeth. He always seemed cheerful and usually hummed a little melody to himself as we worked on the hides. He spoke no English, but we communicated easily with a series of exaggerated gestures involving hands, feet, eyes, lips, and anything else needed to convey meaning.

Naigo and I graded the skins. Naigo taught me that the Eskimo name for the caribou was *tuktu*, and I scribbled the word down on a cigarette package and filed it away for future reference. Word number one in the Eskimo language!

After grading the hides, we bundled them into piles of ten, roped them up, labelled them with the name of the trading post they were destined for, and stacked them ready for shipment.

The next task that faced us was to clear the beach in front of the trading post of all extraneous equipment. All the cargo unloaded from the ship would be landed there and we should need every foot of space.

The day so carefully prepared for arrived at last.

'Duncan! Wake up! C'mon, lad! The ship's in!'

I opened sleep-fogged eyes to find Sandy leaning over the bed. I sat up, struggling into wakefulness, shivering in the chill of the room. I dressed quickly and splashed some cold water from the hand basin onto my face. I was too excited to bother heating wash water.

Sandy was standing in the kitchen gulping down a mug of tea when I passed him on the way out. I grabbed my parka, pushed open the front door—and stopped dead in my tracks. The world was covered with snow!

Large, lazy flakes drifted down from the sky and brushed me with moist tendrils. They clung to my shirt and settled damply on my bare skin. Snow lay everywhere; the ground, the roof of Naigo's house, the blubber shed, everything was blanketed under a soft white layer. It held me spellbound with its beauty, but I realized that beautiful or not, it would be one hell of a day for unloading. Everything would get soaking wet if it was dumped on the beach.

I hurried off to get Naigo and took him across to Sandy, who put him to rounding up the other Eskimos to help unload. The snow was still falling heavily but the sky had grown lighter. I could see the ship anchored about a quarter of a mile off the post. Her lights were on, and there was movement on the decks. Probably the deckhands were out rigging the derricks. A wave of nostalgia swept over me. Three years ago who would have guessed that I would end up on the shores of an Arctic lake watching a ship prepare to unload her cargo. A fur trader!

A small barge churned around the stern of the ship and made for shore. Deeply laden, it breasted through the water.

I opened up the warehouses and turned on all the lights. Best to get as much freight indoors as possible, especially the foodstuffs. I then headed for the beach to meet the incoming barge. Sandy and the first group of Eskimos arrived before the barge reached our little beach. I went over to join them.

He gave me the drill: 'This barge will have the flour aboard, so we'll take it into the warehouse right away. You stand in the warehouse and check off the bags as the Eskimos bring them in. If any are burst or damaged, set them aside so that we can go over them with the purser and claim for the damage. Don't let him get away with anything. You understand?'

The small barge crunched gently onto the snow-covered sand of the beach. The Eskimos surrounded it and began shouldering the bales of flour that comprised the first load. We moved toward the barge to supervise the unloading; the annual shiptime was underway.

We spent two frantic days unloading. On the first morning the snow stopped about noon, and the sun broke through to bathe the settlement in a silver sheen. The reflection glittered on the calm waters of the lake and frosted the ship with sparkling flecks of brightness. The weather was mild.

The beach in front of the post became a trampled morass of slush and sand from the constant passage of the Eskimos going to and from the warehouses with their loads. Much of the supplies and trade goods we unloaded directly onto the beach, the result being a litter of cases and boxes of merchandise strewn in apparent confusion all over the place. But the superficial chaos was misleading. All the bagged goods such as flour, sugar, and rolled oats were carried into the warehouses regardless of how long the barge was delayed, and the only goods unloaded onto the snow of the beach were those in boxes or strong cases that would not absorb the dampness and ruin the contents.

The unloading quickly took on a spontaneous air. After the sun came out, almost every Eskimo in the settlement came down to lend a hand and soon the beach was jammed with people. They laughed and jostled each other in high good-humour, and the light-hearted banter made the physical labour of unloading seem more a game than a task. As each barge arrived at the beach, it was attacked by an army of men, women, and children, the old and the young, the strong and the weak, all sallying forth to seize an item and carry it up to the warehouse or stack it on the beach. Excitement ran high as men vied with one another to see who could carry the heaviest load, and the women cheered them on. The snow and slush were forgotten in the festivity of the moment.

Once he saw that I could handle the unloading, Sandy left the supervision to me. He returned to the house and only reappeared at odd intervals. Once, on that first morning, he came running out in a great fluster, his leather helmet flapping as he ran.

'Duncan!' he cried, 'Duncan! C'mere, lad!' He stopped to catch his breath, face red with exertion. 'My booze is on the ship! My whole supply for the year! I forgot it last year and the damned skipper sailed away with the whole works!' He stopped again, chest heaving, expression worried. 'It's kept in the captain's cabin, Duncan. Go out on the next barge and pick it up, will you? There's a case of rum and a case of whiskey. Sign the bill of lading for it after you make sure everything tallies. And for goodness sake,' he cautioned, 'handle it carefully or we'll be celebrating Hogmanay with water!'

The unloading continued late into the evening darkness. We worked by the light from several gas lanterns, and the flickering shadows created a sense of unreality. Bargeload after bargeload of supplies and fuel were added to the piles already on the beach.

Next day the women and children returned to the beach, but the excitement of the previous afternoon could not be recaptured. The hours passed, and the men grew tired as the work became tedious. Finally there were no more barges to be unloaded. We took a break for a mug-up, then returned with new vigour to begin loading the bales of fur and bundles of deerskins aboard the outgoing barge. These were the last loads of the day.

Some of the Eskimos went out on the last barge to visit the ship, but most of us were too tired. We lay on the piles of freight on the beach smoking cigarettes—tired men, too weary to take part in the traditional leave taking.

Sandy came out of the house and surveyed the mountain of supplies on the beach. He nodded in satisfaction, then came over to join me.

'Well, that's it for another year,' he said. 'We'll need to get all that stuff lifted inside, but we can do that tomorrow. Time for a tot of rum. We deserve one after all this.'

We sat in the living room and drank hot rum while the daylight faded. As Sandy rose to put on the light, the foghorn sounded. We went to the window together and looked out.

The departing ship was underway. Shiptime was over.

2

❄ *With Snow in His Mouth*

One of the first things Sandy Lunan taught me at Baker Lake was to carry a snowknife with me at all times, even around the settlement. When Sandy went out for a walk, he dressed in deerskins, which are much warmer than any whiteman's clothing yet devised, and he carried a snowknife. Even if you lack the knowhow to build an igloo, you can at least cut blocks for a windbreak. An Arctic blizzard isn't really frightening if you are warmly dressed and know what to do. It's only dangerous if you panic, and when you panic, you're halfway dead.

It may seem excessively cautious to carry a snowknife when simply walking around a settlement where there are houses in every direction, but in a real blow at Baker Lake I have seen it snow so hard that one might walk into another man without seeing him. By mid-winter the houses are completely hidden, drifted over by the snow. Sandy and I would string a rope between the trade store and our house, no more than fifty feet apart, to keep us from getting lost during a storm.

One night at Baker Lake a friend working at the meteorological station and I accompanied two young school-teachers to the movies at the DOT (Department of Transport) station. The weather had been calm in the early evening, but by the time the show had ended a furious storm had completely cut off visibility. A power cable ran all the way from the DOT building to the schoolhouse where the girls lived; we thought we could easily follow it. But in the flurry of the wind we not only lost the cable, we got lost ourselves—right in the middle of the settlement. I wasn't particularly worried; I was dressed from head to toe in my deerskins, but the others were wearing ordinary whiteman's clothing, cloth parkas and regular overshoes. They were frightened. The wind drove hard snow granules into our faces like ice bullets, and it felt as if it was cutting the flesh of our cheekbones away. One of the teachers panicked and had to be physically restrained from dashing blindly into the darkness. Yet we might as well have been blind. All we could hear was the moan of the wind and our own laboured breathing. The dogs, dug in against the blow, were unusually silent. We couldn't have been more than a hundred yards from the Hudson's Bay post, but no buildings were distinguishable. We could have been a hundred miles out on the tundra. The feeling of helplessness was frightening.

The whiteman's way is to keep walking in a blizzard to try to keep warm. But the Eskimo will not try to fight the elements and tire himself out. The Eskimo way is to burrow into a snowdrift and let the snow itself protect and insulate him from the bitter wind.

I proposed this, and the others agreed. I held one girl in my arms and the other fellow held the other girl. We got them quieted down, and it seemed not a bad idea after a while.

I tried to explain—reassuringly—that if the worst came to the worst, we could just burrow into one of the drifts and sit out the storm. It wouldn't last more than three or four days, and long before then people in the settlement would become concerned and organize a search. I told them that old Sandy would probably come looking for me if I weren't in by ten o'clock.

But we were like most whitemen—no patience and, by now, incapable of the state of mind that would allow us to make use of the very elements we fought, as an Eskimo would. We elected to venture out and luckily stumbled into an Eskimo shack. The inhabitants told us which way to go to reach the school. Even then, though the school was less than a hundred yards away, we almost missed it.

A recent tragedy at Baker Lake heightened the terror of the experience for the young teachers. A few weeks earlier a young Eskimo schoolboy, about twelve years old, had gone out to get a caribou. It was the fall, and there wasn't yet enough snow to build a snowhouse, but plenty to blow up into a fierce ground blizzard. A big herd of caribou was in the area, only five miles or so from the post. The boy left the settlement with his dog and a rifle. He had never before killed a caribou, and wanted a kill to prove that he was a man.

It was a cold, miserable day. He found the herd and shot true to get his first caribou. Then he tied the carcass to his dog and began to trudge back. But a strong wind had come up and a ground blizzard was blowing in a matter of minutes. The difference of those few minutes doomed him. The young fellow just didn't have enough time to get back to safety.

The storm blew all day and the boy didn't come home. His grandmother, worried, went to the RCMP for help. A group was organized to go out and look for the boy, but the drifting snow had wiped out any tracks. Even for the searchers it would have been suicide to stay out in the storm. Finally, after another day, the wind went down, and we got up more parties to look for the boy. Tracks were in fact discovered where the boy and the dog had walked and the caribou been dragged. We backtracked and found the boy had been coming straight toward the settlement. It seemed that he had followed the wind to get his bearings because he wouldn't have been able to see anything, but just as he neared the settlement the wind must have shifted a bit; he had gone off to the side of the village and just over the rise of a hill a few hundred yards behind it. That was where he was found. He was lying on his back with both mitts off and the wind had blown the parka up over his belly so that the bare flesh was exposed to the cold. His eyes and mouth were packed with snow. His dog was right beside him, happily munching away at the caribou.

The next day, when she was calling roll, the young teacher in whose class the boy had been didn't know what had happened and asked why he wasn't there. One of the children volunteered, 'Oh, he froze to death yesterday.' The teacher almost fainted.

The wild country around Baker Lake could be just as dangerous in the summer if it was challenged by greenhorns. One summer two young whitemen, scientists conducting experiments for the fisheries department, came through the area. Neither had ever been in that kind of rough country before, neither had much experience with canoes—yet there they were in Baker Lake preparing to make a run up the Thelon River to collect different species of fish.

Both Sandy and I were worried about them. They didn't

seem to understand that they had a tough trip ahead of them. We watched while they piled their canoe full until not more than a few inches of freeboard rode above the water. We suggested that they would be well advised to make two trips. But they were late getting started and wanted to get all their equipment across in a hurry. We explained that Baker Lake was about the windiest place in the Arctic, and Sandy, who knew that part of the country like the palm of his hand, stressed the dangers of trying to run up the rapids on the Thelon.

They were lucky enough to get across the lake without a serious blow and they were scared enough by what we had said to portage the rapids. After a month or so of camping out on the river above the rapids, they completed their tests and started back. They decided to shoot the rapids coming down, thereby saving themselves the long, tiresome, difficult portage. They didn't think the rapids very risky.

They made the first stretch of bad water all right, but neglected to look for the main channel through the second stretch; they just let the canoe swing into it and go. They didn't get far before the bow of the canoe dipped under, the stern pushed to one side, and the canoe overturned. One of them grabbed the canoe and hung on. He told us later that he could see his partner struggling in the frothing water and a ten gallon keg of gas bobbing quite close by him. He screamed to his companion to grab the keg, but the shock of the bitterly cold water must have numbed him, for he was never able to reach it.

The one who had held on to the canoe never saw his partner again. He was too busy trying to save himself as the canoe was battered by the rapids. Finally he floated into an eddy at the foot of the rapids minus most of his shirt and jacket and with his shoes and socks ripped off him by the turbulent waters and jagged rocks. He floated close to shore, bruised and exhausted, and just managed to drag himself onto a sand bar as the canoe was swept into the next section of rapids. Once ashore, he recovered enough strength to wander around and set off in what he thought was the right direction to find help. He was walking determinedly inland when a hunting party of Eskimos came across him.

The man who survived blamed himself as leader of the expedition, but his partner had really been the victim of an unforgiving country. The Arctic seldom gives a man a second chance.

3
✳ Uqausiqqut—
Our Way
of Talking

During my years in northern Manitoba I had learned to speak the Cree Indian language fairly well—a relatively easy accomplishment because the sound system of Cree is not difficult and an excellent grammar and dictionary are available.

Once in the Arctic, I naturally wanted to learn Eskimo. I have always felt that not being able to talk person-to-person makes it virtually impossible to appreciate a different culture. Sandy Lunan encouraged me to learn the Eskimo language and customs. 'It's easy to live like a whiteman up here,' he said. 'I want you to learn the Eskimo way, so you will know how they feel about things.'

Sandy spoke Eskimo himself—but with a unique Lunan-esque flavour! When I first arrived I marvelled at what I took to be his great proficiency. I often heard him and Akomalik conversing together. However, after I had been at Baker Lake for about a year and had gained some grasp of the dialect, I realized that there was Eskimo, and there was what Sandy spoke. But no matter how badly he tortured the pronunciation of a word, the Eskimos understood well enough; they had long since grown accustomed to his personal variety of their language.

It was hard going at first. There were only a couple of Eskimos at Baker who had any fluency in English, and they were away from the post out on the traplines, hunting or fishing much of the time. There was a small dictionary, a little red book put out by a Roman Catholic missionary, Father Thibert. Unfortunately the good Father had lived in several places and hadn't bothered to note which dialect a word might come from when he put it into his dictionary. There are many Eskimo dialects and the differences between them, in grammar as well as in vocabulary, can be enormous. An eastern Eskimo can only understand a western Eskimo with great difficulty and vice versa. Even between two settlements as near each other as Coppermine and Paulatuk, the differences could be startling. For example, if one wished to say 'A whiteman arrived yesterday' at Coppermine, the correct expression would be '*qavlunaaq ikpaksaq tikittuq,*' but at Paulatuk one would say '*tanaaluk unnungmi tikittuaq.*'

After I had been using Father Thibert's dictionary for about a month I found so many errors, and the spelling system was so inconsistent, that I couldn't pronounce a single word with any confidence that I would be understood. The only solution was to write my own dictionary.

Gradually I built up my word lists. I would write words down on cigarette packages, scraps of paper, bits of box, anything that was handy. As soon as I picked up a short word that I could remember and whose meaning I could pin down—usually some concrete object such as mug, flour, sugar—I would write it down and study it.

On my trips with Naigo I constantly pestered the poor man, asking 'What is this? What is that?' He was unbelievably patient with me and always gave me the word to write down. I had no systematic spelling system at that time, so I simply wrote the words down as they sounded to my ear. This created enormous problems. Checking back a week later I would find a conglomeration of letters alongside an English translation, impossible to pronounce. I had had no phonetic training, and was merely arranging letters as they seemed correct at the time. Unless the correct pronunciation was still in my memory, I would certainly never find it in my notes.

The obvious first step was to study Eskimo sounds, and work out a system of transliteration whereby one letter would consistently stand for a single sound. Only then could I record Eskimo words with an accurate and systematic orthography which would not vary from one day to the next.

Naturally, I ran into difficulties in working out an accurate spelling system. My background in the English language made me interpret Eskimo sounds in terms of the English sound system, so that in some instances I made too fine a distinction in recording words. For example, Eskimo has only three significant vowels, *a*, *i* and *u*, but because the English alphabet distinguishes five vowels, I normally wrote all five in transcribing Eskimo.

In other instances, I failed to hear the distinction between two separate Eskimo sounds and therefore wrote both with the same letter. Eskimo has two types of *k* sound. One is formed at the front of the mouth and is very similar to the familiar English sound; the other is formed further back in the mouth and has no exact counterpart in English. It was only after my ear had become attuned to Eskimo that I realized what a difference these slight variations meant. I then assigned the letter *k* to the front sound and the letter *q* to the back sound. It was some years before I gained the grasp of Eskimo sound structure that allowed me to distinguish the pronunciation of words I had previously mistaken for homonyms.

The next step was to study the structure of the words themselves and assign a meaning to each element. I took all my little scraps and notes, and re-wrote all the words according to my new spelling system. Then I listed them in separate books—one for the stem words, another for the suffixes (an Eskimo word is composed of a stem plus modifying suffixes), and a third for the grammatical terminations.

Working slowly and on my own, I began to develop a vocabulary and to dissect the words I knew so that I could tell which were stems and which suffixes. From that, I could work out both the grammar and the semantic modifications of the stems. I was lucky in having a good ear for languages. Many words I just picked out of the air, and they would stick in my mind.

An Eskimo called Tagoona, who worked for Canon James and later became the first Eskimo Anglican minister in the Arctic, and who was fluent in English, was a great help to me, but when it came to matters of grammar he was lost. I took to visiting Father Choque, the Catholic missionary. Once a week he would bring out his own notes, which were all written in French, and we would work on Eskimo all evening. He was an able teacher and soon had me deeply involved in the grammar.

I knew, because of my experience with the Cree language, that mere vocabulary is not enough. You can communicate well with two percent of the total vocabulary. But you must control almost one hundred percent of the grammar. So I kept working at it, picking up words from Naigo and Tagoona and the other Eskimos when they came in to trade. I made a point of using the new words I learned, and repeating the old ones to fix them in my mind. Upon learning a word in Eskimo, I tried to use it whenever appropriate. When I wanted a mug I would say, 'Pass me that *tiiturvik*' instead of 'pass me that mug.' When I worked out some new grammatical terminations, I would write them out in large letters and paste them alongside my bed at the trading post. The last thing I would read at night and the first thing in the morning would be what I had written there.

Within a few weeks I was using Eskimo, but mastery of the language came only very gradually. I don't think I could boast fluent Eskimo until I had been in the Arctic three or four years.

When Farley Mowat claims in his books and articles that he went to the Arctic and in a matter of a month or two was able to speak a basic form of Eskimo and discuss shamanism and religion, I just can't believe him. I know that when he came to Baker Lake he didn't communicate at all in Eskimo. The only time I ever heard him say a word in Eskimo was when he said *tuktu* (caribou). It is impossible to master a language, unless it is closely related to one's own, by delving into it for a mere few months—particularly if there is no dictionary or grammar to work from.

The Eskimo's language reveals important aspects of his culture. He will utilize specific terms with fine but highly important variations. We say 'snow', and perhaps modify it with adjectives, but the Eskimo has twenty-five to thirty terms, all meaning snow, but each meaning a specific type of snow.

Choice of precisely the correct word to describe snow on any particular occasion turns out to be of vital importance to people living in a snow environment. When I first went out on the trail at Baker Lake with the Eskimos, to me snow was snow. I didn't care whether I was walking on hard snow or being covered with soft snow. But some snow is just right for building snowhouses; other types of snow can't be used at all in the making of shelter. To a man starting a trip across the Arctic, whose life at some stage of the trip may depend upon finding the right type of snow, it is not enough to tell him there is plenty of the stuff. He must know that there is plenty of *igluksaq* (snow-house-building snow). If someone told him there was nothing but *pukak* (a type of snow granulated like sugar), he would know that he couldn't build shelter. *Masak* is soft, wet snow found in spring when it is thawing. *Ganik* is falling snow, *aput* is snow lying on the ground, *piqtuq* is snow being blown through the air during a ground blizzard, *aqilluqqaq* is a firmish snow but not quite firm enough to build a snowhouse with, *mauya* is a soft, deep snow. There are many more words for different kinds of snow.

There are ten or eleven words for different types of lichens. And mud is of great significance to the Eskimo when he applies it to the runners of his sled. Certain kinds of mud, like skiers' wax, work best in certain types of snow, and the language offers a dozen terms to distinguish between the various kinds of mud. On the other hand, one word suffices in Eskimo for all the hundreds of species of bright summer flowers in the Arctic—*nauttiaq*. Whether it is a tall flower with purple blooms or a tiny flower with yellow petals, to the Eskimo it's *nauttiaq*. The Eskimo has no use for flowers.

As any people do when another culture meets theirs, the Eskimos have adopted many English words, particularly for things strange to their culture, and they have adapted many more. In the Copper Eskimo dialect 'queen' becomes *kuini*; 'minister' *minisitaq*; 'necktie' *niktaq*; 'marmalade' *maamaliit*; 'telephone' *talipuut*. Definite patterns are followed in the adaptation of such words, all of which can be worked out given enough examples.

There is to date no standard orthography in use for the Eskimo dialects. Confronted with a foreign word, people tend to spell it the way it sounds to them in their own tongue. English-speakers write *inuk*, meaning person; the word has usually been spelled *inouk* by French missionaries. Similarly one finds many variants of Eskimo words, and of spellings of Eskimo words, within the same language.

The word *kabloona* is supposedly the Eskimo word meaning 'whiteman', and it is usually explained that the literal meaning of *kabloona* is 'big eyebrows'; since the Eskimo has nearly no eyebrow and the whiteman's eyebrows are usually comparatively large, this seems to make sense. Actually the Eskimo word for whiteman is *gavlunaaq*, which has been anglicized to *kabloona*; but *gavlunaaq* has nothing to do with big eyebrows. The word came from Greenland originally, and meant any man from the south. Since only whitemen came from the south, *qavlunaaq* soon came to mean whiteman. The confusion probably arose from the fact that there is a similar word in the western Arctic, *qavlunaq*, pronounced nearly the same, which means the prominent supraorbital ridge.

Other Eskimo words have been anglicized or corrupted and misunderstood in English. The word *chimo* has gained acceptance and popularity in the southern part of Canada as an Eskimo greeting. To my knowledge, the word does not occur in any Canadian Eskimo dialect, and in fact no Canadian Eskimo word begins with 'ch' as in 'church'.

Because spoken Eskimo sounds so strange to outsiders and because so many nationalities have been involved in exploring the north, visiting or working in the Arctic, with each individual tending to interpret the Eskimo words and names he hears in terms of his own language, many such corruptions have occurred. It is common for an Eskimo name to be spelled three different ways. One form might have been spelled out first by a French missionary, another by a Scottish trader, a third by an English mountie. The federal government's standard orthography, introduced in 1958, will certainly prove of great use when it is generally accepted. Dialectical differences have so far hindered its adoption by the Eskimos.

The word 'Eskimo' itself is a corruption of an Indian word for the people of the Arctic, meaning 'eaters of raw flesh.' Eskimos simply term themselves *innuit*—the people.

4
❄ *People*
Who Live
in Snowhouses

It is becoming increasingly rare to find a teenaged Eskimo in the Canadian Arctic who knows how to build a snowhouse. Most will probably never learn.

The 'igloo' (an adaptation of the Eskimo *iglu* and a term used by southerners only) has been romanticized so much in both fiction and so-called 'fact' books on the North, that their passing is lamented—but only by those who have never actually lived in one.

A snowhouse can indeed be warm and snug, and it is far superior to having no shelter at all. But there simply isn't any comparison between a snowhouse and a proper dwelling, and there is no way that an Eskimo, having lived in a frame house, will ever go back to a snowhouse. One spring in Bathurst Inlet I was camped with a companion about forty-five miles west of the coast. Three or four Eskimo families from Coppermine, travelling to Bathurst, happened by and when they spotted our snowhouse they naturally stopped in.

It was late spring and snowhouses tend to melt at that time of year, a nuisance to their inhabitants. Every once in a while someone, whoever was nearest, had to pick up a fistful of snow and stick it against the spot on the ceiling or high on the wall that was dripping. That would check the dripping for a while; then the snow would be unable to absorb any more moisture and it would fall off with a plop. One would have to dodge quickly or be doused. One of the women from Coppermine, who felt she was among friends and could speak up, said, 'I've lived in a proper house so long I'd forgotten how uncomfortable it is to live in a snowhouse.'

When the weather warms up and the snowhouse starts to drip all over, the bedding is soaked and everything inside the house is damp and cold, it is better to cut away the upper quarter of the house and replace it with the canvas cover from a sled or with caribou skins. The Eskimos often used to build their snowhouses this way in the spring, a type of dwelling they called *nallaqtaq*.

Most Eskimos today live in government low-rental prefab housing, but there are a few locations where the people still live in snowhouses, and Eskimos out on their traplines still build trail snowhouses for overnight use. They certainly served their purpose in the days when the Eskimos had nothing else that could be used for shelter during the winter. The advantage of the snowhouse lies in its ease of construction and its economy. It can be erected anywhere that good snow can be found, be ready for occupancy within a couple of hours at the most, and can be abandoned without loss when it is no longer needed.

The country of the snowhouse Eskimos traditionally lay east of the Mackenzie Delta. The Eskimos of the Delta itself, and to the west, never used snowhouses. They had enough timber to build log cabins; if not, they used driftwood or they put up tents and blocked them with snow for insulation. Not until one reaches Coronation Gulf or farther east does one find true snowhouse country.

On the trail we would build small houses, no larger than necessary to accommodate one or two men. Naigo and I never built anything more elaborate than eight feet across. A large snowhouse, a *qalgi* for a festival or a drum dance, might be up to forty feet long and fifteen feet high, and you would have to stand on a stack of fuel drums to put the final blocks in place in the ceiling. A structure as large as this would require the joint labour of all the men in a settlement; it would be just as sound as a small snowhouse. Once glazed on the inside—it would receive a coat of ice on the underside from the heat of the inside—you could stand right on top of it with no fear of falling through.

My first knowledge of snowhouses came with my initial trips out of Baker Lake with Naigo, while I was serving my apprenticeship under Sandy Lunan. From my observation of

Naigo, so deft and sure, I concluded that building a snowhouse couldn't be very difficult. So when there was free time around the post, I decided to try it for myself.

I bought a proper snowknife from one of the Eskimos, long-bladed like a butcher's knife, and headed out behind the post. I didn't particularly want an audience until I had mastered the technique. I soon discovered that I needed more than a snow-knife. I didn't even know enough to realize that snow of a special consistency was needed. I could get my snowhouse about three blocks high, then the whole thing would crumble.

Until Sandy spoke to me about it, I hadn't realized that my failure had been observed. One day Sandy said, 'I hear you've been trying to build snowhouses.' It seemed that Eskimos passing by with their sleds had noticed and watched me through their binoculars. 'Have you been able to build one yet?' Sandy asked. I had to admit I hadn't. I had to admit that I couldn't seem to master the technique without some Eskimo advice.

So one afternoon Naigo went out with me. I think he was inwardly laughing, but too polite to show it. First he taught me how to locate the proper type of snow for snowhouse construction. It had to be firm enough to cut into blocks but soft enough to enable the blocks to fuse together when they were pushed against each other. If the snow was too hard, or too soft, or too powdery, or granular like salt, then it was useless for snow-blocks. Hard snow could certainly be cut into blocks, but the physical labour involved would soon tire the arms—and produce a snowhouse very cold to live in. Men like Naigo could tell building-snow by the way it sounded underfoot; such snow has a certain creakiness quite recognizable to the educated ear.

Having located the proper type of snow, our next step was to use the snow-probe, an implement somewhat like a thin walking stick, to poke down through the drift and determine if the snow was composed of one or more layers. Naigo taught me to avoid multilayered snow, as blocks cut from this would invariably break along the line between the different layers.

I watched Naigo cut a short, straight line into the drift with his snowknife, then excavate the snow from one side of the cut to leave a flat, vertical face about two feet deep. He then cut two parallel lines to the same depth but about eight feet long from the vertical face. He returned to the hole he had excavated and made a horizontal cut at the bottom of the face. Using his snowknife, he drew a guideline on the surface of the snow about six inches back from the face between the two deep cuts, then made several short jabs down into this guideline. The first snowblock split cleanly away from the face.

Using this technique he cut out about fifteen blocks and placed all but the last one on the surface of the snow to leave an open trench. The last block he placed back in the trench a few feet behind him. Now began the actual construction of the snowhouse.

Using nothing but visual judgement, he placed the blocks from the trench in a circle about seven feet in diameter, then cutting and shaping each block with his snowknife he fitted one against the other and jammed them with a final blow.

When the first row had been completed, still working from the inside, Naigo made a diagonal cut from the bottom of the first block to the top of the third and removed the upper wedge of snow. This left a sloping ramp, the foundation of the second row of blocks, and the key to the formation of a continuously climbing spiral.

This was where I had been going wrong in my attempts to build a snowhouse on my own. I had not observed the vital constructional feature of the ramp when watching the Eskimos build their houses around the post. Instead of forming a spiral of blocks, I had merely placed one row on top of the other with the result that they invariably collapsed.

There was no problem in fitting the blocks together; strangely enough, the higher the walls the easier it became. As the blocks inclined toward the centre, the angle became more acute, and they tended to support each other more readily than in the lower rows. In addition, the blocks were cut smaller, making them easier to handle as the walls rose in height.

Naigo pushed the final block—known as the key block—lengthwise through the gap, turned it horizontal, and trimmed it so that it lowered exactly into place. He cut a low archway in the snowblock left in the trench and emerged. While he had been fitting the blocks, I had been using soft snow to close up all the chinks between them. Our house was finished.

One Eskimo with whom I was to travel a great deal between Gjoa Haven and Spence Bay, Takolik, and who taught me a lot about handling dogs and how to live in the Arctic, was a master at building snowhouses. He could put up a trail house in about thirty-five minutes. Takolik originally came from Cape Dorset on Baffin Island, and the technique of the eastern Eskimos was different from that I had learned. He never used the snowknife to cut out the snowblocks but carried instead an ordinary whiteman's saw and just sawed out blocks of snow as though they were styrofoam. His snowhouses were always big, roomy ones with a full sleeping platform, not the dinky little trail houses most Eskimos built. His sleeping platforms, about twenty inches off the ground, usually took up about half the floor space. The sleeping platform is an important feature of the snowhouse, giving the occupant something to sit on and raising a sleeper up off the ground where the cold air is trapped.

When I first slept in a snowhouse my natural inclination was to lie with my head toward the wall, but Naigo laughingly explained why it was better to sleep the other way around. The reason is highly practical and typical of the Eskimo: a sleeper with his head toward the centre of the room doesn't have to crawl out of his sleeping bag in the morning to get a fire started. He can just reach out of his bag, light the primus stove, shove some snow into the kettle, and the snowhouse will be warm by the time the tea is ready.

I found Eskimo women just as touchy about keeping things in proper order in their houses as white women. From her position at the side of the snowhouse, the Eskimo woman had all her pots and pans, her stove, the stone lamp that burned seal blubber, and all her implements handy—woe betide the man who dared upset her orderly arrangement.

Once when I made a trip east along the coast from Perry River, I came across an Eskimo snowhouse about ten o'clock in the morning. There it was, a solitary snowhouse, sixty miles from the post, probably twenty miles from the nearest neighbours, and when I entered the Eskimo housewife was quite upset and embarrassed. She tried to rouse her husband and bustled around sweeping up the snow floor.

'I'm sorry that things are so untidy,' she said; 'I didn't expect visitors. I was just trying to tidy things up a bit when you came in.' She apologized about her husband being in bed so late in the morning and explained at great length that he had come in late from a hunt the night before and that was why things were in such disorder.

I had to laugh.

5
❄ Ever Northward

About the only thing Sandy Lunan didn't do on time was retire. He was in his sixties when I first came to Baker Lake, but he could and did put in as full a day of work as anyone. He had earned his retirement, and the Company recognized this readily enough and was more than willing to see that he was comfortably fixed. Sandy had, in fact, retired twice, but found retirement frustrating and boring. Each time he came back to Baker Lake. Fur trading had been his life, and Baker Lake his home for thirty years. Like so many men, when the time comes, Sandy literally couldn't retire; he just didn't know what to do with himself.

Finally, however, in the fall of 1959 Sandy made up his mind to leave once and for all. It was comical listening to him trying to rationalize his decision to himself. He kept up a constant grumbling that the place was becoming overrun with whitemen (there were all of twenty or so in the thousand square miles around) and that the country was changing. 'It's too civilized around here,' he complained, 'for an old fur trader.'

On the last day, when the plane came for him, the entire settlement was at the air strip. Sandy uttered barely a word to anyone. He hardly said goodbye to faithful Akomalik, who had taken care of him for so many years. In a loud, hoarse voice he defiantly proclaimed for all to hear: 'Well, I've spent thirty years of my life here, and I'm glad to be leaving this place.' He paused and looked around. 'I've got some money saved up, I'm going to take a trip around the world...I never want to see the Arctic again...' He sniffed loudly and blew his nose, and not a person there was fooled. Everyone could see the old man was on the verge of tears.

Sandy was certainly the finest trader I ever knew in the Arctic. He died just two years after he retired, still an apparently hale man. He would probably have lived another twenty years had he kept working.

After Sandy left, a trader called Bob Griffith came to run the Baker Lake post. He was a first-rate man, but the Company knew I wanted to leave as I had my heart set on a smaller, more isolated post. Baker Lake with its twenty whites was, as Sandy had said, just too civilized for a fur trader.

About five months after Bob took over, the Company transferred me to Spence Bay. I liked the idea. Spence was farther north, one step closer to the type of isolated Arctic post I was aiming for, quite a bit smaller than Baker Lake. It was the home of the so-called Nattilik people. There was a lake behind the Spence Bay settlement named Willersted by the whiteman. The Eskimos had their own name for it. According to an ancient legend of the people there, Willersted was the home of a rare, tiny dwarf seal, so they called the lake Nattilik, meaning 'the one with the seals.' Every now and then an Eskimo would report seeing one of the legendary seals, but no whiteman ever saw one as far as I know. Appropriately enough, the Nattilik people lived mainly by hunting seal.

I arrived at Spence at about the time the annual supply ship came in, and helped unload the year's goods. Then I boarded the ship and went over to Gjoa Haven on King William Island, an outpost of Spence Bay in those days. The idea was that I would check the books there and return to Spence by dogteam after the freeze-up.

The manager at Gjoa Haven was a remarkable little man named George Washington Porter, half-Eskimo, with an Eskimo wife named (of course) Martha. George had done enough things to fill the lives of half-a-dozen men. He had been a cowboy in the States, worked as a seaman on an old-time sailing ship running between the North American west coast and Australia, worked in a Scandinavian sardine factory, and been a US Marine. With almost total recall, he could name exact dates of incidents in his life dating back forty years. His last job before he took over as manager of the Gjoa Haven post had been a stint as pilot aboard the RCMP vessel *St Roche*, when that historic Canadian ship came east making the first trip through the Northwest Passage.

George was a fine fur trader, and he spoke the distinctive Nattilik dialect fluently. The only problem George had was with his accounts. Every trader in the Company had to send out a month-end account by wire in a special code : how many pelts taken, the variety, prices paid, total sales, etc. George had no knack for book work. So part of my job as a clerk assigned to Spence Bay was to go over to Gjoa Haven once a month and fix up George's books.

I liked that little chore. I enjoyed the dogteam travel between the two posts. Those trips did much to teach me how to handle dogs and live on the trail, constituting a sort of graduate course to the training Naigo had given me at Baker Lake.

Takolik came over with his team from Spence Bay to pick me up and we made the return trip from Gjoa Haven to Spence. The run between the two posts was only three or four sleeps in decent weather, and Takolik had a fine team. Occasionally we made a side trip to one of the Distant Early Warning line radar posts to pick up our mail. In those days there were no scheduled flights to Spence Bay, and if we didn't get our mail at the DEW line post, there was no telling when we might. The only planes that ever stopped at Spence Bay were special charters arriving once or twice a year.

My first winter at Spence, I spent only about one week of every month there, a few days with Takolik making the run to Gjoa Haven, about a week there, and back to Spence. Because I didn't happen to get along with the manager at Spence, I was happy to be at Gjoa Haven or on the trail with Takolik.

Takolik would hitch up his team and start us out on a trip, then he would let me take over the dogs. Sometimes we had as many as twenty-three dogs on a fan hitch; we once made seventy miles in a single day. There were some cold trips that winter. We might leave Gjoa Haven at fifty below and arrive at Spence Bay, five sleeps later, at sixty below.

Takolik taught me to navigate in the north, by picking out key landmarks on the horizon for each day's travel. He showed me how to use the line of drifts in the snow to tell direction when I was travelling at night or in the dark months of winter, pointing out that the prevailing winds always packed the hard snow drifts in the same general line. Anyone crossing the land in the dark, even though unable to see any landmarks, could determine the direction of the drifts, and from that his own direction, just by dragging a foot across the drifts.

Takolik and Naigo were both models of patience with the clumsy newcomer. Perhaps they were flattered by my interest, an unusual interest for a whiteman, but still I must have seemed to them woefully ignorant. Never showing their amusement, never embarrassing me when I made dangerous errors, they slowly and carefully taught me how to master the Arctic.

It was at Gjoa Haven that I first met Father Henry, the hero of the famous book by de Poncins on the Arctic, *Kabloona*, and his partner at the mission, Father Goussart. Many an evening we would help ourselves to the sacramental wine and talk about the old days. I never tired of listening to them.

Father Henry was an old man then and had been in the Arctic for many years. He had been in the country before there were any other whites except the Hudson's Bay traders. He was a rugged man but with a face like a saint—very gentle eyes. He had come up from Churchill, travelling alone right up the east coast of Hudson's Bay to Repulse Bay, then across into Pelly Bay, where he was establishing a mission when he met de Poncins. He spent many years at Pelly Bay, then went over to Gjoa Haven to found another mission. He and Father Goussart were two of a kind, always concerned with the good of the Eskimos, visiting their sick, working tirelessly for the benefit of the people. They were splendid examples of the kind of missionaries one could admire in the Arctic. And Father Henry was one of the few missionaries, or whitemen of any calling, who had the sensibility to stay out of a shaman's way.

6
The Perry Islanders

I had been at Spence Bay for about a year when the Company asked me if I would like to go to Perry River. This was a one-man post on the Arctic shore west of Spence Bay, isolated but in good trapping country. The Company knew I liked isolation, and they knew I spoke Eskimo well enough to handle a post where I would be the only whiteman. And—they made no bones about this—they were having trouble at the Perry River post and thought I could perhaps straighten out the problem.

The 'trouble' didn't worry me, and I liked the idea of going to the Perry area, so I agreed to go. The transfer was made speedily because the incumbent manager, a young man named Neil Timberlake, wanted to get out as quickly as possible. Neil was a real gentleman, and he spoke quite good Eskimo, but somehow he had got off on the wrong foot with the people and couldn't correct an awkward situation. In February 1961 I flew into the Perry River post, the arrangement being that I would spend a month with Neil before the Company plane picked him up.

The first task the Company had given me was to find a new name for the settlement. It had originally been built right at the mouth of the Perry River and naturally had taken its name from the river. But the Perry River is muddy, and it was difficult to get fresh water there, so Neil had moved the settlement to a little island which had no English name. But then supply planes often had a hard time finding the post; the pilot would look for it at the mouth of the river where it had been, and where its name suggested it should be, when it was actually eight miles west. The Eskimo name for the island was Innaksarvik, but the Company thought that too awkward, so I suggested we should just change it to Perry Island. That was what we did.

The Company's problem at the Perry Island post proved not so easy to solve. I had already heard a few things about the Perry Island people; they had a very bad reputation. There were seventy-five or eighty Eskimos in the area trading into the post. Not only were they supposed to be a tough bunch and drink a lot, but primarily they were known as killers. A large number were believed to have murdered, and many had been involved in blood feuds in other parts of the Arctic and had come to Perry for refuge. As soon as I arrived I could easily detect people with the Garry Lake dialect, people from the Nattilik country around Gjoa Haven and Spence Bay, and people with the Copper Eskimo dialect of the western Arctic.

I was later to learn that Eskimos differentiate between murder and manslaughter. To them it is murder to kill another without provocation or any real justification. The term manslaughter is applied to killings such as those which are the result of a blood feud. There probably hasn't been a blood feud killing for ten or fifteen years now, at least none that are known to the RCMP, but in the times before the RCMP started policing the North such killings were common.

Every Eskimo I have met has been glad that the RCMP came into the north country and put an end to blood feud killings. When the mounties first arrived in the early 1930s the Eskimos called them *amaruq* (wolf), because they were so tenacious in their efforts to catch any person who had been involved in a killing. Many Eskimos who would previously have committed a vengeance killing gave it up for fear of the police.

Blood feud killings always led to much tension, anxiety and more killing, a continuous round of senseless murder. Many families fled from their homes halfway across the Arctic to escape the consequences. It was not uncommon during the course of a blood feud for eight or nine people to die in the aftermath of one murder.

One major factor that led to murder in the snowhouses was the chronic shortage of women. In the old days when a family could not support an extra child (not an unusual circumstance) they practised infanticide. Normally it was the females who were sacrificed, for the simple reason that a girl could not hunt and therefore was not as valuable to Eskimo society or to the family as a boy. A son was duty bound to provide for his aged parents when he grew up, while the services of a daughter normally passed to another family through marriage. The most common method of infanticide was to put the new-born baby out in the snow for fifteen minutes and allow it to freeze to death. As far as the Eskimos were concerned, that was not murder as long as the child had not been named.

Female infanticide, of course, left an imbalance in the population. In order to get a wife, a man often had either to steal someone else's mate or kill the husband and take over the woman. An Arctic man had to have a woman, not only for sexual purposes, but even more important, to sew up his clothing, repair his mitts, keep his boots in shape, cook and keep the house while he hunted. Life in the Arctic without a woman was rough, in fact for a hunter virtually impossible.

A single killing to win a wife could result in the death of many people. One Eskimo trapper I heard of slaughtered an entire family except the woman he wanted. The RCMP arrested him and he was hanged.

It was by no means the case that all killing ceased with the appearance of the RCMP. Few Eskimos would report a killing and often all the Eskimos would know about a murder but not the RCMP. The Eskimos looked upon a killing as a private matter. Even if his best friend were killed, the average Eskimo would not regard it as his business to interfere. However sorry he might be to see his friend dead, he would view the murder as the affair of the killer and his victim.

Execution was another form of violence. I heard of a very dangerous man, Aqsuq, who lived at Bathurst Inlet, where I was later to be posted. Aqsuq was a powerful hunter and a bully who had killed a number of men, among them the father and brother of a mild trapper named Uqsina. When Aqsuq wanted a woman he took her, and if her husband objected, Aqsuq eliminated him. He defied the entire settlement to do anything about it. Most of the men were so afraid of him that they let him get away with it for a long time. But finally the whole settlement together decided that he had to be killed. They nominated Uqsina to execute him.

The people often took this sort of collective action in Eskimo bands. They would get together and talk it over when someone created a problem, and usually the man designated to carry out the execution would be the nearest relative of the condemned man (thereby preventing the possibility of a blood feud). In this case, since Aqsuq had killed Uqsina's father and brother, it was felt that Uqsina though unrelated to him was the logical executioner.

Uqsina wasn't very happy about this, but the opportunity soon presented itself on a hunting trip. The other men told Uqsina that this was his chance, and that if he didn't do it on this trip, they would. Since Uqsina had been designated to do the job, he would bring shame on himself if he backed down, so he prepared for the killing. Aqsuq had gone back up the trail to look for a dog which had broken loose, and when he returned Uqsina was sitting in his tent with a rifle, waiting. As Aqsuq ducked down to open the flap of the tent, Uqsina shot him in the neck.

No blood feud resulted from this execution. Though Aqsuq's relatives sought vengeance against Uqsina, they found the entire settlement against them.

Uqsina was a mild man and murdered only this once, but he was no stranger to violence. His wife Anangaiq had once been married to another man, but she wanted Uqsina. Seeing her chance one day, she crept up behind her husband and shot him in the head with a rifle. She promptly married Uqsina. Although her son Iksik, one of my hunting partners, was fully aware that his mother had shot his father to go and live with another man, he was raised by Uqsina and never considered it his concern.

Among the Eskimos, a person who consistently displays a violent temper may be considered a potential killer and dangerous to the band, even if he has not hitherto killed anyone. Eskimos think of such a man as being like a grizzly bear—unpredictable—and this frightens them. When fear and dislike of such a man reach a high pitch, execution is resorted to.

I came to know several instances of this at Perry Island and Bathurst Inlet. In each case the executioner—often the man's son—did as the community bid him do, although in one case the son was greatly saddened. He didn't want to kill his father, but he had no choice. He went to his father and explained the situation, and asked, 'Do you want me to shoot you or to strangle you with a thong?' The father just as calmly accepted the community's decision and told his son, 'I'd rather you shot me, but shoot me from behind so that I don't have to look at you when you do it.' The son took his father's own rifle and shot him in the back of the head. In the mores of Eskimo society such killings, and those of people with mental aberrations, were legal executions.

In one quite recent case, a woman was believed to be practising witchcraft. It had long been clear to everyone that she was possessed by spirits, but she suddenly took to blowing her breath at people, something which was universally regarded as threatening to the band. A 'witch' was believed to put people under a spell simply by blowing on them. So out of ignorance and fear, but understandably by their own social reasoning, the people at the settlement decided the old woman must die. Her son and another man executed her. The two men were tried in Spence Bay and given suspended sentences

It was not only excess babies who might be put out of the way. Not many years ago, if a man or woman became too old and feeble to run behind the dogs and could no longer contribute to the family, his or her death might become necessary. Usually in such cases the older people themselves asked a close relative to kill them, a sort of assisted suicide. I have read that the elderly were supposed to walk off into a storm or stay behind in a deserted snowhouse, but I've never personally known of this happening. When the old folks felt that the time had come, they usually asked a favoured son to help them. The old men preferred to be shot, but the old women wanted to be strangled. The garrotting or strangling was accomplished with a loose loop in a sealskin rope dropped around the neck and breaking it.

This kind of thing was a regular feature of Eskimo life until 1949, when the federal government introduced both family allowances and the old-age pension for the Canadian Eskimos. I doubt whether the politicians of the south had any idea at the time just how much benefit they were bringing into the polar country. An extra girl baby suddenly became more of an asset than a debit and was allowed to live. An aged parent represented a financial gain instead of an impossible burden on the family.

Violence has traditionally been a natural way of life to the Eskimo, who puts a very pragmatic value on everything. So it was that caribou would first be crippled in order that they might be driven on three legs to a more convenient place of slaughter; so it was that a new-born girl would be deposited in a snowbank to freeze; so it was that the widow of a man whose head was torn off by a bear could shrug and say, '*Ayurnarmat*' (It can't be helped). I wouldn't say that life is traditionally cheap to an Eskimo, but perhaps it would be correct to suggest that in his old way of life killing came more easily to him than to the typical modern whiteman. Arctic man, after all, lived by killing. One day it would be a caribou, caught in the sights of his rifle, sent shuddering to death, next day a seal or bear, all a simple matter of an infinitesimal squeeze of a finger on the trigger. And no great difference if it was a man between the sights.

During the month I spent with Neil before taking over Perry, I got a good idea of what life would be like. Neil couldn't handle the people. I soon saw the challenge I was in for.

Regularly, about once a week, the Eskimos would come over to the post drunk. They made their own potent brew, and when they didn't have raisins to make it, they would add a spoonful of methyl hydrate to a cup of tea, or use it to spike their brew. All trading posts kept methyl hydrate in stock in those days for use as a primer to light kerosene primus stoves. When it got too cold for the kerosene to catch fire, a little methyl would fire up at any temperature. So the Eskimos had easy access to the stuff, and they had quickly learned to fire themselves up with it as well. In fact, it was very dangerous; sometimes when they got drunk they were careless about the methyl, and would take it straight. Naturally, it would then burn their guts out or cause blindness. Many Eskimos were blinded or killed in this stupid way.

The Eskimos, well intoxicated, would come across from their snowhouses to the post, ten and sometimes twenty at a time, a pretty rough bunch. Sometimes they would be in a jovial mood, but moments later they would turn ugly, and Neil was plain scared of them. They would often ask Neil for booze. We didn't stock liquor in the posts, although every manager had his own personal supply and the Eskimos knew this; but as far as I knew or saw, Neil never gave them any. Anyway, they would be drunk enough when they came in. Sometimes they would have a bottle or jug of their home brew with them and Neil would take a few drinks. Under the circumstances, it was a mistake for him to drink with these people. A wise manager didn't bully the Eskimos, but he knew he had to have their respect.

Another thing I particularly didn't approve of was that when I arrived at Perry, almost all the Eskimos, every family except two, were living right on the post. February is a good month for fur, so they should all have been out trapping, like the people at Baker and ꟶpence and other settlements. Instead, they were loafing around the post and drawing welfare—in fact, living entirely on welfare. At a small post like Perry, an isolated settlement where he was the only whiteman, the trader always had the additional duty of handling welfare for the people, on behalf of the government. This matter was something I quickly gave some thought to, feeling that it could and should be corrected—both on principle and for the people's good.

One cheering thing I did notice about the Perry Island people; there seemed to be a remarkable number of attractive young women from about eighteen to twenty-five, quite out of proportion to the number of men.

The month before Neil left was well spent. I met most of the Eskimos. And with Neil still in authority I had time to observe the difficulties and to consider what moves I might make and how I should make them. We went over the accounts and took inventory. I got a good bit of additional information over and above what Neil told me from the book on the Eskimos in the area, a kind of character reference book which each post maintains, a record as to whether a man is a good trapper, how many furs he has taken each year for the past ten years or so, how good he is at paying off his debts; in short, what kind of man he is—practically everything that might be of help not only in running the post well, but also to a new manager coming in to take over a post. Together we went over all the Eskimos in the area, and Neil pointed out the troublemakers. There seemed to be quite a few of them.

One problem at Perry was our post servant, a man named Angulaalik. A post servant in those days was an Eskimo who did the chores around the trading post: he handled the dogs, took care of them and drove them on trips for a manager who didn't know how; he skinned out the hides and baled them up; and in general did the odd jobs that were necessary and helpful to the manager, as Naigo did at Baker Lake.

As post servant at Perry, Angulaalik was paid one hundred dollars a month plus fifteen barrels of fuel oil for his house. The Company had built a house for him about a hundred yards from the post, and he and his family were the only Eskimos not living in snowhouses. On the face of it, Angulaalik's status in the community appeared to be excellent, but it was actually a rather touchy situation for him. He had been in charge of the post at Perry when it had no resident white manager and was administered as an outpost from Cambridge Bay. Then, two years before I arrived, he had killed a local man called Utuittuq. For the Company that was enough, particularly since the people in the area grew increasingly afraid of Angulaalik after Utuittuq's death, and that wasn't good for business.

I found it hard to believe that Angulaalik was a murderer. He was a small man with a charming smile, the kind of smile that flashes from a toothpaste advertisement. Neil described him as a fine trapper and hunter, a man of very strong will, which he easily imposed on the other Eskimos, a man accustomed to having things his own way. I knew that he was strong for his stature, but basically he seemed a gentle man. Yet I was warned that Angulaalik and his family were the basis of much of the trouble at Perry.

An RCMP corporal later told me that the force knew of five killings Angulaalik had been involved in, and I heard higher numbers from other sources. I documented a few killings myself, but some had to be classed as doubtful because they took place so long ago that no one could say for sure who had struck the fatal blow. We did, however, establish beyond question that he was one of two men involved on several occasions when there had been a killing.

One of the favourite techniques among Eskimos of disposing of an enemy used to require two killers working together. The pair would come up on either side of their victim, seize both his arms, lift him into the air and then thrust the victim's own snowknife in under the armpit. Efficient and virtually foolproof, I was told. But the Utuittuq killing had been a sloppy, almost accidental, casual thing, as death often is in the Arctic. I eventually heard a detailed account of this killing from Utuittuq's daughter, Niksaaktuq.

At the time of the killing, Perry River was an outpost of the Hudson's Bay Company trading post at Cambridge Bay. Angulaalik was running it for the Company, so he was a man of considerable importance in the tribe. A young Eskimo named Iqquk, aged thirteen, had been stealing from the store. Angulaalik got to know about this and bawled him out, but Iqquk wouldn't stop. Angulaalik warned him there would be real trouble if he stole anything more.

A few days later the Eskimos held a drum dance. When Angulaalik arrived Iqquk's father, Utuittuq, a big tough man much bigger than Angulaalik, jumped on Angulaalik for giving his son a bad time.

Everyone had been drinking home brew, so when Utuittuq fell on Angulaalik it looked as if a dangerous fight was in the offing. To everyone's surprise Angulaalik backed down, a most unusual and difficult thing for him to do since he was boss in Perry River. He quietly left the party and returned to his own house. Utuittuq followed him out but stopped short of entering Angulaalik's home. Eskimos believe that a man killed in his own house will surely haunt the killer.

Utuittuq stood in the snow in some wonder as he watched Angulaalik retire into his house. After a while Angulaalik returned to the party and again Utuittuq, now a bit tighter and more confident of himself, loudly tried to start an argument with him. Once again Angulaalik went back to his own house. But he wanted to dance and to enjoy the home brew, so he kept going back hoping that Utuittuq would tire of bothering him.

On one of his trips back to his own house, Angulaalik picked up a small pocketknife with a three-inch blade and stuck it down the front of his pants. When he entered the party Utuittuq came after him again, and Angulaalik pulled the knife. Utuittuq sneered at him. He made a grab at Angulaalik, and Angulaalik stabbed him ineffectually. Utuittuq was wearing heavy skins and the knife just nicked him on the upper left arm. It looked as if Utuittuq was going to get the best of Angulaalik, so the smaller man tried again, and again failed to get the knife into Utuittuq even though he made a thrust directly at Utuittuq's heart.

Utuittuq was a strong man, and he wrestled Angulaalik nearly off balance; then Angulaalik stepped right up to his tormentor and shoved the knife into Utuittuq's stomach, slitting him open like a hunter gutting a caribou. It wasn't a deep cut into the vitals, because the knife blade was too short, but it slit open the entire abdominal wall. Niksaaktuq related with typical Eskimo graphicness how her father just stood there, shocked, looking down at the blood spurting between his fingers as he pressed his hands against the long wound. Then he took his hands away and all his intestines fell out with a whoosh, just as when a hunter guts a caribou and his knife punctures the membrane around the stomach.

Then Utuittuq panicked and ran out of the house screaming and falling over his own trailing intestine. No one wanted to touch him; the blood of a dying man is taboo, and the others were afraid to help him. Besides, most of them were pretty drunk by then, and didn't want to become involved in a murder for fear another blood feud might start. Some of the Eskimos told me that it wasn't a bad cut, certainly not a fatal wound if only Utuittuq hadn't panicked. They thought that he had actually killed himself by panicking and messing up his own entrails. Niksaaktuq led her father back into the house and tried to do the best she could. He died early in the morning.

Angulaalik was truly sad. '*Tuqutani qiavagaa,*' it was said of him (he cried often for the one he killed). Utuittuq had been regarded as a good man, not a troublemaker, but he had hit the home brew hard that night.

Angulaalik was arrested by the RCMP and stood trial before the Honourable Justice John H. Sissons, the famed first circuit court judge of the NWT, and was let off. Niksaaktuq, who might have been understandably prejudiced, and some of the other Eskimos believed that he was let off because he was the trader, because he had powerful friends and money. Eskimos often think of whitemen as being able to break the law with impunity in the Eskimos' country.

Others said that no one dared testify against Angulaalik because they were afraid of causing a blood feud. They were afraid that if someone testified against Angulaalik and that testimony led to a conviction with capital punishment, it would have been the duty of Angulaalik's nearest blood relative to take vengeance. Some of Angulaalik's earlier killings had been the result of blood feuds, and his father had been killed in just such a dispute.

Neil suggested that the real trouble with Angulaalik was that he simply couldn't take the reduction in status from outpost manager to post servant, and felt the loss of face very keenly. As manager, he had been the big shot of the area, and suddenly he had been reduced to the status of a whiteman's hired hand. Fiercely proud as he was, he was proving his independence by never turning up for work in the mornings. Understanding this, I nevertheless thought it was only right and proper that Angulaalik should work if he expected to be paid, and I intended to make an issue of this immediately, so that not only Angulaalik but all the Eskimos would know just who ran the post.

Early in March a Company charter plane stopped in overnight to pick up Neil. On the afternoon of the plane's arrival, I made a point of speaking privately to Angulaalik, telling him that I was in charge now and that I wanted him to be at work at nine o'clock the following morning.

The plane left with Neil about eight-thirty the next morning, and quite a number of the Eskimos came to see the plane off. As it disappeared over the horizon I was relieved at the prospect of being on my own at last and fully in charge of the post. At the same time I couldn't help reflecting that there was no other whiteman closer than Cambridge Bay, a good two hundred miles to the northwest. I was alone with a group of Eskimos who had reputations for lawlessness unmatched in the Arctic.

Most of the Eskimos came into the post store to trade after the plane left, but Angulaalik hadn't shown up as I had requested, and then I realized he had not been among the group that gathered for the plane's departure. It was just nine o'clock, so I sent one of the Eskimos up to Angulaalik's house with the instruction, 'Tell Angulaalik to come right now to the post. We're going to start work.'

Angulaalik didn't show up. At about eleven o'clock, I sent another man to his house. I told this courier to say to Angulaalik: 'If you don't get down to the post right away, then you're no longer working for the Hudson's Bay Company.'

Angulaalik finally deigned to appear, all toothy smile as though nothing at all had happened. I jumped him on the spot, in front of everyone. This was something I didn't like doing, but I knew that in a situation like this I had to be firm from the beginning. So I set into Angulaalik with a first-rate tongue lashing, and told him if he wanted to work for the Company and earn his hundred dollars a month and his fuel oil, then he had to be at the post every morning at nine o'clock.

All the other Eskimos stood round, watching and listening in silence, but they were looking sidelong at each other and obviously wondering how Angulaalik would take this. Angulaalik's wife was standing beside him, so it was particularly embarrassing for him. When I had finished laying down the law to him, I looked around for the most lowly chore I could give him, and ordered him over to the house to fill the kitchen stove with fuel oil.

Angulaalik hardly said a word. He was jittering with nervousness. He had clearly not expected such a confrontation, and I'm sure he hadn't realized till then how well I could speak and understand Eskimo. Irvana, his wife, stayed in the background.

Angulaalik went into the house and filled the stove, and then I told him to go into my living room, and I quickly finished trading with the remaining Eskimos. Then I went over to my house, and with just the two of us there I calmly and quietly emphasized that I expected him to be at the post at nine o'clock every morning. I explained carefully that if he came late, he would be docked a dollar and a half for each hour. I dropped my outraged tone because I had already embarrassed him enough to last for six months.

But Angulaalik was determined to show his independence, and he frequently turned up late for work. Every time he did so I would tell him, 'All right, I've docked you two dollars today,' or three and a half, or four dollars, or whatever it came to. I wanted him to understand that while his business was his own, if he wanted to work for the Company, then I called the tune and the Company came first.

At the end of the month Angulaalik wanted to buy some trade goods for his wife and family, but out of all his month's wages he had only fifteen dollars coming to him. I showed him the books, the record I had kept of the times he came in late or not at all, explaining once more that fifteen dollars was all he had earned and I was not going to pay him unless he worked. That finally did it. The shock of having his hundred dollars dwindle to fifteen put the point across to him. From then on he showed up at nine. Then I was able to explain to him that if I had no tasks for him, he was free to return home, but only after checking in with me first.

Meantime, while I was dealing with Angulaalik as an individual, there was the annoying fact that an entire settlement full of healthy hunters and trappers was on welfare. They had drawn their welfare ration just before I arrived, and had all the supplies they needed for a while so there was little I could do. But I wanted to get those people out trapping. I called a meeting of all the people living in the settlement, asking them to come over to the post. As could have been expected, there were only two families out trapping.

I said, 'Look, you've just had a ration; you're all well off for food. Now I want you to know that you get no more welfare here.' I scolded them: 'You're not doing anything but sitting around the post. You're making home brew and causing trouble. Now I'm not a missionary nor a policeman: if you want to drink, go ahead and drink, I don't care. But if you drink, don't come to my post. Don't cause any trouble for me—get out and go to work.'

With that warning I cut them off welfare, and naturally there was a lot of complaining about that. I heard plenty of comment from some of the Eskimos, especially from those Neil had warned me were the troublemakers. That particular bunch kept on coming over to the post and made no move to go out trapping. They kept on making home brew and getting drunk, and every now and then a few would stagger into my house or the post. I would politely ask them to leave, and if they didn't I would escort them outside—never anything violent. I just took hold of them gently but firmly and put them out, saying, 'Off you go now; come and visit me when you're sober.' Truly I enjoyed having them visit me, but I didn't want them drunk.

They kept up their brewing, and then began to get low on food and other necessities. They started coming in and asking for welfare. 'Okay,' I said. 'We've still got a few weeks of trapping season left. You get some fur, and I'll trade with you. Then you can have anything you want.'

They said: 'We've got nothing to go trapping with—no food, no supplies.'

I reminded them: 'I told you two weeks ago to get out and trap; you still had food left then; you still had your welfare supplies, and you wouldn't go. Now I'm showing you I mean what I say. And I say, go and earn your own living.'

They didn't like it, but there was nothing else for it; they had to go trapping, and finally they all went except Angulaalik, who stayed around the post to earn his money there, even though he was one of the best trappers in the whole region, and was permitted by the Company to go trapping whenever he liked.

With all of them out on the land we at last began to get some fur, the first fur in any quantity for months at the Perry Island post. When the trapping ended, I still wouldn't let them hang around the post and revert to their previous state. I wasn't playing the heavy-handed dictator, but I suggested to them in a friendly way that it would be better for everyone if they kept up their good work and went after seal now that the white fox season was finished.

However, they were still drinking heavily after I had been at the post a couple of months. I decided that my easiest move was just to cut off the sale of raisins, with which they had been making their brew. There was still a lot of trouble in the settlement: there were fights, and some people, women included, had been beaten up, and a few times families came across and asked me for protection. I warned them that if they kept on getting drunk by using methyl hydrate, I would cut that off too. 'You'll just have to start your primus stoves with scraps of paper,' I told them. Still, even this didn't lead to much less drinking.

I remember one typical incident that occurred when two families came in one evening. I had invited them over because they had told me they didn't like to join in the heavy drinking when Angulaalik and his son-in-law, Tupilliqqut, and the other toughs in the settlement cooked up a brew. They were always invited over and were afraid to refuse.

This was the situation when Paniuyaq and Ulikattak and their wives visited me that particular evening. We sat around and ate hardtack biscuits, drank tea, and talked, a typical quiet, social evening in the Arctic. About nine thirty I went out to the shed to turn the power plant off. It took me ten or fifteen minutes to complete the chore.

When I returned to the house I found Paniuyaq and Ulikattak, their wives and a couple of their kids all standing with their backs up against the wall of the living room, terrified. Three men had come in—Angulaalik, Tupilliqqut and another called Uqalitaaraaluk, all three of them somewhat drunk. Three of the worst troublemakers in the settlement.

I said: 'You look as if you've been drinking.'

Tupilliqqut, a small man but powerfully built and still in his prime at forty-five, answered back with a cocky air: 'Sure we've been drinking, nothing wrong with that.'

'No,' I said, 'there's nothing wrong with that. If you want to drink in your home, go right ahead. But I'm telling you now that if you want to drink, you might as well leave here and come back when you're sober.'

Tupilliqqut became angry and snapped back at me, 'We're not scared of you.' He added, 'Angulaalik's not scared of you either, and he's killed lots of men.' Angulaalik nodded in agreement.

I knew that this was going to be a real test, and that if I backed down from these three men I might as well leave the post. The Eskimos would run over me just as they had run over Neil. I actually felt no fear—there was nothing very dramatic in the situation. I just knew I was right, and I knew I could make the three of them buckle under.

I went right up to Angulaalik, face to face, and challenged him. 'Do you want to kill me?'

Angulaalik dropped his head a bit; he paused for a second, and then said, 'No, no, *mitaanginnaqtunga* (I'm just joking); I don't want to kill anyone; *mitaanginnaqtunga*.'

'Okay, that's fine.' And I turned to Tupilliqqut. 'How about you?'

'No, no, I'm just joking too,' he said. 'I don't want to make any trouble at all.'

'Well, that's fine. I don't go looking for trouble, but when I tell you to leave my post, I want you to leave.'

Then I turned to Uqalitaaraaluk. I was going to ask him the same question when Tupilliqqut butted in and said, 'Uqaak, don't talk back to the whiteman. We don't want any trouble with the whiteman.'

So I said, 'Okay then, the three of you go away now, and come back when you're sober.' I turned to Angulaalik. 'Angulaalik, I want you here at nine o'clock in the morning.'

This got Angulaalik's back up. 'Hmm...well, I don't have to work for the Hudson's Bay Company. I can go trapping.'

'If you want to go trapping, go right ahead,' I said. 'If you don't work for the Company, we won't have to pay you, and I can easily get someone else.' Then I put in a sharp dig: 'We can get a younger man, too.'

This made Angulaalik pretty chippy, and he looked right at me and said, 'I don't have to work for the Company. When I was trapping at McAlpine Lake, my sled was always full of fur. I got lots of foxes; I had so many that they used to spill off my sled.' I found out later that this was true; he was a tremendous trapper.

'You go ahead to the Adelaide Peninsula, Angulaalik,' I returned. 'At least then you won't be bothering me here. You're more trouble than you're worth.'

This stung him and he fired back: 'Okay, okay; you're the whiteman; you can say anything you like. I'll go back tonight and I'll burn my house and then I'll go trapping.'

The three of them were standing at the door by this time, and beside them was a counter that had some drawers. I yanked open one of the drawers, pulled out a box of matches, and handed them to Angulaalik. 'Here!' I said, and automatically his hand came out. I shoved the box of matches in his hand. 'Go ahead. Burn your house down, go trapping.'

He was so startled to have his bluff called that he dropped the box of matches and hung his head down. Then he smiled, but didn't look me in the eye, and said: 'No, I'm just joking, you know. I've had a bit to drink, and I just feel happy. I don't really want to burn my house down.'

I sent them on their way and that was that. Paniuyak and Ulikattak and their wives had been watching all the time, and I felt a moment of real exultation because I knew that they would tell everybody. This incident would go right around the settlement.

Several people came straight round to the post next day. They immediately opened the conversation: 'I hear you had a bit of a run-in with Angulaalik and his friends last night.'

'Yes, nothing much.'

Soon they got around to asking, 'Do you mind if we visit you next time they cook up a brew?'

'Not at all,' I replied, 'you come any time. Then you don't have to get drunk like the others.' I explained to them, 'I'm a Scotsman and I've always liked a drink once in a while; there's nothing wrong with having a drink. But when you drink too much you get into fights; your women are beaten up—that's no way to be living.' I pounded my point in. 'When you drink all the time, no one goes trapping. You're just bumming, living just like children, off the government and the whiteman.' I knew I was pushing my luck a bit, but I felt I had them on the run.

It seemed to me that Perry Island was very much like a sea-port town in that it attracted outcasts from all over the Arctic. Many of the Eskimos had come there for safety after killing someone, fleeing from possible revenge at the hands of their victims' relatives. When I began to get the details about their backgrounds I found there was only one man, Paniuyaq, who hadn't committed at least one killing. And Angulaalik was indeed known to have killed a lot of men. It seemed that after humiliating him in front of the other Eskimos it was a good idea to be careful. He was clearly nervous in my presence and I sometimes had the feeling that if I turned my back, he might hit me over the head or put a knife into me. The only whiteman in a settlement simply doesn't take any chances; he is a fool if he isn't cautious with a bunch like the Perry Islanders.

At the same time, however, I didn't want to miss any chance to get them back on the beam, so I had to try putting down the bullies, jacking up the laggards, cutting off brew supplies and welfare funds.

At any rate, so far I had been successful. The Eskimos went trapping, and when they returned to the post they would spend only a day or so purchasing supplies and then go back out. They would come into my house, and the drinking seemed to be on the decrease. There was suddenly a tremendous difference in the atmosphere of the post that was very encouraging.

Additionally, there were all the chores that every trader has at an Arctic post. As soon as the snow disappeared we had our painting to do. All through the Arctic the Company's buildings are painted the same, trim white buildings with red roofs. Every winter the storms blow hard against the buildings, and the snow is almost entirely frost granules like blowing sand, scouring the paint right off the buildings. Every spring, before the fly season came along in June, we would have to re-paint all exteriors. There was the dock to rebuild too, steps to repair and paint, and so forth. On top of that, I wanted to clear away a jumble of rocks and boulders around the post.

Even Angulaalik was out sealing by then, and I was on my own. I did go out to the sealing camps a couple of times to visit the hunters because they were doing a very poor job on the sealskins. They didn't scrape them properly, so the skins had the black inner epidermis on them, and they were oily. I had to train the Perry people to do a better job on the sealskins the way the Spence Bay people did them, really clean them to leave a creamy white skin. This would bring a better price to the hunters themselves.

While I was alone at the settlement I took good advantage of my time. During the daytime there was the work around the post, and at night I put together my notes on the Eskimo language, brought them up to date, and wrote them up in orderly form.

But it wasn't all work. I went out with the Eskimos seal hunting by canoe after the ice went out, just as I had at Spence Bay, and sometimes I would take my canoe out alone on a calm day. I would go out a few miles from the post and then sit there and drift, sometimes as much as eight or ten miles from the post, on beautiful calm, blue seas, with a brilliant sky, no clouds, and twenty-four hours of sunlight. The Perry River region was splendid goose country. I would just lie back in my canoe and watch the birds—geese flying overhead, swans, ducks, loons—the place was one of the greatest nesting grounds on the North American continent.

So summer passed, without any untoward incidents.

7
A Fight for Life

In the fall of 1961 a man named Uakuak returned to Perry Island. Uakuak was Angulaalik's stepson, but he had been raised by Angulaalik as though he were actually his own flesh and blood. A powerful, aggressive man of thirty-five years or so, he had been away for a year working at a DEW line site. I knew his reputation as a true Eskimo bully, the toughest of them all at Perry. He was not a lazy man, not one to live off welfare. He was a topnotch hunter and trapper and provided well for his family, but he was one of those natural rebels among men who have to challenge the order of things. If someone put up a sign that said no smoking, Uakuak would lean against it and smoke. When he came back to Perry and moved in with Angulaalik, I resolved to keep an eye on him.

Uakuak brought a hoard of rum with him from the DEW line, and the Eskimos at Perry went on a drinking spree again. He also brought back a lot of yeast cakes, something we no longer carried in the store because the Eskimos didn't make whiteman's bread, just bannock. Neil Timberlake had stocked it because he made regular bread (as I had done at previous posts), and he had given the Eskimos yeast for their brew, but that was another thing I had promptly cut off. They polished off the rum in short order and got going again making home brew with Uakuak's yeast cakes.

Uakuak, of course, had heard about me from the other Eskimos. I had been at Perry for seven or eight months, and it was now the fall of the year, just before freeze-up. One evening after I had finished supper, around seven o'clock, I was in my house washing up the dishes. Uakuak and his wife came in. She was a nice girl, about eight months pregnant at the time and very much intimidated by Uakuak. They were both pretty drunk. Uakuak was carrying a bottle of home brew, and he wanted to give me a drink.

I declined. 'No thanks, I don't want a drink. I don't drink very much. I don't care much for home brew, anyway, because it can make people go blind.'

Uakuak would talk normally for a while, then he would turn belligerent. He was not drunk enough to have lost control of himself, but he was drunk enough to show a mean streak. He said: 'I hear you have been pushing people out of the house when they come to visit you. I hear if they've had a drink or two you just push them out.'

'I don't push them out unless they won't go when I ask them,' I replied.

He stuck his chest out and said, 'Well, I'm not going to go.'

I thought that perhaps I could talk him out of this with my usual line: 'Look, why don't you just go home and finish off your drink there and then come back to visit me when you're sober?'

'No, I want some whisky.'

We got into a childish argument. I said, 'You're not getting any whisky from me, I don't have any whisky.'

'Well, you've got liquor here.'

'No, I don't have any liquor.'

'I know you do.' He looked hard at me. 'People don't like you, and particularly me—I don't like you at all. I used to come here when the last manager was here, and he was a good man. He always gave me whisky, and sometimes he even gave me a bottle to take back so my wife and I could drink it at home.'

'Well, that was his business, but managers are different. The last manager might have given you all sorts of things, but I'm not the last manager, and I'm not giving you any whisky.'

Then he got mad. 'Don't talk to me like that,' he said.

I flared up a little myself. 'You're in my house. How would you feel if I came over to your house and started talking to you like that? You wouldn't like it.'

'I'd give a man whisky if he came to my house.'

'Well, that's your business. I'm not giving you any here . . . .'

So you might as well go now.'

He braced himself. 'If you want me to go out of the house, put me out. You come and take me and put me out. Push me out like you pushed out those other people.'

I tried to be patient with him. 'I don't want to push you out.' I just thought he was in an argumentative mood, as drunks so often are. I turned away from him as if the argument were finished, and went back to the stove where I kept the dish towels. I was going to pick up my dish towel again and finish the dishes I had been washing when Uakuak and his wife came in. But Uakuak leapt in front of me and shoved his arms out wide and wouldn't let me pass.

So I said to him, '*Asivarit*,' which is a polite request. 'Excuse me.'

He crouched as though to spring at me and snapped, 'I'm not letting you past.'

I was beginning to get fed up, and a little angry, and I snapped right back at him, '*Taillait*—Get out of the way!' and no politeness about that.

He moved one step aside, and when I pushed past him and got the dish towel, he sneered the equivalent of 'You really think you're quite a man, don't you!' He moved around and stood in front of me again. 'Come on, I want to see you put me out. You've put out a lot of people. People have told me about you, and nobody in this place likes you.'

He was daring me, but I held my temper. 'I'm here to do a job. I want everyone to be friendly. I hunt and trap with the people, and visit their houses. If a man's wife is sick, I come and help her and give her medicine. If someone gets hurt, I help patch them up.'

He gave ground grudgingly and admitted, 'Well, some people like you, but not all.'

I said, 'It isn't good to argue like this. You come back, you and your wife, when you are sober, and we'll have a visit.'

At this his belligerence returned, and he cried, 'Try me! You're scared of me—come on, try me!' He stuck his face up close to mine and said, 'Come on, take me up like this,' and he grabbed himself by the shirt front and repeated his challenge, 'Come on, take me like this and put me out.'

I said, 'No, I'm not going to take you,' and by this time I was nervous and wary of a real fight coming. He was a big man, as tall as I and very broad in the chest, hard as a bear. I knew he was a powerful man.

His wife hadn't opened her mouth once all this time. She stood there and watched. I thought she might be able to talk sense to him, so I turned to her. 'Tell your husband to go home and not make trouble here.'

That was a mistake and I should have known better; it made him furious. 'Don't talk to my wife,' he said, and the next thing I knew he had jumped forward and grabbed me by the wrist and throat and thrown me back against the wall.

My blood up, I let fly and caught him flush in the mouth. I don't think he was expecting it. All the time I had been backing down, or so it seemed to him. He had been challenging me and daring me all the way, and it was natural for him to interpret my reluctance as fear. But when he threw me like that, as far as I was concerned we were through talking.

He went flying and fell over on his back. I jumped on top of him, and as I was kneeling over him I hit him once more, another good one.

When the action began his wife started up and cried out to me, 'Don't fight him, don't fight him. He'll kill you!'

I paid no attention to her, because I had him down, though my stomach was churning, all knotted and heaving. I knew this man was dangerous, and all around were dangerous people; it was a nerve-wracking experience. I realized there was no way I could get out of it; after he grabbed me, I knew I was in for a full-scale battle.

When I struck him, the blow split his mouth. He lay back on the floor as though he couldn't quite believe he was there with me on top of him. He licked his lip where it was cut, and said in amazement, 'You made me bleed.'

'Yeah,' I said, 'but you started it.'

He licked his lip again. Then he announced, 'Well, I'm going to get up and go home,' in a strangely quiet voice.

'That's fine. If you don't make any trouble for me, I won't make any for you.' I felt relieved, and yet I still waited to make sure he meant it. It seemed somehow too easy. Anyway, I certainly didn't want to get involved in a real fight.

There is an enormous difference between fighting an Eskimo and fighting a whiteman. When two Eskimos get into conflict with each other, invariably—ninety-nine times out of a hundred—one man will back down right away and say, 'I don't want to fight you. I'm afraid of you.' Eskimos are not ashamed or afraid to admit this. Obviously, if one man is bigger and tougher than the other, there is no shame in backing down; it's simply the wiser move. Another major difference is that a whiteman may say, 'I'm going to kill you,' but of course he rarely means it literally. When an Eskimo gets into a fight, he means it and the fight is total. It isn't a matter of shoving or wrestling around or even just trying to inflict some damage. In most cases an Eskimo fight will end in a killing.

I got up off Uakuak and stepped back a bit. He at once jumped to his feet and made a lunge for me. Fortunately, I was wary enough for him not to catch me off guard, and just as in a movie I automatically swung and hit him at exactly the moment he jumped me, catching him flush on the side of the jaw. His head snapped round so hard that his neck made a sharp cracking noise, and he went down as if he had been pole-axed. The force of his attack combined with my blow knocked him cold.

My heart leapt into my throat; when I heard his neck crack I thought I had killed him. My hands and arms were shaking and I felt sick. I knelt across him again, shook him and slapped his cheeks and listened for his heartbeat. I had visions of being hauled up in court for killing an Eskimo. Then after what seemed an interminable moment, he drew in a gasp of breath. I was so relieved I could have kissed him.

He lay there on the floor, and as consciousness returned he said, '*Sinnaktulirama*—I feel dreamy.'

Still a bit shaky myself, I said, 'No, you're not dreaming.'

He turned his head and looked up at me with a blank expression, as if he were stone cold sober. In a perfectly calm, almost casual voice he said, 'I'm going to go home, and I'm going to get my rifle, and I'm going to come back here and kill you.' His lack of expression and complete lack of menace somehow made it all the more terrifying.

I was properly nervous by now, but I wasn't going to back down. I kept my voice just as low and replied, 'Okay. You get your rifle, and if you come back here with it I'm going to kill you first.'

He said, 'We'll see,' and turned to his wife. 'Help me up.' I stepped towards him to give him a hand.

'Get back! Get back from me!' he shouted. 'Don't put a hand on me.'

I stood back a bit, and he started to rise. He got up onto his haunches, then suddenly he kicked out with his feet and caught me in the pit of the stomach and knocked me back against the stove. I put both arms back to break my fall. I was in my shirt sleeves with cuffs rolled up and the stove was blazing hot. I ended up sprawled over the stove, both arms burned from elbow to wrist.

I came off raging mad. I went at Uakuak and smashed him up against the wall and really went to town on him. I kept him in one spot, pounding his face again and again. He had no chance to recover his wits or strength. I slammed him repeatedly, kneed him and kicked him as if we were in a dockfront brawl. I was scared stiff that he would overpower me or reach for a kitchen knife if he had the chance. I was fighting with the strength of fear and the muscle of desperation.

There was a patch of blood on the floor and splatters all over one wall and even on the ceiling. All I suffered were the burns on my arms and some skinned knuckles; Uakuak never actually hit me at all. He would try to punch at me, but like most Eskimos he wasn't a boxer or a fighter with his fists. Eskimos wrestle or use a knife or gun. He was twice as strong as I was, and if he had got me down he would have strangled me. Perhaps my fright gave me extra strength. I felt I was literally fighting for my life.

I was hitting him with my right hand, so hard and so often that I could feel it beginning to weaken. I switched to my left hand, not nearly as effective, but enough to keep the initiative.

Uakuak began to sag against the wall as I kept knocking away at him, but once more he started to recover and pull himself upright, so I let fly again with my left hand. I slammed the side of his forehead; he went flying sideways, half-knocked, half-slipped over to one side, and caught his head on the kitchen counter. The sharp edge whacked him right on the temple, and he was out cold again.

This time I didn't wait for him to come round. I flung open the two doors to the storm porch, the inner kitchen door and the storm door, grabbed Uakuak by the feet, and dragged him out onto the porch. Then I took his wife by the arm and shoved her out with him—I wasn't feeling at all like being polite. I picked up Uakuak's bottle of home brew and threw it after him.

I figured that Uakuak was going to come right back in, fighting mad; he was already coming to with the shock of the cool air. I slammed both doors shut and latched the inside kitchen door. I raced into my bedroom where I snatched my shotgun and two shells. Sure enough, I could hear Uakuak on the porch, and heard him pounding on the door as I raced back into the kitchen. Uakuak had smashed the window panes of the two doors and was reaching through, trying to get at the bolt on the inside of the door, his arms covered with blood from the broken glass.

I shoved the two shells into the gun and clicked the double barrel closed. When he heard the clicking of the gun, Uakuak froze.

'Get your hands away from that door or I'll kill you right now!' I cried. I do believe I was scared enough to pull the trigger. He took one look and shot off the porch.

The whole thing, the argument and the fight, had started around seven o'clock when Uakuak and his wife had come in; it was ten past nine when they were pushed out. I noticed the time—and that I was shaking like a leaf.

It was dark outside, of course. I saw Uakuak pass by my house in the light from the windows, and then he was swallowed up in the darkness. I didn't dare go outside; I just kept watching through the window. I saw Angulaalik's door open and Uakuak and his wife go in.

I knew the Eskimos had been having a party at Angulaalik's house. As soon as they were inside, I dashed over to the store. We never locked the store, but I ran over to close it up in case the Eskimos decided to help themselves to the guns. I loaded up a 30-30 rifle, my .22, and another one besides. I was sure that since I had beaten the tar out of Angulaalik's stepson, some of his friends would certainly retaliate. They were drunk, and they would be angry, and they were quite capable of killing me.

I flew around the house; I put the easy chair up against the front door, pulled down all the blinds and curtains, and doused the lights. I took an axe and my ice dagger and placed them on top of my bookcase beside the door. This would do as a starter.

Then I got on the radio. I knew I was in a serious situation, and wanted to know I could have help if I needed it. I called the

DOT in Cambridge Bay and asked for the RCMP. I explained that I had had a fight with Uakuak and had laid him out a few times. I told them there had been no serious injuries—yet.

'If he comes through that door with a rifle, I'm going to kill him,' I said. 'I wanted you to know; if something does happen, that's how it started.' Whether I ended up in a graveyard or in court, I wanted someone to know what had happened.

The RCMP officer tried to calm me down. 'Take it easy, Duncan. We know this man Uakuak, and he's a rough character, but whatever you do, don't shoot anyone unless you're in physical danger of being killed yourself, unless you're acting in self-defence.' He went on, 'We've a plane on hand, and we'll be down first thing in the morning, as soon as there's light. So just take it easy. The DOT will monitor your frequency all night; if you have any trouble, give them a call.'

The house was completely dark except for the transmitter's red light, indicating that the radio was on. I was as prepared as I could be, but never felt so alone in my life. It was windy that night, just enough to obscure the sounds outside. I would peek out round the side of the curtain and look towards Angulaalik's house. The moon dodged in and out of clouds, and shadows kept catching my eye. I was sure the whole settlement was about to attack; the worst fates came into my head, my imagination working overtime.

An hour or so passed. The rifle, loaded and cocked, lay across my lap. All of a sudden, I heard a bang at the door. I leapt straight up along with my jangled nerves and palpitating heart! There was nobody to be seen, but I was sure my murderers had come to carry out the deed. In the silence that followed I listened to my heart thumping, then footsteps moving off the porch, then ominous silence returned.

Someone testing me out, I thought, seeing if I was ready.

A couple of hours went by with no more visitors or suspicious noises. I was becoming tired, and went into the bedroom. My bed stood against one wall, right opposite a window. Outside, beyond the window, the ground sloped upwards away from the house. In that bed I would be a sitting duck. All the Eskimos had been in the house countless times; they all knew my bed was right in line with the window. I picked up the pillows and one or two blankets, and put them down in a corner of the living room—a corner without a view, you can be sure. Lying down on this makeshift bed with the shotgun between my knees, I tried to calm down.

It must have been midnight or one o'clock. I could hear the radio humming and buzzing, so I turned it off, hoping I would have enough time to reach Cambridge Bay before anyone could break into the house. The last thing I did before settling down was to take several empty tin cans from the garbage and stand them one on top of another in front of each door. Should I fall asleep while someone tried to ease his way into the house, they would act as an alarm.

I had dozed off for perhaps an hour or so when I was awakened by a banging noise on the side of the house. Once again I came bolt upright, shotgun in hand. It sounded as if someone was banging his hand against the wall of the house, I couldn't imagine why. The noise was repeated several times at intervals, but since nothing happened after that, I went off to sleep again. To my annoyance, I discovered next day that I had been frightened half out of my wits by a broken clothesline flapping in the wind.

When I next awoke I heard a *chuk-chuk-chuk* off beyond the house. By now it was six in the morning and there was just enough light to see Angulaalik and Uakuak, their wives and children and a pile of gear taking off out towards the bay. That was the last I saw of most of them until Christmas.

The first man to come across to the post next morning was Tupilliqqut, Angulaalik's son-in-law. He came into the house and looked around. He took it all in, the blood on the wall, the floor and the ceiling, and grinned knowingly at me.

'*Tuktutpit?*' ('Did you kill a caribou?')

'I had a fight with Uakuak.'

'Yes, we heard about it. We were in Angulaalik's house last night when Uakuak came in.' To my surprise, Tupilliqqut sounded pleased. He said, 'We were in there last night when he came in, and his face was a mess of bruises, and he had two big black eyes, and there was blood all over him.' He added, 'The people are glad.'

While I listened in astonishment he went on, 'The people are glad because Uakuak was such a bully. He took my son and beat him once.'

An old woman had come in, and she told me, '*Quanaqquq.*' ('You make me feel grateful.') And from everything I heard that day, it seemed that Uakuak had long been the real bully of the settlement. People were greatly relieved that he had at last been cut down to size.

Uakuak never came back while I was at Perry Island, I suppose because he had lost face in that fight. Angulaalik returned to Perry with his family just before Christmas and said Uakuak had gone on to Cambridge Bay.

When Angulaalik did reappear after his long absence, he seemed quite nervous when he walked into the post a few days later. I asked him where he had been.

'I went trapping down in the Perry River country,' he said.

'I hope you don't expect any pay, since you haven't been working here for a long time.'

'Oh no,' he said. 'I wouldn't expect that.'

The battle with Uakuak was never mentioned between us, then or ever.

Just after the fight, the Arctic divisional manager for the Company and the general manager of the Company came through the area on an inspection trip. While they had been in Gjoa Haven they had heard of the incident. Since all posts in the Arctic are tuned in on the radio, everyone knew of the time I had had that night. The RCMP had called me next morning to find out what had happened, and to tell me that a plane was ready if it was needed. I was happy to be able to tell them that it was all over and that I was still in one piece.

The Company's Arctic divisional manager came to Perry Island to see me. 'Would you like another post?' he asked. 'I know this is a rough place. Neil Timberlake and the manager before him had trouble here. If you want to get out. . . .'

I thanked him, but declined the offer. Those first few months had been tough. I had been hard with the Perry people, with those who tried to make trouble. But when things settled down I didn't have one incident in four years. I honestly grew to love the Perry Island people, and will always think of them as the best people I ever worked with in the Arctic.

It was the Perry Islanders who took me most into their confidence. It was among them that I was accepted as an Eskimo. At Perry Island I put together my first dogteam and learned to travel with dogs on my own. It was there that I became fluent in Eskimo, when I realized that I had answered back in Eskimo for the first time without having to translate it in my mind. It was there that I saw and came to understand shamanism and witchcraft; learned and shared in many ancient Eskimo ways; was taught to harpoon seal in the old way, and to hunt caribou.

After Uakuak left, the people all went out trapping, and before the winter was out they were turning in more fur than posts three times as large; we had it good from then on. And one of the best results—we never distributed another penny of welfare while I was at Perry. The drunkenness and rowdiness came to a stop, everyone got out and worked and the place revived itself.

At Perry I was on my own a good deal of the time. I was my own boss, and I pursued my trapping in earnest. I had trapped before with Naigo at Baker Lake and with Takolik at Spence Bay, but this was different. These were my own traps; I wasn't just helping someone else.

I bought my dogs from Angulaalik, and as time went on we became close friends. We held each other in mutual respect. It was remarkable, in view of our initial relationship, that Angulaalik was the first man at Perry to whom I offered a drink.

8
❄ Tikirluk

White visitors were a rarity at Perry Island. The
Company supply ship normally came in for a day or two each
summer, but some summers the ice didn't break up in the
straits to the east, and the ship could not get through. Few
scheduled flights crossed the Arctic in those days, and only
the odd charter plane ever dropped in at Perry. It was not
unusual for eight or ten months to pass without a guest.
Naturally, when a plane did show up and buzz the little
settlement before landing, everyone rushed to greet it. Any
arrival was exciting to the Eskimos, and to me just as much.
Visitors brought welcome news of the outside world in far more
detail than we received on our skimpy shortwave radio broad-
casts. Although I was enjoying and profiting from the opportunity to perfect my command of the Eskimo language, it was
a treat to speak English now and then. In addition, most
visitors thoughtfully brought with them the backlog of mail
which had been accumulating at other Arctic points until a
plane could get into Perry. Many travellers who knew conditions
in the North brought greatly appreciated gifts of fresh fruit or
the odd crock of rum or good Scotch.

Only one fact consistently disappointed me. The drop-in
visitors were never women. Once an old northern friend
stopped off for an hour at Perry on his way from Coppermine
to Cambridge Bay. When he stepped out of the noisy little
Otter aircraft in front of my post, he greeted me with a mailbag
and announced, 'Duncan, I've brought you your mail.' To my

own consternation I heard myself blurt, 'You didn't bring a female?'

On one occasion we were blessed by a female visitor, a young white nurse from Cambridge Bay, and the first white woman I had seen in nearly a year. I was extremely attentive to her, which did not escape the careful notice of the Eskimos. Two or three days after the girl had returned to Cambridge Bay, I was sitting in my living room writing a letter when Ikpakuhak, one of the friendliest of the Eskimos at Perry, came in to visit me.

Ikpakuhak prepared himself a cup of tea and made one for me too, and after watching my labours he asked politely, 'Are you writing to a woman?'

I said that I was writing to the nurse who had visited us.

'Is that your girl friend?' he asked.

'No, she's not my girl friend, but I just thought I'd drop her a line.'

'Well, why don't you take her as a wife?' he pursued. I hadn't realized the Eskimos were concerned about my status as a single man. Certainly it didn't worry me. I replied, 'Oh, I don't think a white woman would like to live here, it's too lonely. She wouldn't like that.'

We talked a few more moments, and then Ikpakuhak went home and I forgot about the matter. But, as I was to learn shortly, he did not.

Early the next morning—it must have been no more than five or six o'clock—I was awakened by the sound of my outside door being opened. I drowsily opened my eyes to find two Eskimos, Ikpakuhak and Tupilliqqut, all dressed for travel in full deerskins, standing by my bed. Ikpakuhak, seeing that I had awakened, said abruptly, 'Yesterday you were writing to your girl friend, weren't you?'

Ikpakuhak was known as a man who pursued an objective with great singleness of purpose, and perhaps it was knowing this that kept me from finding the juxtaposition of subject and circumstance unduly strange. I said, 'If you mean that nurse, well, she's not really my girl friend.'

Undeterred, Ikpakuhak persisted. 'Well, do you want to get married?'

As a matter of fact, I didn't particularly. Trying to rub the sleep out of my eyes and make some sense out of this early morning social hour, and without thinking about it, I just said,

'Well, sure I wouldn't mind getting married. It's a tough life when you're alone and a man gets lonely without a woman.'

Ikpakuhak was almost quivering with eagerness. He sat down on the edge of my bed and said, 'You'd like to get married, then!'

I shrugged: 'Of course. I'm a man you know.'

He shifted around and looked at his companion with an expression of triumph, and then he said to me, 'Well, I've been talking to Tupilliqqut. We were thinking that you might like to have a wife. Tupiiq and I were thinking…how would you like to marry my niece?'

I stammered, 'Your niece? Which one is that?'

'Tikirluk.'

'Tikirluk?' I couldn't quite place which girl they meant.

Tupilliqqut said, 'Amirairniq's sister—the one who is living with her adopted father, Uqalitaaraaluk.'

Finally I knew which girl they meant. I was thunderstruck. Tikirluk was a very pretty girl—and all of thirteen years old!

I hastily protested, 'Oh, I couldn't marry Tikirluk; she's much too young!'

Tupilliqqut straightened that out in a hurry. 'Oh, she's not too young,' he said. 'She's got pubic hair already and her breasts are nicely developed.' This may have been true; she certainly seemed well advanced for a girl so young. I had noticed that, all right.

Suddenly I sensed the disturbing possibility that I might end up a married man. I thought fast how to get out of this and yet be diplomatic and not hurt their feelings. After all this was a genuine, honest offer out of the goodness of their hearts, with no strings attached.

So I thought a minute, and then said, with an air of regret but authority, 'Well, you know, among the whitemen you can't marry a girl until she's eighteen.'

Ikpakuhak said, 'Oh, that's all right; she'll be eighteen soon enough.' I was almost certain she couldn't be over thirteen.

I tried another tack. 'Well, I can't marry a girl that young—the police would take me off to jail.' I didn't know if that was true or not, but it seemed likely to impress Ikpakuhak. I added quickly, 'Oh, I wouldn't mind marrying Tikirluk. She's certainly a nice girl, a nice-looking girl too.'

Her uncle beamed at this and agreed. 'Oh yes, she is, and she's a good seamstress, too; she's really good at sewing.' To the Eskimos this was the clincher; to them a fine stitch is even more important than physical attractiveness. 'She's really a good worker,' he went on. 'She could make you some nice things.'

I began to backpedal some more. 'I'm sure she could, but the thing that worries me if I married her...and I wouldn't mind marrying Tikirluk, you know...she's too young. If I married her the police would surely arrest me.'

Ikpakuhak had an easy answer for that; I should have foreseen it. He reassured me. 'Well, no one here is going to tell the RCMP; the police don't need to know.' Obviously feeling that he had scored a decisive point, he rushed confidently on. 'I'll tell you what; if you like her and you want her, she can move over here with you today. I'll go now and tell her.' He got up from my bed, and so did I—in a hurry. He said, 'You can just use her until she gets older and then you can marry her in the whiteman's way when she is old enough.'

A magnanimous offer, but I put a hand on Ikpakuhak's arm to restrain him. 'Oh no,' I said hurriedly, 'don't do that. Don't tell her yet. I mean, she couldn't move in here. If the police...' My voice trailed off. I visualized these two well-intentioned Eskimos bringing that sweet little girl across and moving her in with me lock, stock and barrel. The divisional manager of the Hudson's Bay Company enters to find me living with a thirteen-year-old girl!

So I quickly shifted ground. 'No,' I said, 'I couldn't do that. Even if the police didn't find out, my boss from the Hudson's Bay Company, he comes here every year, you know—he'd find out, and then I'd be in trouble with him.'

Ikpakuhak thought about this; then he shrugged and asked, 'Do you want a mug-up?'

I was flooded with relief. 'Yes, I would very much.'

We sat at the kitchen table with our morning tea, and Ikpakuhak and Tupilliqqut explained that they were all dressed in their deerskins to go out early for a hunt, but had been worrying about me, a poor single man without a woman, and had stopped by to suggest their solution.

'We'd really like you to stay here,' Ikpakuhak said.

That was a gratifying thing to hear. I had heard often enough that people didn't like me at Perry. I smiled, but made it plain that Tikirluk was not for me.

So good old Ikpakuhak came up with a new tack of his own. He turned to Tupilliqqut and said, 'Hey, Tupiiq, why don't you let him borrow Kuptana?' Kuptana was Tupilliqqut's wife, a girl of about twenty-one, and one of the group of very attractive young women I had noticed around Perry when I first arrived there. Now my ears pricked up.

When Ikpakuhak presented this idea he used the Eskimo word *atullagliuk*, which literally means 'allow to use temporarily.' Tupiiq would have been a poor poker player. I could read the dismay in his face, and it was easy to see that he didn't think this was such a good idea at all. I was sure that he and Ikpakuhak hadn't talked about this when they planned their little visit. But Tupilliqqut was on a spot. He obviously didn't want to go along, but he didn't want to embarrass his friend either by saying no. So I took him off the hook. I said, 'Oh no, that's all right. I can get by without having a wife. I'm doing all right.'

Ikpakuhak didn't buy this. 'Oh no,' he said, 'you're a real man and you can't live all the time without a woman. A man needs someone to do his sewing, and fix his boots, and cook for him. A man needs a woman to keep him warm in bed.'

We finally eased off the subject, and my two concerned friends went off on their hunt. I hoped that the matter was ended, because while I appreciated the genuine interest and regard for me that had prompted Ikpakuhak's offer, I really had no intention of getting married then, particularly to a girl barely out of childhood.

That evening I saw their dogteams coming back into the settlement, and within five minutes, still in his deerskins, Ikpakuhak stood before me taking up exactly where he had left off.

'We've been talking with the others,' he said, 'and we heard that a white man can marry a girl as soon as they stop paying her family allowance.' All the Eskimos knew about the family allowance paid by the government for each child in the family, and that it stops when the child is sixteen. Tupilliqqut, perhaps anxious to keep the talk from turning to any temporary borrowing of Kuptana again, was all ready to be helpful. He suggested, 'You could just get Tikirluk to move in with you until she's sixteen. That's only two or three years away.'

Ikpakuhak pointed out; 'We don't know just when she was born, anyhow.'

I could see I was back in it again. Ikpakuhak hurriedly pounded the last nail in: 'We asked Tikirluk about it, and she's glad. She's very pleased that she can move in with you. Oh, she's quite willing.' He and Tupilliqqut looked at me expectantly.

Again I could foresee all kinds of trouble. I ticked off in my mind: the Company, the missionaries, the police, everybody I could think of, except Tikirluk and my friends here. The time for diplomacy had passed. With a determined look at Ikpakuhak and Tupilliqqut, I uttered just one word: 'No.'

That, mercifully, ended the matter, but thereafter Tikirluk was especially friendly, and indeed she was far from unattractive to me. But marriage being the serious matter it is, I was careful to avoid such situations for some time afterwards.

9
❄ *Drum Dance*

Christmas time in the Arctic is about the only time of the year when a man feels the keen loneliness of real isolation. Sitting by himself in his post, hundreds of miles from any other settlement, perhaps a howling blizzard outside, there sits the trader fiddling with his radio. All he can get are Christmas carols and news of festivities—all over the world he imagines people together, sharing the joy of the occasion with each other. He is all alone with a bottle of rum.

That is why traders in the Arctic have always gone along with the idea of a big Christmas party for the Eskimos. It has always been customary at trading posts for the Eskimos to come in at Christmas from their traplines for a party after the winter trading session. There would be a feast, a big mug-up, and games, rifle shoots, dogteam races, all kinds of Eskimo sports and, of course, a drum dance.

Before the whiteman came with his odd ideas and customs, Eskimos never celebrated Christmas or New Year. They did hold, however, a mid-winter celebration at about that time, when they first saw *Aagyuuk*.

Aagyuuk refers to two relatively unimportant stars in the northern skies, part of the Eagle constellation: one small, rather faint star and directly below it a much larger one. They are first seen around early January, in the morning when the sky is lightening. There is no sun yet that far north, but the Eskimos know that when they see *Aagyuuk*, it will only be a matter of seven or eight sleeps until the sun appears on the horizon again. The long, dark days of winter will have reached a turning point; *Aagyuuk* is a promise that the warm, bright summer will return—good reason for a celebration in the Arctic.

After the whiteman came, the missionaries, of course, made a point of celebrating Christmas, so by the time I reached the Arctic, Christmas had become a festive occasion among the Eskimos. When I was at Perry Island the tradition was well established. The Eskimos came in, bringing along any skins they had to trade, and the women bought new bolts of cloth and made bright, fresh coverings of calico for their parkas, and sewed up new Christmas things for the men. The Eskimos built a *qalgi*, a huge snowhouse where everyone could dance and enjoy the old games. My part was to provide a feast for everyone.

Some of the people brought in caribou, and the women all went over to Irvana's house and cooked up a great stew. We borrowed copper vats, the kind used to wash clothes in, from the store. We filled three or four of these with rice from my own mess supply and caribou and *patiq* (the marrow from caribou leg bones), and boiled it all up together into enough stew to feed the entire settlement. I gave the women plenty of flour and salt to make a huge mess of bannock. The feast was held in the *qalgi*, and our games inside and out—three-legged races, dogteam races for the kids and the women as well as for the men. The tangle of excited dogs and yelling children was something to see.

A sealskin thong was stretched across the interior of the big snowhouse, passed through the walls and tied to sleds that braced against the exterior. Inside, the thong made an impro-vised trapeze. Men, women and children all vied in performing tricks on the trapeze, one agile young man even walking it like a tightrope.

Everyone tried a turn at *ayagaq*, which appears tantalizingly easy but turns out to be frustratingly difficult. *Ayagaq* is a hand game in which a small bone, taken from the flipper of a bearded seal, is pierced. The prepared bone is then attached by a one-foot thong to a pencil-sized stick or bone. Holding the stick, the player tries to flip the pierced bone into the air in such a manner that it can be caught on the end of the stick. It's harder than it sounds.

Another old Eskimo contest was a game called *nullugaut*. A

thong is hung from the ceiling and fastened to the floor so it stays taut. In the centre, about shoulder-high, is an eye made from a piece of bone with a hole bored through it. Four or five people stand around with short spear-like sticks and stab at the hole to see who can get the point of his spear in first.

A dozen versions of tug-of-war and tests of strength were played, individual, pairs and team versions, arm tug-of-war, hand tug-of-war and even finger pulls. These were games that Eskimos had played for generations when it was too dark out or too stormy to hunt, or sometimes perhaps when there was plenty of food for everyone, and it seemed unnecessary to hunt any more. If they couldn't go hunting and there was plenty to eat, they played.

The greatest of the ancient games, of course, is cat's cradle. Every child, man and woman had mastered hundreds of varieties of string figures. The older people especially were marvellously dexterous. It was a custom that one never made string figures in the sunlight, only during the dark part of winter.

When night came it was time for the drum dance. There was always some horsing around before the dancing started, a preliminary bit of fun to get everyone in a good mood. I took over as master of ceremonies, and when everyone was seated in the *qalgi,* I said: 'Tonight, before the dancing starts, I have devised a contest to find the strongest men in this settlement. Now I want the three strongest men among you up here, but I'm not going to pick them out; it is not for me to say which ones they are.' As I knew it would, this created a hubbub. All the men immediately became terribly modest, saying, 'Oh not me, I'm not really very strong. So and so's much stronger than I am,' the usual way Eskimos politely talk themselves down.

I quieted them and said, 'Okay then, we'll let the women pick out the strongest men,' and of course this caused more excitement. Some shouted for this one and some that one until finally they agreed on three of the biggest and toughest of the hunters and trappers.

I got the three nominees out in the middle of the *qalgi,* all looking tremendously husky in their bulky deerskins, but smiling sheepishly, not sure of what I was going to make them do. I brought out a cardboard box and held it up. 'Now, the one who finishes first in this contest will be the strongest.' They all watched intently as I opened the box and handed each a baby bottle full of milk, nipples all prepared. I gave a bottle to each man. The sight of those three strong, tough-looking Eskimos sucking away on their bottles brought gales of laughter from the crowd. The comments from the audience were strong, too.

Irvana shouted: 'Look at that man, I wouldn't mind having him at my breast!' And someone else: 'What kind of a husband have you got there, anyway? Look at him—he's just a big baby. He couldn't do anything for a woman. How could a big baby like that make children?' Everyone was soon in a great mood for the dancing.

There is no special time for a drum dance. Eskimos may call one any time people get together and feel like one, just as white people might decide to get up a party. It might be held in a *qalgi*, or out in the open when the weather is mild, or in the trading post itself.

The significance of the drum dance is not in the beating of the drum, but in the words of the songs. When a person sings a drum dance song, he sings his own original composition—his *pisiq*. It is usually the story of some specific happening in his life, a great hunt, or a bad winter of starvation, some important event in his experience. A man's wife may sing his song, but other people cannot sing it unless he gives them permission. Sometimes men become song partners and will exchange songs and sing about each other. This is a device to overcome the Eskimos' natural modesty, which would prevent them from seeming to boast of their own accomplishments. Then there is the *atuut*, a general song that everyone can join in, a sort of community song.

Before the singer begins a drum dance song, he announces whose song it is. Everyone sits around and someone, perhaps a woman, will get up and start the dancing. When the singer starts drumming, he holds the drum—like a huge tambourine, one-sided, perhaps three feet in diameter—with the finished side facing out. The performer beats against the skin, keeping the drum close in against his body and beating a rhythm while he bounces up and down and turns from side to side, sometimes in a circle so that everyone can see. When he goes into the actual song, he turns the drum round, swings it and beats on the frame made of bone rather than on the skin. The spectators encourage the drummer with shouts of '*Nivliqtiriarit, nivliq-tiriarit!*' ('Cry out with joy, cry out with joy!')

As each drummer takes a turn, and it becomes warmer in the snowhouse, people leap to their feet to dance, sometimes more than one at the same time. It is not the kind of drum dance white people might see at Cambridge Bay or Inuvik today. As the dance got going, and the temperature higher, we would strip to the waist, men and women alike. Everyone is excited and caught up in the noise. A real Eskimo drum dance can be highly provocative.

If a man is drum dancing and has his eye on a woman, he will dance for her, the rhythm and the words are directed to her. Often her husband will urge her on. He'll say, 'Go on, get up and dance with him.' Sometimes the tension and excitement builds up so high that a woman and her drummer will simply leave the scene. The drum dance is a primitive thing, with the beat of the drum throbbing out, and at its height the words don't matter very much.

The songs often revive memories of dead people whom many who are present have known, memories of times everyone has lived through. There is always someone in every settlement who knows all the words and will lead the song, and everyone sits and sways and sings them out together, like a sing-along. Angulaalik was very good at leading songs.

But the star of our parties and dances at Perry was always old Arnayak, the wife of the shaman Alikammiq. This remarkable woman served as the mental archive of the tribe. Not only did she remember all that had happened to members of the band there, but she was the repository for all the fantastic stories and legends that the people treasured, and which were the only existing history of their ancestors. An essential part of every drum dance was the break in the dancing in which Arnayak would tell a legend or tale.

I remember one drum dance at Perry that went right on into the early hours of the morning. There was a girl that I had been paying my attentions to. The flirtation was returned. At Perry and other places in the Arctic, the white trader enjoys a place of prestige in the Eskimo community and Eskimo girls consider him a good catch, permanent or temporary. This girl's husband was away, and we danced until we were pretty worked up, and then discreetly left the dance. She came up to the trading post with me and we made love that night.

I learned something about Eskimo women from that girl. A shy man had best not get involved with an Eskimo woman. The next morning this girl went back to her own house and bragged all over the settlement about her night with the trader —in clinical detail.

10
❄ A Furtrade Bachelor

There is a widespread belief that a man has only to go to the Arctic, and the first Eskimo he meets will happily turn his wife over to him for the night. There was indeed at one time, and there remains still in some of the more isolated settlements, a system of wife exchange among the Eskimos, but it was rarely established on a casual basis, and there were always certain social niceties and boundaries to be observed. The custom might better be termed spouse exchange because in many cases the wife, not the husband, initiated the exchange.

This custom used to be accepted, even preferred community behaviour among the Eskimos, and was practised throughout the Arctic. When I was at Perry Island every adult man had an exchange wife, and every woman an exchange husband. There was no question of adultery, or any feeling of 'shame'. In fact, Eskimos thought it shameful, or at least strange, if a man or woman did not have an exchange partner. In white society today, if a teenage girl isn't dating, her mother wonders what is wrong with her and pushes her to get into the swim, to be like everyone else. Similarly, in Eskimo society there was family pressure on young people to obtain exchange mates. The mother of a young bride, perhaps uncertain of her new son-in-law's ability to keep the larder full, might impress upon her daughter the advantage of a liaison with an older, more experienced hunter.

Such relationships did not exclude single people. A man or woman who had lost a mate, by death or desertion, might become involved in a triangle exchange with a married couple. Occasionally young unmarried men and women entered such a relationship.

Sound sociological reasons contributed to the growth and perpetuation of the system, and not the least important was self-preservation. Up to twenty or thirty years ago Eskimos were as bad as the MacDonalds and the Campbells when it came to blood feuds. If Anaqqarniq killed Simigiaq, the next of kin to Simigiaq was duty bound to take revenge on Anaqqarniq, and so on as long as there was anyone left in either family. As we have seen, kinship relationships and blood feuds played a major role in Eskimo life. An Eskimo who was without kin to avenge any wrong done him was exposed and vulnerable. If he travelled to strange territory to hunt or trade, he could fall into a dangerous situation, alone among strangers who might, and generally did, covet anything from his dogteam to his harpoon, and were sometimes more than willing to kill him to get what they wanted. With no kin to avenge his death, he could be murdered with impunity.

To prevent this, the Eskimos evolved spouse exchange as a kind of insurance policy. When a man travelled in distant regions he always took his wife with him, and when they reached a strange settlement, the visitor automatically arranged a wife exchange with one of the local residents, thus establishing the all-important kinship relationship. He acquired all his wife's exchange husband's family as his kin, and they became bound to avenge any injury done to the visitor. It was no longer safe to rob or harm the traveller.

According to Eskimo belief, moulded to fit the circumstances, a one-night stand would never result in pregnancy. Accordingly, a single act of intercourse with a non-spouse had little significance to the immediate family.

Whenever wife or spouse exchange took place within the same band or settlement, choice was virtually unrestricted except for the important taboo of incest. As long as a man or woman chose someone outside his or her kinship circle, any arrangement agreeable to the persons concerned was possible.

Within a tribe or settlement, spouse exchange sometimes developed as a purely sexual thing. One man might like another's wife, and his wife in turn might have her eyes on the other husband, and if feelings proved to be mutual, an exchange was easily established. Among the Eskimos I knew at Perry Island and in some other villages, the average length of a spouse exchange relationship was about two years, but such extramarital fidelity was unusual.

The Eskimo attitude towards the custom and towards sex generally is well illustrated by Iqaluut and his wife Qungayuna, an older couple I knew at Bathurst Inlet. One year a missionary came down from Cambridge Bay to hold some services, and he was surprised and pleased at the number of Eskimos who attended. He had brought along his record books and said that he hoped to baptize some of the older Eskimos who had never undergone that sacrament. The missionary wanted to visit his potential converts, and asked me to act as interpreter. One of our first stops was the home of Iqaluut and Qungayuna.

'Well, you seemed to enjoy the services,' the missionary began. After some small talk he asked, 'Would you like me to baptize you so that we will know for sure that you are an Anglican?'

To the missionary's surprise Iqaluut promptly declined: 'Oh no, I don't want to get baptized, and I don't want my wife baptized either.'

'Why not? You are Anglicans. You came to the services.'

'If we get baptized, then we can no longer exchange mates,' said Iqaluut. He and his wife believed that if they were baptized they would have to follow the ways of the missionary, and all Eskimos knew that missionaries frowned on wife exchange.

To make the point clear, Qungayuna, giggling and laughing, butted in: 'That's right. It gets awfully boring when you've just got one man all the time.'

To them it was a poor man who could only attract one woman, and a useless woman who failed to have several admirers.

In my own case it was a beautiful and brazen girl, Niksaaktuq, wife of the young hunter Nasarlulik and daughter-in-law of the shaman at Perry, who initiated the exchange. Almost from the time of my arrival at Perry, Niksaaktuq had flirted provocatively with me. For that matter, so had several other women in the settlement. I was flattered, but I realized that I was considered unusual not because of my appealing Scottish face or my splendid physique, but simply because as the only whiteman in the place, and as the trader, I had enormous prestige. I was something new, a whiteman who spoke Eskimo and who made it obvious that the attention of girls was pleasing.

But I moved slowly. I was neither naive nor celibate, but during my first days at Perry my time was fully engaged in getting the post back on its feet. I was unsure of local customs and dared not risk an already precarious position by committing a social gaffe.

But Niksaaktuq was a delightful girl and I was soon sure she was making a real play for me. Once when I was visiting with Nasarlulik and his mother Arnayak, Niksaaktuq made a point of joking in a rather risqué way with me, smiling and teasing in little ways that women everywhere instinctively use. When Nasarlulik and I left, I discovered I had forgotten my mitts and went back to get them, telling Nasarlulik I would catch up with him in a minute. Niksaaktuq handed the mitts to me, and when our hands touched she held on to mine, looked knowingly into my face, and smiled. Neither of us said a word, but I knew for sure that this girl was interested.

I was interested too. Very much. Niksaaktuq had caught my eye my very first day at Perry Island. She was an extremely good-looking girl with a beautiful body, slim and vibrant. Although she was only twenty or twenty-one, she had already been involved with eight or nine different men in spouse exchanges.

She had a trick of scratching her instep with the toe of her other foot. I thought she must have a very itchy foot, but later discovered she was using an old Eskimo custom to signal to me that she was interested in a sexual liaison. I was willing all right, but I didn't know quite what to do about it.

Fortunately Niksaaktuq was neither as faint-hearted nor as inhibited as I was. During the next couple of months she made the most of every opportunity to see me, even when Nasarlulik was there. Whenever her husband's back was turned Niksaaktuq would smile at me and try to catch my eye, or she might scuff her mukluk suggestively. When they came over to the post to trade she always seemed to find some opportunity to touch me. I didn't object—to be strictly honest, I tried to make it easier for this to happen. The big problem for me was that I really liked Nasarlulik. We got along well, hunting together, joking and laughing to the point where the other Eskimos called us *kipaqatiqiik* (joking partners), which meant we were close friends.

Finally, the situation came to a head. We had been on a trip together, and when we got back I asked Nasarlulik and Niksaaktuq to come over and have a mug-up with me as soon as they had their dogs chained and their gear stowed away. When they arrived I went to the kitchen to get the tea ready. Niksaaktuq came up behind me, put both arms around me and pulled me back against her. Nasarlulik had plopped down on the chesterfield in the living room, just around the corner from us and barely out of sight where we stood by the stove. I turned round and Niksaaktuq put her hands to my face and pulled my head down to her and rubbed noses with me. The Perry Island people didn't engage in kissing, but they certainly knew how to rub noses, and rubbing noses can be very exciting if it is done the right way with the right noses. First this saucy girl just held the side of her nose against mine. That is considered just affectionate; but when she pressed the side of her nose against the side of mine and started rubbing, then that is not only considered passionate—it is!

She was busy leading the nose rubbing, and I was busy trying to see where Nasarlulik was, when she reached into her parka and brought out a little slip of folded paper which she handed me. I stepped away from her and into the tiny adjacent washroom to see what was on the paper. She had written in Eskimo syllabics three words, *Piyumaguvit uiga kanngunaittuq* ('If you want something, my husband won't be embarrassing'). What it really meant was, 'If you want to go to bed with me, ask my husband for his permission, and he won't embarrass you by saying no.' This was a proposal for a wife-exchange relationship.

As soon as I read it I understood the proposal but lacked the confidence. Never before had I asked a man for permission to take his wife to bed. It might have been easier if I hadn't liked Nasarlulik so much. I was worried that we should both end up badly embarrassed. I was fully aware that Naksaaktuq shared none of my doubts, but not only did I hesitate to go behind my friend's back, I also knew such an action might be dangerous. Loss of face when our activities became known might force Nasarlulik to strike out at me. Normally a man would never ask for an exchange relationship unless he were virtually certain the woman's husband would agree. Nor would he risk an illicit arrangement unless he was prepared for a violent reaction. Of course, in this instance, Niksaaktuq had prepared the way with Nasarlulik, but I didn't know that for certain. I just stalled as though nothing had happened.

I went back into the living room with the tea, and Niksaaktuq smiled expectantly at me and Nasarlulik smiled expectantly at me, and I just grinned back at them. I was thinking furiously to myself. I well knew Niksaaktuq's reputation as an impetuous and headstrong girl, and I wondered if this was something she had cooked up on her own, or if, as she implied, her husband knew about it and was in agreement. I didn't want to move too fast in spite of Niksaaktuq's reassuring note. I thought that if Nasarlulik did turn me down, it would mean he suspected I had been friendly with him only because I wanted his wife, which wasn't true at all.

So we sat there and drank our tea in silence, each trying to think of something to say. Every once in a while Nasarlulik and Niksaaktuq would flash pregnant smiles at me and make little comments that could be taken two ways. At ten o'clock I excused myself while I made my nightly message broadcast. It was then that I received orders, heard any news that was on the air, and relayed my own messages. Nasarlulik went to the bathroom and Niksaaktuq followed me into the radio room where I was twiddling the dials to tune in the Cambridge Bay station. I stood up to reach for something, and that bold girl threw her arms around my neck, then suddenly reached down and grabbed me by the genitals. Being only human, I grabbed her back—and just then the Cambridge Bay station came on. I had to sit down and answer their call. All the time I was talking to Cambridge Bay, Niksaaktuq was caressing my face until Nasarlulik came back. Then she stopped, and we went into the kitchen and all sat around the little table there.

Niksaaktuq had another of her little notes ready. This time it read, 'What are you waiting for? Ask my husband!'

I was still too embarrassed, so I folded the note up and stuck it in my pocket. She laughed and said '*Kanngusuktutit?*' (Are you shy?)

'Oh, no,' I replied, and cleared my throat.

'Well, go ahead, do what I asked you to do.'

I didn't know what to do. Somehow Nasarlulik seemed to have become nothing more than an onlooker in this little game between his wife and friend. Then Niksaaktuq picked up her pencil and wrote out another little note, and in the next half hour or so she wrote six or seven little notes and passed them over to me while we made small talk. Some of them I looked at and some I just folded over and shoved in my pocket. I began to devote my exclusive attention to Nasarlulik. I was about to fold another note without reading it and stick it in my pocket with the others, but Niksaaktuq could take no more.

'Give it to me,' she ordered. 'Go on and ask my husband. Don't be shy. Go ahead and ask my husband.' She grabbed the note out of my hand and gave it to Nasarlulik.

Her husband opened the note, looked up and smiled. I was sure it was a smile of relief because now the little comedy was over. Obviously he had known all along what was going on. This had all been talked over beforehand between the two of them.

He asked me plainly, 'Do you desire my wife?'

I still played it cautiously, and said, 'Oh, she's very desirable. Any man would desire her, a woman as good-looking as your wife.'

'Do you like her?' he persisted.

'Sure I like her.'

Then looking right at me, and with Niksaaktuq hanging on every word, he said, 'Do you want to make love with her?'

I was still very cautious. 'Well, she's not my wife, you know.'

Nasarlulik grinned and said, 'Well, Niksaaktuq likes you, and I like you too, so if you want to get my wife (and that was the term he used), 'then go ahead.'

Still uneasy, I tried to be amiable. 'Okay, that's great...'

'Fine,' he said, 'Where do you want to get her?'

'Well, in my bed,' I blurted. There wasn't anywhere else to go. Niksaaktuq jumped up—'Come on, let's go, let's go.'

Off we went while Nasarlulik stayed in the kitchen. The bedroom was just off the kitchen, and there wasn't even a door. It was all wide open. I was in there with Niksaaktuq, not feeling the least bit romantically inclined, with her husband sitting a couple of arm's lengths away in the kitchen. But Niksaaktuq had no such inhibitions. She was trying to hurry me up. Down came her pants and bloomers and everything else, and she jumped into bed. So I got undressed and into bed too, but I still had a strange feeling. 'What about your husband? He didn't go home.'

'Oh, he'll be all right in the kitchen,' said Niksaaktuq.

Nature took its course. We were a bit noisy about it, because Niksaaktuq was just as eager as could be. The thing I most remember is her comment: 'You like me, even though I'm an Eskimo.' I have never heard any other Eskimo say that.

We got up, dressed and went back to the kitchen, and I was a little embarrassed thinking of the noise we had made. Nasarlulik was standing there; he had cleaned up all the dishes and was drying them. He turned to me with a smile and asked, 'Are you feeling better now?'

'Much better,' I smiled.

'I'm glad.' Then he explained, 'Niksaaktuq likes you, and I like you. Niksaaktuq kept telling me that we should share, because you are such a nice fellow, but I didn't want to say anything, because I didn't know how you felt about her.'

We sat down and had another mug-up; then they went home.

By the next day the news had spread. Niksaaktuq was proud to be the first woman in the settlement to 'get' me. She was just like a man who makes love to a beautiful woman and feels so good about it that he wants everyone to know. In typical Eskimo fashion she described to anyone who would listen the entire event, from beginning to end. It didn't make any difference whether men or women or both were listening, Niksaaktuq went into minute detail. Before noon every Eskimo in the settlement had heard all about us. Amirairniq, the young husband of Tuiligaaryuk, who liked to hang around the post, came in and said, 'I hear you slept with Niksaaktuq last night.'

I said that was true.

'How was she?' he asked. 'Was she good? Did she bounce up and down or did she just lie there?'

'She was good,' I replied.

Amirairniq nodded. 'You know that she is Tupilliqqut's exchange wife?'

I said I knew that, and he said, 'Well, she told Nasarlulik this morning that she doesn't want to exchange with Tupilliqqut again.'

Amirairniq said that Niksaaktuq had been all around the settlement that morning, casually bringing up the subject in numerous conversations—it just happened that the trader wanted her, and she just happened to be there, and one thing had led to another, an exchange had happened, a sharing taken place.

After a while Niksaaktuq arrived with Kuptana, Tupilliq-qut's wife, another very good-looking girl who had been Niksaaktuq's chief rival for me. I hadn't objected to them competing; it made me feel good. I was surprised to see them together, but I soon realized why Niksaaktuq had brought her competitor along. The two of them sat down in my living room and had a mug-up, and Niksaaktuq said to me, '*Kina nuliasut?*' ('Who's your exchange wife?' Modern young Eskimos would translate it as 'Who's your girl friend?')

I looked at her and said, 'I don't know.'

She bristled. 'What do you mean you don't know? Who did you make love with last night?'

'You', I said.

She turned triumphantly to Kuptana as she said to me, 'Well, then I'm your exchange wife.' Her smile of triumph was all woman.

Tupilliqqut didn't think much of what I had done, taking his girl away from him, but there wasn't anything he could do. He came over to the post the next day and opened with a remark I was beginning to hear over and over again. 'I hear you made love with Niksaaktuq.'

I said that was right.

'You know she is my exchange wife?' He turned away and looked out of the window.

'Yes, I knew that.' I added carefully, 'Nasarlulik agreed to it.'

He just said, 'Oh.' Then, 'You know, I really like her.'

I said, after a pause, 'I do too.'

'Oh, I see,' he said. That was all I ever heard on the matter from Tupilliqqut.

Every time after that when Nasarlulik or I made a trip, we would wind up at a camp together and we would share Niksaaktuq. Up at his trapping camp there would be Arnayak, his old blind mother, the two kids, Nasarlulik, Niksaaktuq and myself. We would all sleep on the sleeping platform together. At one end would be Arnayak, then me, Niksaaktuq, Nasarlulik, and then the two kids. Several times we made love in that situation. If it seems strange making love to a girl with her husband seven inches from your right knee and her mother-in-law seven inches from your left knee, then that is just another inhibition to be overcome. Everyone politely pretends to be asleep, but all ears are wide open. I can't say it really helped my sexual performance; on the other hand, it didn't stop me.

I didn't know how long this arrangement might last. It seemed that Niksaaktuq was a natural man collector. Among her partners was her father-in-law himself, the shaman. Normally such an alliance would have been taboo because of the kinship factor, but a shaman lies outside all taboos.

Niksaaktuq didn't like Alikammiq, but the shaman was a strong-willed man who dominated the family, including his son and his daughter-in-law. Niksaaktuq was frightened of him, and Nasarlulik could hardly object. One night Alikammiq had wanted Niksaaktuq and simply taken her. I knew that Nasarlulik felt repressed by him, but I didn't know why until after his death when Niksaaktuq told me about it. She said she hadn't wanted to make love to her father-in-law, but that he had forced himself on her. It was close to rape; Alikammiq just bullied her mentally until she gave in.

Nasarlulik and I spent more and more of our time together, hunting and trapping and working together as a unit. When two men share a wife, each has definite responsibilities. If, for instance, Nasarlulik had fallen sick, it would have been up to me to look after him and his family, including his old mother and any children there might be. In turn, if anything happened to me it was Nasarlulik's responsibility to see that I was provided for. If I had had a wife and family, he would have taken care of them until I was able to work again.

At Perry Island, two men who share one wife are called *angutauqatigiik*, and they will become as close as brothers. They will share every confidence with each other, all of each other's problems and troubles. When Nasarlulik was worried by anything, he usually came and told me. Once he confided that he was glad he had agreed to share Niksaaktuq with me; before she fooled around with too many men, but now she had settled down. She knew that other girls around the settlement, like Kuptana, would like to have me and that if she flirted elsewhere, I might look for another girl.

As my exchange wife, Niksaaktuq performed many duties. She did a lot of cooking for me, baking bannock and boiling stews when I was busy at the post. She took care of my clothing, which is no small matter for a man in the Arctic. Any Eskimo woman will try to outdo the others in making elaborate boots and *kamiks*, or the handsomest parka with the best stitching. No one outdid Niksaaktuq. She turned out beautiful clothing for me, embroidered *mukluks*, a caribou parka, perfectly tailored.

When she first began sewing for me, like most Eskimo women, she simply measured me with her eyes to get the proportions. Eskimo women have keen eyes for that sort of thing and seldom make a mistake, but Niksaaktuq decided she must measure me more carefully. She said I was a bit lopsided, probably because I was a whiteman, and produced a short piece of string to measure me with. I was puzzled how she expected to get accurate measurements with that, but she tied it around my head, across the forehead. I didn't see how that helped unless she was going to make me a hat. She called me silly and said that everyone knew a man's height is always three times the circumference of his head. That was all the measuring she did and everything fitted exactly.

Like couples the world over, Eskimos have their share of marital problems. One day Angulaalik came to the post about nine in the morning sporting a terrific shiner. He kept his head turned away from me to one side but several Eskimos had been in already, and they had told me what happened. The previous night Angulaalik, who must have been in his middle or late fifties, had sneaked over to Nasarlulik's house and made love to the blind, hunchbacked Arnayak. Old Arnayak was reputed to be a real sex-pot. Irvana had found out and given her husband his black eye.

Soon Irvana came over to the trading post. She was a very attractive woman, much younger than Angulaalik, and intelligent into the bargain. Arnayak, proud as punch over what had happened, had gone all round the settlement blathering about the events of the night before. Irvana said she was mad at Arnayak too, but there was nothing she could do about that. Eskimos are taught to respect the older generation. Irvana told me about it all, then reached out and squeezed my foot. 'Don't tell my husband I told you.'

I promised I wouldn't and she returned to her house. I thought no more of it.

Early the next morning I heard Angulaalik's team going past my window, the usual rattle-rattle-bang of the sled and dogs excited and yapping. The noise half-awakened me. I noticed that it was only five o'clock. A few minutes later, I heard my front door open and footsteps coming into the house. I opened my eyes just a slit to see Irvana standing beside the bed.

Seeing me awake she said, 'You've frequently desired me?'

My eyes widened, and I answered, 'Because you are desirable.'

She hesitated another moment: 'You always tell me you think I am good-looking, so I came over.'

Then she waited no longer. She climbed into bed with me and we made love. At that particular moment I was all for it. But later I began to have serious misgivings, remembering the gentle Angulaalik's past.

By this time several months had gone by since Niksaaktuq and I had become exchange mates, and I had learned a great deal about the dos and don'ts of the spouse-exchange system. I knew the risk involved in going to bed with Irvana behind Angulaalik's back. I had no agreement or arrangement with Angulaalik as I did with Nasarlulik. The only factor in my favour was that Irvana had come to me; I had not pursued her. Eskimos are quite understanding and tolerant of such little human foibles as errant sex, and I was banking on this, but at the same time was fully cognizant of the fact that Angulaalik might feel obliged to kill me to defend his honour. It was ticklish.

Irvana sneaked out, but in a few minutes she was back and worried herself: 'I wonder if people will see me leaving? It might be better if you didn't gossip about this.' I assured Irvana that I had no intention whatever of gossiping, on that or any future occasion.

Soon afterwards, around Christmas, a couple of Eskimos came down from Cambridge Bay. They brought some yeast with them, and made some home brew for a party at Angulaalik's house. This was nothing like the drunken brawls staged there before, just a good party. But the next morning one of Irvana's daughters, Tuiligaaryuk, came over to the post, giggling and laughing.

'Oh-oh, oh-oh, you've been making love with my mother.'

Thunderstruck, I demanded, 'How do you know that?'

'Because last night Angulaalik and Irvana got tight and she told him that you two had been making love.'

The fat was in the fire. I have to admit I was nervous.

Later in the day Irvana came over to explain. 'I had to tell him,' she said, 'I had *satqara isuirmat*' ('something wrong with my breastbone', which is to say a guilty conscience).

I watched out for Angulaalik, but he didn't come to the post that day. The next morning he arrived at the usual time, but he wouldn't look me in the eye. Finally he said, 'Do you like my wife?'

I knew I might as well admit it. 'Yes,' I said, 'I do.'

He said, 'Well, she likes you, you know, and she told me she's been coming over here when I've been away.'

I admitted that too.

'Well, I just wanted to let you know that it's all right,' said Angulaalik.

I gave a sigh of relief. So we sat down and had a mug-up and talked about women.

Angulaalik was in a mood to philosophize. 'Women are strange. They always like to fool around,' he said. 'I know that the first time Irvana came over here she did it to get revenge on me because I made love with Arnayak. She told me that.'

My curiosity got the better of me. 'How was Arnayak, anyhow?'

'Oooh,' he said, rolling his eyes, 'she was good. That's why Irvana was mad. Everyone knows that Arnayak is good in bed.' I had to remind myself that he was talking about a blind woman, at least fifty-five, and hunchbacked.

So we sat there like any couple of cronies, laughing and talking. Angulaalik said, 'If you like my wife, go ahead whenever you feel like it, because I like you, and you've always been good to us.' With a shake of his head he added: 'I'm an old man now, and can't satisfy her as I used to.' He was close to twenty-five years older than she was.

So life was pleasant at Perry Island. Niksaaktuq was my exchange wife, and others were always willing. Eskimos don't think of sex in the romantic way we do. An Eskimo woman doesn't fall head over heels in love, as we would say. Marriage is a practical matter to her, and sex is something else again.

Niksaaktuq and I became very close and affectionate as time went on. Our relationship was very much like a marriage. She was the most help to me in learning and perfecting the language —the Copper Eskimo dialect. It is natural to lie in bed and talk after making love. Niksaaktuq had a good ear for the shades of meaning and pronunciation that make so much difference. I began to feel that I was really learning to think in Eskimo. And then I could say things to her I would never say to a casual friend, even in bed. Sometimes, when I had been working on my accounts, Niksaaktuq would bring me a mug of tea and just stand there with her arm on my shoulder. Sexuality is listening and touching and wanting to make the other person happy, and Niksaaktuq's ways were very sexual.

I should never have become involved in wife exchange if I hadn't practically adopted the Eskimo way of life. The fact that I spoke their language made a world of difference. Some of the early explorers and many of the fur traders in particular took Eskimo wives or mistresses for a period, and there are many half-white Eskimos in the Arctic today. But that situation has changed. There are few isolated settlements today where the old Eskimo way of life continues. Missionaries, the RCMP, government workers and other whites flocking to the Arctic, the swift movement of Eskimos off the land to the larger villages and towns, and the almost universal education of the children in white schools—all have contributed to what amounts to a new culture in the North. I knew that the missionaries frowned on me for having Niksaaktuq as a shared wife. But what I did, the way I lived, was within the context of the Eskimo society in which I lived, not to be sneered at or scorned by outsiders.

When Niksaaktuq became pregnant, Nasarlulik and I didn't know which of us was the father. Niksaaktuq just kept smiling and assuring me, 'I know it is going to be yours. He'll be born with a nose like yours. You wait and see.' Eskimos believe that every child takes after the father, so they think they can always tell who the father is.

There is no word in Eskimo for illegitimate child. The child of any union belongs to the mother, so it becomes relatively meaningless who the father is. The child is raised by the mother and her husband, and when the child is old enough to understand, it is told who the real father is. Everyone knows, and there is no shame. Identifying the real father enables the incest taboos to be kept.

The matter of kinship has always been vital to the Eskimos. When two strange Eskimos meet in the middle of the tundra, the first thing they do is sit down and have a mug-up and try to find out if they are related in any way. Whenever a new family comes to a region, there is a great cross-examination until everyone is satisfied that all kinship ties are established. A relationship will be identified if any exists.

The Eskimos proved quite right about children taking after their fathers as far as Niksaaktuq's baby was concerned. There was no mistaking; I was the father. Before the birth of the baby, Nasarlulik and Niksaaktuq went to Cambridge Bay for a visit, and the child was born there. Before they returned to Perry, I had been transferred by the Company to a new trading post at Bathurst Inlet, so it was a long time before I was able to see my daughter. But Father Menez, one of the most decent missionaries I ever knew, who saw the child in Cambridge Bay, had no hesitation in confirming my fatherhood to me. 'Don't try to deny it,' he said gaily. 'Everyone knows it is your baby.'

The last thing in my mind was to deny it. I was very proud. My daughter was named Utuittuq, which had been the name of Niksaaktuq's father, one of the men killed by Angulaalik. But little Utuittuq was weak as a baby. She caught the flu when she was still tiny and very nearly died. So Niksaaktuq and Nasarlulik renamed her, as the custom decrees when someone has a brush with death. Her new name was Qummiq, which literally means a thing that one grips between one's knees. But Eskimo names are relatively meaningless. They are also all asexual. After our daughter got her new name, her health improved rapidly and she has developed into a lovely little girl.

Niksaaktuq's mother, Aaruattiaq, and her second husband, Tupilak, had no children. By Eskimo custom, when a couple want a child and can't have their own, they often adopt a grandchild. Niksaaktuq and Nasarlulik didn't want to give Qummiq to them, but Aaruattiaq begged them; she was getting old and wanted the company of a child. An Eskimo daughter can't really stand up to her mother; it simply isn't good manners to go against the wishes of an older woman, so finally Qummiq went to live with her grandparents and now lives in Cambridge Bay. Niksaaktuq and Nasarlulik eventually moved to Gjoa Haven, where they live today.

Qummiq was not my first—or my last—northern child. Young Eskimo women are at least as eager as young white women. A man isolated in an environment where there are only native women, where he never sees a white woman, doesn't take long to adjust to native standards of beauty. He will soon find that he appreciates their striking looks, and he can always find a girl to sleep with. The problem is which one.

We were all very close at Perry Island. The people had come to that little settlement from all over the Arctic—it was a most cosmopolitan place. We all became related or tied in one way or another, through seal partnerships or wife exchange. We were like one big family; and I was fortunate enough to be considered a member.

11

❋ *Birth,*
Death
and Marriage

Irvana was pregnant again, and Angulaalik was hoping to have another son. Of Irvana's eight living children only one was a boy. Angulaalik feared that something might happen to his lone son, and he would have no one to whom he could teach his ancient knowledge. It never occurred to him to teach his daughters.

One day an Eskimo came into the post for help—'Come quickly—Irvana's having trouble and Angulaalik thinks she is losing the baby.' Normally at such a time the person called would be the shaman, but at this time we had only a young apprentice shaman at Perry Island, so Angulaalik wanted me. He knew that I handled many medical problems and had a stock of medicines.

When I reached their house a very worried-looking Irvana cried, 'I just burst and all the fluid came out, and I think the baby's died, because I can't feel it kicking any more.' Wanting a boy so badly, and having talked themselves into thinking this baby would be a boy, Angulaalik and Irvana were even more upset than might normally be expected at the thought of losing the baby. Angulaalik was worried that he might not have another son before he grew too old, although certainly there were no signs of this happening yet. Irvana produced a new baby almost every year and by this time had borne eleven children, not all of them by Angulaalik.

Clearly the sac had burst and the fluid drained, but this looked to me like a case of false labour. Irvana was obsessed with the idea that the child was dead because she no longer felt it kicking. I told her to quit worrying. 'We can fix that easily,' I told her. 'The whitemen have a special medicine for that.' I hurried back to the post and got out the Company medical manual. I found there wasn't much I could do about false labour, but I could certainly do something to set Irvana's mind at rest.

I grabbed a couple of two-twenty-twos (a mild sedative rather like aspirin) and a mortar and pestle.

Once back at Angulaalik's house, I asked him to prepare some powdered milk. With elaborate ceremony I put the two-twenty-twos in the mortar and poured a little milk on them and ground them into a paste. This I took to Irvana, pausing for effect as she reached for it. 'It is a very powerful medicine,' I cautioned, 'so be ready for a quick reaction.'

She downed it bravely in one big gulp, and a moment later her face lit up and she said, 'Oh yes, I can feel how strong it is going down me.'

I was congratulating myself for this display of the power of suggestion when Irvana gave a gasp and grabbed her stomach. 'The baby kicked!'

Angulaalik jumped up with a big smile on his face and said, 'Are you sure?'

'Yes,' she said, 'he kicked again.' When she referred to the baby she used the term *nutaraksaqquk* (our baby-to-be); Eskimos never say 'baby' until the child is actually born.

Angulaalik turned to me and thanked me and said, 'Well, maybe you'd better stay till it comes.'

Irvana herself was the midwife for most of the women in the settlement, but with her own baby coming she called in Illiviuyaq, the wife of Paniuyaq. She didn't really want Illiviuyaq because she was untidy and dirty. However, at the time Illiviuyaq happened to be the only woman at the trading post since all the others were out with their families in hunting camps. But she was a good-natured, motherly woman. As soon as Irvana had calmed down I returned to the post. The next morning word was sent that Irvana was in labour.

So I went over to Angulaalik's house again, and found Irvana on the bed sitting back on her haunches with her knees bent underneath her. She was already sweating and contracting and obviously in the beginning throes of labour. So we sat there,

Angulaalik and I, and watched Irvana. Illiviuyaq was there too, bustling around the house. Every now and then she would come over and press Irvana's stomach and ask, 'How do you feel now?'

With eleven kids under her belt, so to speak, this was old stuff to Irvana. She wasn't worried any more about the baby being dead. But still the baby hung on and hung on and wouldn't come out. The labour pains were coming closer together but still there was no sign of the baby. Irvana said, 'He doesn't want to come out; he is shy.'

'Well, it must be that this baby-to-be is a girl, then,' said Angulaalik. 'If it were a boy, he would know how much we wanted him and would come out. If it's a girl, she knows that we don't want her; she doesn't want to come out.'

The labour dragged on and on and the pains became worse. Eskimos believe that if a child is slow to be born, it means that it knows the house is dirty or that the midwife is dirty. In this case the house was spotless, so Angulaalik sent Illiviuyaq into the other room and very politely suggested that perhaps she should wash her hands. He asked her if she was menstruating. She assured him she was not. According to the Eskimos, a menstruating woman is very dangerous to a child about to be born.

Irvana called us back. 'I felt him moving.' She rose up on her knees. Angulaalik had placed a bar across the foot of the bed, and she held on to the bar, gripped it hard as the pains came, and rose up on her knees again. A new caribou skin had been put underneath her so that when the baby came out the first thing it would see would be a new, clean caribou skin. When the baby started to come, Irvana hiked her dress up and tucked it around her breasts; now Illiviuyaq pressed forcibly on her stomach. I was afraid that she was pressing so hard she might damage the baby, but she knew what she was doing.

At last the baby began to slip out, in the normal position, head first. The Eskimos believe a breech birth is bad, that it is very unlucky when a baby is born feet first. So when Irvana's child started to come naturally, it was a good sign right away. Irvana and Illiviuyaq cradled their arms and caught it so that neither its head nor its body touched any part of the sleeping platform. That is a taboo. The baby is not allowed to touch even the new caribou skin until it has been cleaned up.

The baby had a loop of the umbilical cord wrapped around

its neck and its face was a dark bluish-red colour. It wasn't noticeably breathing. Irvana quickly picked it up and unwrapped the cord from its neck and then handed the baby to Illiviuyaq, who took it by the back of the neck with one hand and by the feet with the other and shook it vigorously. When the baby didn't cry right away, Angulaalik came over and stood by it and sang a birthing song to it, a special little chant specially for new-born children. This is supposed to induce the child to give voice for the first time. The midwife was already shaking the daylights out of the poor baby to make it cry, but the father still had to sing to it. As Angulaalik chanted, Illiviuyaq kept on shaking the baby, and in another moment or so it burst into a yell.

When the baby uttered its first cry everyone shouted, '*Tamayya inuuliqtuq!*' ('Here it is! It is starting to live!')

Then Irvana, with Illiviuyaq's help, took some caribou sinew and bound off the umbilical cord, both close to the baby and close to herself, and with an *ulu* which had been specially cleaned she sliced the cord.

The baby was a girl after all. Because it was a female child, Illiviuyaq took the skin of the *siksik* (ground squirrel) and wiped the baby carefully all over. Eskimos consider ground squirrels to be very attractive animals. The skin of the *siksik* is always used to clean female babies, so that they will be pretty too. If the child had been a boy, Illiviuyaq would have used the skin from the forehead of the bull caribou, the *pangniq*. She had both ready, of course, just in case. The Eskimos believe that if a baby boy is cleaned with the *pangniq* he will grow up to be a good hunter and kill many bull caribou.

The person who first cleans a baby in this way, whether it is the midwife as in this case, or someone else, is called the *uaqti* (the cleaning person or washing woman). That relationship, closely equivalent to our system of designating a godfather or godmother, lasts the life of the child, and any Eskimo knows who his *uaqti* was.

There are other rituals, too, which used to be followed but which are dying out. With this child Angulaalik did something that normally is done only for a male child. He took the beak of a yellow-bellied loon (*tuullik*) and touched it to the mouth of the child and turned it all around, just touching the mouth. This is to make the child a good singer, particularly to give it a beautiful voice for the songs of the drum dance.

After the child had been washed and dried off by its *uaqti,* it was given its name; an Eskimo baby is not considered a human being until it has been named. Irvana and Angulaalik named her Uqalitaaraq. After she was named, she was given her first clothing, and certain little amulets and good luck pieces, *atataq,* were fastened to her clothing.

With a male child it was common to take two little bones from the foot of a wolf, pierce and string them together, and tie them to the clothing. That would give the child, when it grew up, staying power on the hunt. He would be as persistent as the wolf in hunting. Sometimes a ptarmigan feather would be used so that the hunter-to-be would have crouching ability, the ability to blend in with the background and so be hidden from his prey. The hair of a fox would ensure agility. Very good indeed would be the hair of the weasel, the ermine, considered by the Eskimos to be the most bloodthirsty killer in the Arctic; such a good luck *atataq* would make the man-to-be a great killer of game. In the case of a girl, various amulets ensured that she would grow up to be a fine seamstress or the bearer of many strong sons.

Because this was a girl, Angulaalik now had to obey certain taboos. Had it been a boy, then Irvana would have had to observe the taboos. Oddly, the birth taboos are much like the death taboos. The person under taboo is not allowed to do any work at all, and especially no work connected with either bones or ice. Angulaalik was forbidden to break any bone to get out the marrow, or to cut up ice to make a window in a snow-house or to melt for drinking or making tea. The birth taboo had to be followed until the *mikslaq* (umbilicus) healed up. If the taboo was broken, the baby would die.

In the spring of 1961, an X-ray plane came to Perry Island from Cambridge Bay, and the government health nurses X-rayed all the Eskimos in the area except one family who were out hunting. That plane brought trouble with it, or perhaps the trouble came as a result of a combination of things. Someone on the plane brought flu germs to Perry.

The Perry Islanders had been out of contact with whites all winter, and they had no immunity. They went down like flies. At first Alikammiq, the shaman, and I went around ministering to the ill. There seemed little cause for alarm—most people just had colds and sniffles; but things quickly became much worse, and sufferers started running high temperatures.

Everyone in the area was there for the X-ray plane and had built their snowhouses all around the trading post. Alikammiq started going around all the snowhouses, using the *qilayuq* (head lifting) method of shamanizing to discover the cause or person responsible for the epidemic. Then he went down too, and I was left the only healthy person out of the whole band of eighty or more.

I had a stock of medicine for such emergencies, and like Alikammiq began making the rounds of the snowhouses, dosing everyone with the same series of shots and pills. After a while I found people were getting worse, so I decided to get on the radio and call Cambridge Bay for help. Possibly the nursing station there could send a plane with someone who could help. But I found my batteries were down, and when I went out to run the power plant to recharge them, it had just started when it went right out—something wrong inside. Normally I could repair almost anything that happened to the little generator, but this time I couldn't locate the trouble. Without the power plant there was no way I could reach Cambridge Bay and advise of the epidemic at Perry Island.

By now many people were seriously sick, running fevers up to 105 and 106. We had to wrap Irvana in sheets with ice to try to bring her temperature down. Between calls I stripped down the power plant, trying to get it going again so I could call for help. When that failed I cooked up big vats of soup and caribou stew. I put the pots on a little sled and hauled them around with me everywhere I went. I was literally the only person on his feet. I was run ragged.

All the dogs had to be fed too. I would make my last call at twelve o'clock at night to give penicillin shots; it would take me an hour or so to get around; then I would have a couple of hours' sleep, and at four in the morning I would make my next round with the shots. I had started out with sulphadiazine but soon ran out of that—we hadn't anticipated a major epidemic. I turned to oral penicillin until that too was gone, and then began giving penicillin intravenously. Then the first person died, a boy. At the snowhouses I didn't mention the death; in an epidemic like this, I have found more than once, Eskimos just seem to give up hope if discouraged.

Many of them had tied a thong around their heads—one of the methods used by the Eskimos to ward off the evil spirit when the shaman is not available. The shaman himself, Alikammiq, not only had the flu, but he was complaining of severe back pain. Finally, he wasn't even able to answer when I spoke to him.

Somehow the other Eskimos knew that the powerful old shaman was dying. Angulaalik and the others, most of them really quite ill, came out of their houses down to Alikammiq's house. It is an Eskimo custom that if a friend or someone they know well is dying, they will try to see him before the breath leaves his body. I did not protest that they should not be out of their beds themselves. I realized it would do no good. Alikammiq was the second victim of the epidemic.

Angulaalik and Alikammiq had been close friends for years and had even shared wives at one time. When Angulaalik saw that his friend was dead, he broke down. His head dropped down between his knees, and I thought perhaps he had fainted; he was very ill himself. Then his head came up, and he uttered a terrible, stricken wail. The cry swelled up from all the people in the room, a cry so heart-breaking and full of despair that I myself felt their loss.

In the course of the next week, four more people died. Altogether six people died in that epidemic, five adults and a child.

On the thirteenth day of the epidemic, an Eskimo arrived from Cambridge Bay by dogteam. He didn't know anything about our trouble. As soon as I saw him I got him away from the settlement to keep him from being exposed to the sickness. I gave him my fresh dogs and told him to get back to Cambridge Bay as fast as he could. I wrote out a letter describing our plight to show them. 'If you can't find a nurse, give it to any whiteman you see, at a DEW line station or anywhere, but tell them that a lot of people are going to die here if we don't get help.' The fellow took off immediately; he didn't even spend the night in Perry Island. I watched him go and hoped he wouldn't come down with the flu on the way back.

Fortunately no one else died and several people began to show improvement. The worst was over by the seventeenth day—the day a plane arrived. Our messenger had made a remarkably fast run and the people at Cambridge had responded immediately. They sent a couple of nurses, and a man to fix my power plant. Five of the sick were flown to Cambridge Bay for treatment at the nursing station. Two of the most serious cases were flown on to the hospital in Edmonton.

The death rituals for Alikammiq were followed very closely since he had been such a great shaman. As a sharing-husband with Alikammiq's son Nasarlulik, I was considered a relative and expected to take part in these rituals.

When a person dies, the body remains in the house on the sleeping platform for four days. The women who actually live in that snowhouse, who are members of that household, observe the death taboos for five days; all male relatives follow the taboos for four days. During this period neither men nor women can take part in sewing or sawing of any material. They cannot hammer anything, and they must not break any bones. If the meat of caribou or seal is eaten, the bones must not be broken to get at the marrow. During the entire period the women must remain on the sleeping platform. It is taboo for a woman's feet to touch the floor of the snowhouse.

At the end of the fourth day the body of the dead man is dressed in his cleanest clothes. The body of Alikammiq was wrapped in deerskins and thongs were lashed around it to make sure he didn't pop out. (The taboo on sewing even prevents the women from sewing the body into its caribou shroud.) Nasarlulik and I had to dress the old man. By this time Alikammiq's body was frozen stiff because we had no heat in the snowhouse since his death. If we had, the body would have been putrid.

It was now time to 'bury' Alikammiq. We laid his body on a sled with his head in the direction that we would travel toward his burial place. We hitched up only four dogs.

Eskimos are not buried in the sense that they are put into the ground. No one could dig into ground frozen rock-hard. They are laid to rest at a spot which they pick before their death. Nasarlulik knew where Alikammiq's place was and took us to a gravel bar up on the side of the inlet overlooking the sea.

We lifted the shrouded body, just Nasarlulik and I, and we walked around in the direction the sun takes in the sky. We walked in a wide circle three times around the place where we were going to leave Alikammiq. Then we laid him down with his head facing toward the west.

His son made a little hole in the skins which were wrapped around him, close to his head. This allowed his soul to escape. In all my time with the Eskimos I have never heard them talk specifically about an afterlife. The Eskimos around Perry Island and Bathurst Inlet seemed very vague about any such concept. However, Nasarlulik explained to me that his father's soul would wander near the body and stay in that area until a new-born child in the settlement had been named for him. Until such time as this was done, Alikammiq's spirit would get restless and make trouble for the band.

Leaving the body, we walked another circle around it, then went back to the settlement. It was against the taboo to look back. We just left the body there on top of the bare ground without a marker. Wolves and foxes would clean up the body, and smaller animals like lemmings and mice finish the cleaning of the bones. Sometimes, only a few days after such a 'burial', one may see rib bones, leg bones or a skull picked clean already. Just as it was taboo to look back at the grave, no one was allowed to look at or visit the body again until at least one day had passed. Even after the remains had been scattered by the animals, that place would be known as *alikammip iluvra,* Alikammiq's resting place.

Both birth and death customs were stronger than marriage customs among the Copper Eskimos, at least among those around Perry Island and the Bathurst Inlet region. The Copper Eskimos actually preferred cross-cousin marriages, a relationship that was tabooed as incest among some of the more easterly bands. Many marriages were arranged at birth. If two brothers had children, a boy and a girl, it was automatically assumed that the two would marry when they were old enough. Sometimes this caused a problem. In the case of the death of either, the survivor in this child pairing would have no mate until such time as another family might have a baby that could take the place of the dead one. This sometimes resulted in a troublesome age disparity.

However, if all went well, when a young pair reached the ripe age of sixteen or seventeen, the boy had to go and spend a year working for his prospective father-in-law. All that he hunted and trapped in that period went to the future father-in-law. During that year the young couple would live together in a sort of trial marriage. If, at the end of the year, the father-in-law was convinced that the young man could support his daughter, then the 'bridegroom' was allowed to take her back to his own family, or they set up housekeeping on their own. If they had not hit it off during the trial period, severance was simple. The young man or woman just said '*Avitara*' ('I break off with you') and that was that.

There was no marriage ceremony as such. During the year of trial marriage, others could tell whether it was going well or not. If it was, they would refer to the girl as 'his wife' and the young man as 'her husband.'

Even though the young couple might be betrothed at birth, they didn't get together until the girl had started menstruating and her body had begun to develop. Sometimes during the trial marriage period a baby might be born, but this never bothered the Eskimos in the old days.

These patterns are all changing rapidly now that Eskimo boys and girls are becoming educated in the whiteman's ways. Today it is not uncommon in a settlement to find an eighteen- or twenty-year-old girl still without a husband, something which would have been unthinkable not many years ago. Modern Eskimo girls, with more education than previous generations, want the whiteman's way of marriage. They want romance, love—the kind of thing they see in the movies and observe from the white boys and girls around them.

There is evidence in the North that the old Eskimo way may have been the better way. There was a time when a boy and a girl married, and they each naturally expected to do the things that must be done, took pride in each other and looked naturally for affection from each other. They might not have known 'love' in the modern whiteman's sense, but more often than not, they grew to hold for each other a deep, true care. Not so many in those days found it necessary to say '*Avitara*.'

12
❄ The
Immortals

Alikammiq, an inoffensive, mild-looking little man, had been one of the greatest of the Eskimo shamans in the days before the whiteman drove these ancient practitioners underground. Oddly enough, it was not his ability to walk on water, nor his feat of flying to the moon, not even his return from the dead that won him fame with his own people. The Eskimos all agreed that the fact that he could casually cut off his own leg, wave it in the air for all to see, then re-attach it and walk away, put him in a class by himself.

Walking on water didn't count for much. Any close observer of nature—as every Eskimo is—could see certain insects perform this stunt; it followed quite logically that given the right circumstances, man could do likewise. As for flying through the skies without wings or motor, every Eskimo boy knows that all good shamans do this, and that the really talented ones can fly to the moon whenever they want—and return the same night.

It has long been common knowledge in the land of the Arctic people that it is virtually impossible to kill a shaman. Even when they appear to be dead and have been laid out on the tundra in their best skins for the scavengers to pick over, a proper shaman will very likely rise on the third or fourth day from his resting place and return to confound those who thought he was taken care of.

Alikammiq's feat of cutting off his own leg and then putting it back on was a display that every Eskimo at Perry Island, with the possible exception of one female agnostic, stood ready to swear to having witnessed. If, when questioned individually, they admitted that they hadn't actually seen it happen, they could at least name one person who had witnessed the event and could vouch for its authenticity.

Many of the people at Perry Island recalled with considerable glee the time a whiteman, a new police constable, came to Perry Island from Cambridge Bay. Hearing about this particular talent possessed by Alikammiq, he swore that no such heathen shenanigans would take him in.

He went with a group of Perry Islanders to Alikammiq's settlement by the mouth of the Perry River where the shaman lived with some other hunters. New in the country and new to its ways, the young policeman flatly refused to believe the stories of the shaman. He told Alikammiq that he had heard of his self-amputation, and that he for one knew it to be a ruse. He brazenly suggested that Alikammiq was probably not even a proper shaman.

Naturally, Alikammiq could not stand for such things being said. Not only were they rude, but they were uttered in the presence of seven or eight Eskimos in Alikammiq's own settlement. This left Alikammiq with no choice but to prove his claims; he could not let the policeman's ill-mannered challenge go unanswered.

He grabbed a snowknife stuck in the wall of the snowhouse and turned to his antagonist.

'Here, take this,' he said, handing the snowknife, butt-end first, to the policeman.

'Now,' he continued, putting his foot up on the sleeping platform so that his leg was right in front of the startled whiteman, 'if you don't believe me, go ahead and cut my leg right off here.' He pointed just above his knee.

According to the Eskimos who were there, the young constable was nonplussed. He was so unnerved at this unusual offer that he dropped the snowknife. They say that from that time on he never doubted Alikammiq again—or at least, he never said so publicly.

The Eskimos often cited this incident as proof that Alikammiq could indeed cut off his leg and restore it. But to me the story seemed a beautiful example of the shaman's grasp of practical psychology. Alikammiq had pulled a magnificent bluff—one he knew he would get away with.

There was the lone whiteman, perhaps no more than twenty-two or twenty-three years old, hundreds of miles from the help of his own kind, new to the country and suddenly aware that he was among a group of very tough people, most of whom were already annoyed at him for insulting their respected shaman. If he had taken the knife and cut into Alikammiq's leg, the chances are he would never have escaped to enjoy his piece of oneupmanship. He wouldn't, either, have been the first RCMP to be killed by the Eskimos.

I never ceased to be amazed at the phenomenal range of abilities credited to the shamans. They turned at will into polar bears or birds; they could become small enough to slip through a keyhole or make themselves disappear entirely; they healed the sick, flew to the moon, changed the weather, found caribou or seal, and used every trick I ever heard of in the way of ventriloquism, hypnotism and sleight-of-hand.

Eskimos don't just believe that shamans can fly; they know it. There is a crater west of Perry Island which, Eskimos will explain, marks the spot where two great shamans collided in mid-air and fell to the ground. When the United States first crash-landed a rocket on the moon, I thought this a tremendous feat, and I excitedly told the Eskimos about it. They listened to me politely but I could tell they were amused rather than amazed. Finally one man spoke up.

'Yes,' he said, 'that is good, but the shamans have always been able to go to the moon.' He thought me a bit dull to consider a rocket to the moon so remarkable.

Not every shaman can fly. Only superior shamans fly and when they do so, they are careful to take off outside the range of sight of ordinary people, perhaps behind a hill. For the flight to be successful, they must take off from a patch of snow where there are no tracks of any kind, human or animal. And no shaman can fly with any piece of metal on his body—a knife or even a button will make flight impossible.

Although shamans take their leave in secret, they can be seen once they are in flight. The sighting of a meteor or shooting star was sure evidence that Alikammiq was in the sky.

A trip to the moon is never a frivolous undertaking. The most common motive would seem to be to help a barren woman have a child. When a woman has been married several years but has not had a child, she seeks help just as a white woman might. The Eskimo woman approaches the shaman. The shaman enters a trance and, after summoning his helping spirits, takes off on a magical flight to the moon. There he picks up a child for the woman and hurries back with it. His modest remuneration for the service is the privilege of spending the night with that woman in her bed. There are certainly those who would argue that the flight to the moon had little to do with the procurement of the baby, but an Eskimo will assure anyone who enquires that babies never result from a single sexual encounter.

Some consider a shaman's 'immortality' his most outstanding characteristic. On occasion a shaman has been seemingly 'killed', perhaps in a duel with another Eskimo over the favours of a woman (the shamans are as mortal as any man in their desires). Everyone knew, however, that even when the shaman met his 'death' in such a manner, he would return to life within three or four days and, more often than not, take revenge on those who had 'slain' him. It was this acceptance of the shaman's ability to rise from the dead that always made it easy for Eskimos to understand the Christian Jesus's rise from his sepulchre. They see nothing extraordinary in it at all.

The Perry River people would tell of a duel that Alikammiq fought with two men who 'fatally' shot him with their rifles. His relatives took Alikammiq's body and laid it out for the waiting period decreed by the death taboos. Sure enough, on the third day he came back to life, and he and his family hunted down his assailants. One was killed; the other narrowly escaped.

According to Eskimo belief it is almost impossible for an ordinary man to kill a shaman. The only man who can is another, more powerful shaman. If a shaman should die, it indicates that another shaman has put a spell on him. His death would never simply be attributed to old age or illness.

Of no small benefit to the shaman's longevity is the hole in the centre of his chest, and his ability to move that hole to any part of his body at will. Alikammiq once gave a practical demonstration in a dispute with a man named Savgut. When the argument turned ugly, the two decided to settle their differences with rifles.

Alikammiq challenged Savgut: 'Shoot me!'

Savgut did just that. Only a few feet away from Alikammiq,

he levelled his weapon at his chest and fired. Nothing happened. Witnesses claim that they saw the snow puff up behind Alikammiq where the bullet landed, but the old shaman was unharmed. He in turn raised his rifle and coolly shot off part of Savgut's ear. Savgut fled the area with his family and dared not return. Those present swear that Savgut shot Alikammiq right through the chest from a range of not more than three or four feet. He could not have missed. The bullet went through Alikammiq's body and out the back: Alikammiq had quickly shifted the hole in his chest so that the bullet passed harmlessly through without touching him. What other explanation could there be?

Another incident was reported to me by a man who said he had actually thrust a seal harpoon through Alikammiq's chest without hurting him. Qingarullikkaaq, an old trapper and hunter, had shown some scepticism about the shaman's capabilities; so, in a roomful of people, Alikammiq dared him.

He invited the sceptic to plunge a knife or any weapon into him. The only handy object happened to be a harpoon. Alikammiq continued to challenge him, so Qingarullikkaaq grabbed the weapon and jabbed it with a powerful thrust right through Alikammiq's chest. Other witnesses told me they actually saw this, and claim that the harpoon head came out of Alikammiq's back.

There was considerable difficulty in removing the harpoon from Alikammiq's body. Qingarullikkaaq told me that he personally pulled out the shaft of the harpoon after they had cut the head off. It felt as if he were pulling a harpoon from a seal.

Alikammiq lifted his parka. There was a hole in it where the harpoon had passed through, and a bruise on his chest just where his ribs met—but no wound and no bleeding. Qingarullikkaaq was convinced and never doubted Alikammiq again. Some time later, Alikammiq's skill as a healer saved Qingarullikkaaq's life.

Sometimes the shamans would use their powers to play tricks on the whitemen, often in an impish way. Once Alikammiq and another shaman, Aittauraaluk, decided to visit the police at Cambridge Bay. They looked inside the police office and saw a constable working at his desk, a young fellow in his stockinged feet, wearing suspenders over his long underwear. The two shamans were in a playful mood, so they assumed tiny shapes, slipped in through the keyhole and suddenly materialized in front of the surprised constable. When he looked up astonished, they disappeared up the chimney and stood laughing on the roof. The policeman rushed outside, but was unable to see the two pranksters, because they had made themselves invisible again. The constable, it is said, doesn't know what happened to this day.

Many times the shamans have performed amazing tricks just to demonstrate their powers. A favourite trick of the great shaman Utuggauq, who was noted for his ability to foretell where caribou would be found, was to swallow the ear of a caribou and then pass it out through the wall of his stomach. He would first wet the ear thoroughly, then hold his head back and swallow hard, making certain everyone could see him gulping down the ear. Then he would straighten up and pat his stomach and ask someone to lift up his parka carefully. There, lo and behold, was the caribou ear, still wet, stuck to his skin right next to his navel.

On one occasion, at a dance festival in the *qalgi*, Utuggauq and Aittauraaluk put on a magic display. They stood together in the centre of the floor with the people all around them on tiers against the walls. Aittauraaluk and Utuggauq stood about six feet apart, heads back, and took turns changing into polar bears. Each did this by first making a pair of fangs grow in his mouth. These fangs projected visibly out of the mouth when the shaman raised his head, disappeared when he lowered his head and reappeared growing in the mouth of his partner who stood opposite. So great was the power of suggestion engendered by these top-notch shamans that all who saw them were absolutely convinced.

Every shaman, according to Eskimo belief, has the ability to take on the form of an animal, any animal, as quick as a flash. In fact some otherwise ordinary people can do the same. Some have this ability to a very great degree: old Eskimo legends frequently describe such happenings—a man becomes a wolverine, or a woman falls in love with and marries a man in the form of a goose. Certain whitemen are said to be able to turn into wolves.

But however many tricks he might be called upon to perform, storms to shift from their course, or murders to circumvent, the true role of the shaman is that of a healer...a faith healer. I have spoken many times to Eskimos about shamans, and they have always compared them to physicians rather than to missionaries in the whiteman's culture. When an Eskimo hears about a doctor operating on someone, he will say that the shaman, too, 'opens' people to remove the evil spirit. That is, the shaman will not literally operate on a sick Eskimo, but will draw out the cause of the sickness.

I did not understand what a shaman was to the Eskimos until I had been in the Arctic for several years. Nor did I understand their full function, nor appreciate their power until I lived with the Perry Island people. A shaman is for the most part a trapper and a hunter, just like ordinary men, but with his vital difference. He is not a 'medicine man'. He is not feared by other Eskimos, though he is held in awe. He is not a witch doctor. His prime responsibility is to cure sickness, and in doing so, he deals with the supernatural.

Angulaalik was one of the first to tell me in detail of the shamans' healing abilities. He told a story about the great shaman Utuggauq. A woman who had suffered a painful arm for some months finally decided to seek the shaman's help. Utuggauq agreed to try and relieve the pain. Everyone in the settlement gathered to watch.

After carefully examining the woman, he told her he would remove the pain by 'sucking it out.' He laid the woman on her back with her arms above her head and told her to clench her fist. When the arm was rigid, he rubbed it vigorously and placed his mouth over the sore spot, sucking very hard. He did not go into the usual trance. Angulaalik explained that he was watching closely, both because of a professional interest as a one-time shaman himself, and because Utuggauq was acting in an unusual way, 'like one who couldn't be believed.' The shaman continued to suck on the arm, apparently withdrawing something. He spat into his hand and held it out for all the onlookers to see. In his hand were small, pebble-like objects, some of them quite large. He dipped them into the oil of the blubber lamp and threw them out into the open air, indicating that they were now harmless. This was a type of shamanizing that Angulaalik had never seen before, yet it appeared successful. The woman was completely cured and was never again troubled by pains in her arm. Utuggauq slept with the woman that night, presumably his fee for the treatment.

During the period I spent at Perry Island, there occurred a case of what proved to be rheumatic fever. At the time I thought it was just a bad case of flu and set about treating the man, Qingarullikkaaq, as best I could. In those days all Hudson's Bay men at isolated posts doubled as doctors, handling virtually all medical services for the people of the area. I wasn't certain what it was that afflicted Qingarullikkaaq, but knew he was in bad shape with a temperature of 104 degrees. I dosed him with antibiotics, sulphadiazene and penicillin, but he showed no improvement. I was at a loss as to what to do next.

Qingarullikkaaq's wife decided he needed the help of the shaman, and invited me to attend a session that night with Alikammiq. Naturally I was delighted and excited; little is now ever seen of the practice of shamanism. Here, in the Perry River country, were some of the few shamans left who practised openly. That night in Qingarullikkaaq's snowhouse there were five of us watching the sick man and Alikammiq.

Eskimos believe that all sickness and death are the work of a supernatural spirit, an evil spirit, known in the Perry Island dialect as the *agiuqtuq*. When someone dies, his name must be passed on, preferably to his own newborn child, but at least to a newborn child of a relative in the region. If there is no newborn child available, then the name will be passed on to a newborn pup. If this is not done within one winter of the death, then that name turns into an *agiuqtuq*, and will cause sickness or death among humans and dogs alike. Illness is attributed to an *agiuqtuq* from one of the victim's relatives who perhaps unknowingly has broken a taboo.

The shaman acts as an intermediary between the natural world and the supernatural world, the world of spirits. The first step in a case such as Qingarullikkaaq's is for the shaman to find out from whom this particular evil spirit is coming. To do this the shaman holds a seance, goes into a self-induced trance and summons his helping spirits, his familiars, to aid him in locating the *agiuqtuq* responsible.

This is what Alikammiq did. Qingarullikkaaq was lying on his back on the snow platform. Alikammiq crouched down on the floor of the snowhouse and began bobbing up and down, bending and dipping from the waist, calling on his helping spirits. Spirits are just like mortals in one respect. They like to visit around, and a shaman can never be sure where they may be off to.

Gradually Alikammiq assembled his spirits. Each new spirit that possessed him would seem more frightening and dangerous than the last. The watchers grew very tense. When the shaman felt that all his familiar spirits were assembled, he proceeded with the *qilayuq* method (head-lifting) to learn which spirit was causing the sickness.

Alikammiq tied a sealskin thong around Qingarullikkaaq's head. Standing beside the man, with a tight grip on the thong, Alikammiq began a series of questions that required a yes or no answer. The sick person would reply, acting unconsciously, by headweight alone. If the answer was no, the head would lift up by the thong easily. If the answer was yes, the head would be difficult to lift.

Chattering away in the shaman language, bowing his knees as he pulled on the thong, Alikammiq would exhale strongly, almost gasping. It was remarkable to see the change that had come over Alikammiq as he operated under the trance. In everyday life around the settlement, the little shaman was a somewhat timid person, very quiet by nature. But as his familiar spirits took control of him, he underwent a total personality change. He loudly challenged us to 'try him' (by thrusting a knife into his body), and twice he lapsed into an imitation of a polar bear, indicating that the spirit of the animal had completely overtaken him.

The questions continued for almost an hour; always the head lifted easily and the answer was no. Finally Alikammiq struck on the name of a dead relative—Qingarullikkaaq's head became very heavy and it was all Alikammiq could do to budge it. The identity of the *agiuqtuq* was revealed.

The tension in the snowhouse was broken by sudden exclamations. Even I could remember that the name of the *agiuqtuq* had not been passed on to anyone in the settlement, not even to one of the dogs.

Yet, even with this success, Alikammiq's work was not done. As sometimes happens, Qingarullikkaaq did not get better. It appeared that the shaman must go on to the second phase of the ritual. When a man fails to recover from his illness once the identity of the evil spirit is known, the Eskimos say that his soul has already left him, stolen by the spirit. The shaman must attack the thief for the soul to return home.

Next day Alikammiq once more summoned his familiar spirits. Then he took a long sealskin thong and tied it around Qingarullikkaaq's parka, which was of ordinary caribouskin. He took the parka outside the snowhouse, left it there, and came back inside with the end of the thong. He prepared to fight a tug of war with the *agiuqtuq* for possession of the parka. Making himself the anchor man, Alikammiq asked two other men to help pull. Together they would attempt to pull the parka back inside the snowhouse, thereby winning the soul of the sick man and assuring his good health. If the thong should break under the strain, the sick man would die.

The latter seemed the likely outcome to me. Qingarullikkaaq's condition was worsening; his temperature was now at 106 degrees. I suspected that the wily old shaman would save face by looping the thong around some steadfast object outside, cut it so as to make it break when pulled, and resign the family to his patient's death in spite of his efforts.

Back in the snowhouse Alikammiq and his helpers had stripped down to their undershirts. They braced themselves as the shaman gave the call to pull. I was sitting beside Irvana not more than three feet away from the porch opening of the snowhouse. I had a clear view of the parka outside on the snow, the three men inside the snowhouse, and the sealskin thong between them. I was sure that I was about to discover where the sham in shamanism was.

The men pulled with obvious strength. I could see the veins and corded muscles on their arms stand out as they strained, pulling the cord in bit by bit, hand over hand. The thong stretched taut, and I expected it to break at any moment.

Incredibly, the parka eased its way towards the door. I watched it like a hawk, seeing but unbelieving. Any ordinary caribou parka weighs two or three pounds at the most; there is virtually no weight to a sealskin thong. There was a simple explanation if one accepted Eskimo belief. Pulling hard against the men was the *agiuqtuq*. The men themselves were not amazed at its strength, nor at the fact that they could see nothing of the adversary. They knew that the *agiuqtuq* was a formless, frameless being, composed purely of blood and totally invisible to all eyes but the shaman's.

Heaving and gasping for breath, they finally pulled the parka completely into the snowhouse. There was an audible sigh of relief, and the men sank back on their haunches. The parka was lifted off the floor to the sleeping platform where Qingarullikkaaq lay. My eyes never strayed from the parka. I casually walked over and picked it up. Nothing unusual! It was an empty parka, no weights, only the thong tied to it—yet I had seen three men use all their strength to pull it into the snow-house.

There was a celebration that night; it seemed Qingarullikkaaq would now get well, and by this time I was as strong a believer as the Eskimos. By the next day, his temperature had dropped.

Still the recovery was not fast enough to suit Alikammiq. He was not convinced that Qingarullikkaaq's soul had been completely recovered. We returned to the snowhouse a third time, as the shaman prepared to do battle with the evil spirit.

Alikammiq armed himself with a tiny wooden bow and arrow, just like a child's toy, only four inches in length, and a wooden dagger. With these he would face the spirit alone in a fight too frightening to be viewed by others.

We sat huddled inside the snowhouse while Alikammiq crawled out onto the low snowporch to fight for Qingarullikkaaq's soul. Presently we heard groans and shouts, apparently the sounds of the struggle. Fearful screams followed, and with a shout in his own voice Alikammiq reappeared at the door of the snowhouse, his hands and clothes bloodied. The blood was recognized by the Eskimos as that of the slain *agiuqtuq*, now visible to all. The shaman had emerged the victor.

Within a few days, Qingarullikkaaq, whom I had expected to die in spite of massive doses of the whiteman's medicine and the efforts of his shaman, was on his feet.

Few whitemen, and no missionary as far as I know, have seen a shaman's séance. They now operate largely underground, but they are active and are believed by a good number of Eskimos and apparently by some whitemen. There was an incident at Cambridge Bay in which the RCMP sought a shaman's help after a fruitless investigation of a theft. Following the shaman's directions, they eventually captured the thief and recovered the stolen property.

Alikammiq was undoubtedly one of the greatest shamans of his time. When I met him he was about fifty years of age, married to the blind and hunchbacked Arnayak. Handicapped as a result of an accident when she was a young woman, she was one of the few such afflicted among the Eskimos to survive. It was from her that I learned much about shamanism and how one is selected as a shaman.

Most are chosen as young boys to be a shaman's apprentice. Generally they are children who do not behave normally, perhaps crying and wailing more than is expected, or wandering off alone. In describing them Arnayak used the term *nakimayuq*, an expression also used in describing the behaviour of a rabid animal. She was careful to avoid any terms used to denote insanity or mental aberration. Such children are considered normal mentally, but abnormal in outward physical behaviour.

An apprentice's training does not start until he is *qauyimmakkami* (aware of himself). Up to a certain stage of childhood Eskimos see children as acting instinctively, quite without reason. By about the age of five or six, however, the child begins to rationalize and he is ready for training.

The difficult shaman language is the first thing an apprentice must master, along with the many songs and chants in the shaman's repertoire. Many expressions and phrases are so ancient that their exact meaning is lost to the oldest of shamans.

By the age of thirteen or fourteen, the apprentice shaman is ready to take part in séances. By this time he must be skilled in ventriloquism, convincing in the power of suggestion and able to divert the attention of his closest observers. If the shaman is not so clever, a good many tricks can be seen through easily. Obviously a great deal of his ritual is for the sole purpose of creating atmosphere, not unlike the musical background or incense pot of the Christian church. And no matter how skilled the apprentice may become, he is not considered a full shaman until he is a mature man.

Surprisingly, missionaries and shamans frequently get on well together, although the missionaries try their best to sway Eskimos from their shamanistic beliefs. Whenever the good Father Lou Menez came down to Perry River, he would question me closely and look through my notes on shamanism. He realized that if he were going to win the population to his religion, he had to know more about their current faith. He did make a few conversions, and even counted Alikammiq and

Arnayak among their number.

I have my doubts whether such conversions meant very much. Most Eskimos at Perry River were nominally Anglicans. When the Anglican missionary arrived at the settlement they would all attend the services, but my observation was that they were all pagans. Belief in shamanism and spirits was strong and generations old. Christianity was popular when the missionary was there; the next day he would be gone and his religion with him.

Anthropologists and others who have lived in the Arctic for only brief periods have written that the Eskimos see spirits in all things, in weather, rocks, animals, and so on. This, as far as I can determine, is not true. Rather, the Eskimo observes taboos connected with natural events such as childbirth or death, so as to avoid invoking the wrath of spirits. If a man, knowingly or unknowingly, breaks such a taboo—and there are countless such—then the hunting may be bad or the weather turn against the people. It is then that the shaman is asked to use his powers to find out who has broken the taboo and to tell the people what must be done to rectify the situation. In the case of an individual committing an offence in full knowledge of what he is doing, then the shaman can assign punishment to the guilty.

But there are limitations on the power of the shamans. They must not interfere in people's private affairs, because, after all, they are just ordinary people themselves in most ways. They make their living by hunting and trapping and do not live off their shamanizing, although they may receive favours and gifts for their successes. They do not occupy any special place in the settlement tribe hierarchy except that which is earned on the basis of their ability. It is the shaman's duty to help people; it is not his job to cast spells on others, or to use his abilities for personal power or gain. A shaman does not practise witchcraft, though witchcraft, according to Eskimo belief, is available to anyone who cares to indulge.

Many tales of the powers of shamans are told by Eskimos at Perry River and Bathurst Inlet. The events may have taken place years ago, but the people believe them still.

13
A New Name for Paniuyaq

One of those who had to be taken all the way to Charles Camsell Hospital in Edmonton during the Perry Island flu epidemic had been a man named Paniuyaq. He was kept there several months before being allowed to return. When he did get back to Perry all seemed to be well, and he and his partner, Iminngaaq, left right away for their hunting camp some twenty-four miles from the trading post. There Paniuyaq's family joined him.

The summer bloomed and faded into fall, and it wasn't a summer we were sorry to have done with. There had been trouble with ice and great difficulty in bringing the annual supply ship into the harbour at all. Then, early in the fall, long before freeze-up was normally due, a great field of ice drifted into the southern shores of Queen Maud Gulf, covering the entire sea. As far as the horizon all we could see was a mass of moving ice, blocking and choking off our harbour, the river and the inlet.

I was alone at the post on the island when Iminngaaq unexpectedly arrived. He said he had walked in from his camp, hiking way inland to a point where he could ford the Perry River and then in to the post to tell me that Paniuyaq had suffered a relapse and was very sick. He thought Paniuyaq might be going to die.

I got the nursing station at Cambridge on the radio. Iminngaaq described how Paniuyaq's knees and shoulder joints had all swollen up. His throat was giving him a lot of trouble. I passed all these symptoms on to the nursing station.

We advised Cambridge that we couldn't get to Paniuyaq because of all the shifting ice. They sent a plane out, circled low over Paniuyaq's camp but found they couldn't land because there wasn't enough open water for the plane. There was no way they could get to him, so the plane flew back over the trading post and dropped a message letting me know.

They asked if I thought there was any chance of getting a team of dogs and going overland, picking Paniuyaq up and bringing him back to the trading post. They had observed a clear stretch of water in the bay near the post and believed they could get in there on their floats if we could bring him that far. The problem was that for all the ice, we had no snow cover on the ground yet, and dragging a heavy sled across dry land is a terrible job. I was doubtful whether the dogs could do it. Iminngaaq and I decided to have a look at the ice in the channel. Given a reasonable chance, we would attempt to take the sled over the ice to Paniuyaq's camp.

We hitched up my dogs and took the sled down to the edge of the ice field. We tied sealskin boots on the dogs' feet so they wouldn't be lacerated by the candle ice and also to give the dogs better traction on the ice. We figured that if the dogs fell into the water, they wouldn't all fall in at once and those still on the floe could pull the others out. Our sled was a big twenty-two-footer, which meant that it was long enough to bridge the open stretches from ice floe to ice floe. We thought we'd try it.

At first we went gingerly; the dogs would leap onto a small ice floe, and it would tip. Some floes were only six or seven inches thick, others were three or four feet thick, but they were all tipsy, moving in the water at the least pressure and sliding in every direction. Yet we soon discovered that sitting on the sled we were relatively safe. We felt very insecure, but the length of the sled made it easier than we had expected. The long runners would extend over one or two of the smaller floes, and just as we began to sink, the dogs would be scrambling ahead and pulling us onto the next one; then, as that one went down under our weight, we would reach the next. It was all right as long as we kept going; we just seemed to be moving on a continually sinking carpet. Every now and then we would hit a big ice floe, one that might stretch a hundred and fifty feet or so, and we would catch our breath.

We decided that as long as things were going so well in the channel, there was no point in going onto the land, where we should have to help the dogs drag the sled over gravel, sand and rock. So we continued over the ice. There were some alarming moments, but we kept going.

The first serious trouble confronted us at the mouth of the Perry River. There the fresh water flowing into the sea had worn away the ice, and the water looked black and dangerous. We had no choice but to skirt around it and head out to sea, where the ice appeared to be more firmly packed. All the time this ice was moving, grinding, shifting around. It wasn't packed ice or solid ice, just a mass of constantly moving floes. We went way out, beyond some islands.

Just as we had left the islands behind, the wind came up and began to push the ice, threatening to move it offshore altogether. There we would be, drifting with no canoe, nothing, just drifting out to sea with thirteen sled dogs. We quickly scooted over to the biggest ice floe we could find and sat tight there for a while to see what was going to happen.

The wind seemed to be definitely pushing the ice away from the shore. We had to make a dash for shore before it was too late. Yet the nearer we worked our way to the shore, the more open water we found. There was an open channel at least a hundred yards wide separating the ice and the shoreline.

We thought perhaps the ice might still be jammed against the shore farther east, so we pushed along in that direction, still fortunately the direction of the camp. By now we had been out on the ice the entire day. It had taken us nine or ten hours to cover about twenty miles, with an empty sled. All I had brought along was some medicine, drugs and a grub box. Just in case we couldn't get back with Paniuyaq, I wanted to have some stuff to attempt to treat whatever his ailment proved to be.

To our relief, as we kept pushing east, riding up one floe and down the next as they bobbed in the sea, the wind switched, and a little farther along we found the ice was pushed in against the shore. No time was wasted in making for shore and soon afterwards we sighted Iminngaaq's camp.

Illiviuyaq, Paniuyaq's wife, fixed us a mug-up of tea while I examined her husband. He looked bad, and from his symptoms I suspected rheumatic fever. Though I had never had any experience before with rheumatic fever, I decided to treat him for it. I gave him some drugs, and we watched him for any change. After two or three days I could see no improvement, and was beginning to feel it was beyond me. After all I was a fur-trader, not a doctor. I thought we had better take the risk of getting him back to the post and from there to the nursing station at Cambridge Bay for proper treatment.

The wind was still blowing in toward the shore and packing the ice well. We got Paniuyaq into a sleeping bag, well bundled up, laid some caribou skins on top of the sled, and off we went again. For the first ten miles or so we found the ice packed in so tightly by the wind and tide that we had virtually no trouble. At the mouth of the river, however, we once again ran into problems. A large lead or break in the ice had been opened by the river's current, and again we had to detour out to sea seven or eight miles. Coming back in we ran into difficult ice floes on the other side of the river, because all the islets out there had kept the water more or less open.

At one point we thought we had had it. The back of the sled went right down in the water, a good six feet, slipping off one of the floes. Only the fact that the dogs were able to keep on their feet, scrambling forward, kept the sled from going on to the bottom. Paniuyaq was sitting up forward and hanging on for dear life. We had wanted to lash him on the sled to keep him from falling off, but he had asked us not to just in case the sled did slip into the water. We had attached long ropes to the sled in case it had to be pulled out, but I was certain a bath in that icy water would have meant the end of our patient.

Once back at the post, our troubles were not over. Before a plane could set out from Cambridge Bay, a storm came up, pushing the ice inshore, clogging the strip of clear water on which the craft could land. Iminngaaq felt he should return to his camp to take care of the women and children of the two families, and he made the trip back on foot.

I was alone on Perry Island with the sick man, but Cambridge Bay called back and the nursing station had figured out from the symptoms I had relayed to them that Paniuyaq probably had rheumatic fever. My confidence was restored when they confirmed my diagnosis. They told me to put him on anti-biotics, and for ten days I nursed him, shooting him full of antibiotics every day. At last he began to get better.

About then Iminngaaq and the two families arrived back at

the post. They had left their sled in camp and made pack saddles for the dogs to carry supplies and had walked back to the post.

Paniuyaq moved out of my bed into his own tent. He went off the needle and on pills. Then, because he felt so much better, he stopped taking the medicine entirely. He seemed to be feeling fine, but almost as soon as he quit the pills he suffered another relapse, this time worse than ever.

We started him all over again on the antibiotics and the pills. By now I had been working on him more than two weeks. This time I made him stick with the pills, taking them for a full week after he seemed entirely cured, just to make sure.

About a week later I was skinning out a caribou when Illiviuyaq, Paniuyaq's wife, dropped by for a visit. We talked while I finished the caribou, and later had a mug-up. The conversation turned to Paniuyaq's illness.

'Paniuyaq wants you to name him,' she said.

I didn't understand.

She said, 'He wants you to name him again, because he was so sick.'

Usually the renaming of a person is the function of the shaman, the man who cured the sick person. It hit me suddenly that Illiviuyaq must have associated me in her mind with the shaman, because I had cured her husband. In her eyes, at least, I had kept him alive.

As though reading my mind, she said, 'He would have died if you hadn't nursed him. We're so grateful to you, and he would like you to give him his new name.'

It was a rare honour to give this man a new name. Paniuyaq and Illiviuyaq had been the first to befriend me at Perry Island when I first arrived there and we had always been close.

'All right,' I said, 'I'll name him, and I'll give him a good strong name that will keep him healthy...I'll call him Nanuq— the polar bear.'

The next day the new Nanuq came in with her and thanked me. He said he felt much better with his new name, and added, 'If you ever want to use my wife—you're a single man and we know you need a woman sometimes—you can have her. I know you like women.'

I thought that was very nice of him, but his wife wasn't a particularly attractive woman. I just thanked him and said,

'Well, yes, whenever I feel like it, I'll let you know.' But I never did.

From that time on Nanuq addressed me by a quasi-kinship term—he called me Attiaqsiga, which roughly means 'the one who named me,' and I called him Attiara (the one I named). He hardly ever called me Taqak. He carries the name Nanuq to this day. He lives in Cambridge Bay now and as far as I know hasn't been sick a day since he acquired it.

14

❋ 'You're a Real Eskimo!'

When the white fox trapping season ended at Perry Island, around the last week of March, all the Eskimos who had been living out on the traplines drifted back to the post. A day or two spent turning in their fox pelts and trading for the staples they needed, time for a few mug-ups, time to sit around and visit a bit, and they were ready for the annual spring seal hunt out on the sea ice. This time I convinced myself I should go with them. Since everyone was going, there would be nothing urgent to do at the post, I told myself, but to be truthful, I wanted to learn the Eskimo way of hunting seal with harpoons. Angulaalik had promised to teach me, and this seemed the best opportunity to learn.

There was a great bustle and stir of preparatory activity as the men repaired the long, heavy freight sleds, patched up dog harnesses, filed new heads for harpoons. Finally one morning, to the accompaniment of the shouting of the men, the scampering of the kids, the yelping of excited dogs, and the busy scurrying of the hard-working women, we were ready to go. The entire settlement simply loaded up and moved out as if in a demented dogteam drag race.

I had driven past spring seal hunting camps on the ice and even stopped in to visit with the hunters on some of my trips along the coast, but I didn't know the first thing about this kind of hunting. I had been out in my canoe in the summer both at Spence Bay and at Perry and killed seal with my .22 rifle, but was well aware that was entirely different.

It was a fresh spring morning, a bit of a mist hanging over the coast, but with a good hot sun high above doing its best to burn through the haze. We spread out across the landscape, eighteen families, each with its own dogteam and entourage, keeping a proper distance between teams so there wouldn't be too many dog fights and following the leaders, Angulaalik and another experienced hunter named Kuvluruq.

Twenty miles out from the coast and just off the tip of a little island called Uummannaq, Angulaalik stopped his team. He knew exactly what he was looking for, of course, and had pulled up by an *aayuraq,* an open lead or break in the sea ice, which is caused by the shifting pressures of the ice, and has frozen over again. Such pressures also help to create the jumbled-up, topsy-turvey slabs of rough ice that make such good hiding places for seal dens and breathing holes. Leads like the *aayuraq* where we had stopped freeze over and break open again many times, but such places usually have thinner ice than the ordinary sea ice, often no more than three or four feet thick. Seal tend to congregate along breaks like this, where it is comparatively easy for them to keep open their vital breathing holes.

Angulaalik and some of the older hunters studied the *aayuraq* and decided to set up camp right there, leaving Kuvluruq to take half the families and search farther out for another good campsite. Eight families and I stayed with Angulaalik.

Within moments, the confusion of our departure from Perry was more than matched by the confusion of setting up a new camp on the sea ice. Each family immediately started cutting out snowblocks and building its own snowhouse. I erected mine next to Angulaalik's, but just as I was putting the finishing touches to it, I was disconcerted to notice that mine was the only full snowhouse. The others were all building partial snowhouses called *nallaqtaq,* similar to an ordinary snowhouse except that the top snowblocks are not put in place. Instead, once the walls are head-high, a caribouskin sled cover is thrown over the open top to make the roof. I should have watched the others instead of trying to impress them with the speed of my snowhouse-building technique. These people were old hands at setting up spring camps, and they well knew one thing I had overlooked: warm weather would melt those top blocks of snow and a full house such as I built would cave in—

as in fact mine did later on.

No one gave any directions as to where to build. Each family's house was built wherever it seemed desirable with no apparent order or pattern, yet the result was a camp that formed a sort of rough semi-circle with the houses spaced about fifteen feet apart. All were set side-on to the prevailing northeast wind and each had a low snow porch or entrance and a snowblock windbreak.

The older children took charge of staking and chaining the teams behind the houses, since the dogs would have little work to do the next few weeks, except those special dogs that had been trained to hunt seal. The sleds were unloaded by the women, who took their stoves, cooking pots and bedding skins inside the new snowhouses. We men sorted out our hunting gear. Harpoon shafts were stuck in the snow right alongside the porches, and the *tutiriaq* (caribouskin bags), with the special seal hunting tools that each of us carried, were laid on top of the porches with a thong tying them to the harpoon shaft so they wouldn't blow away if a storm came up. The sleds, after being emptied, were pulled up alongside the houses out of the way, and the kids were put to packing snow around them to prevent the mud and ice on the runners from melting as the weather grew warmer.

The women bustled back and forth between the houses, visiting, gossiping, helping each other, and deciding among themselves who would boil up the caribou for the evening meal. Children cooked up some dog food and fed the howling teams. Somehow, everything was put in order. All the houses were finished, all the hunting equipment was made ready, and everyone was snug and content in a new house and with a full belly. The new camp settled down to sleep.

Early next morning all the hunters set out on foot to find the seal. There were ten in our party, including myself and three teenagers who I was sure knew more about what they were doing than I did. We peeled off across the ice, our seal dogs straining and sniffing at the ends of their long leashes. Each of us carried our own harpoon and the *tutiriaq* containing all our gear. The sun was bearing down on us as we tramped across the ice. We were dressed from head to foot in caribouskin even though it was warm when we were walking. The temperature was actually below zero and we should soon have become chilled without caribouskin clothing.

We followed the *aayuraq* farther out to sea, looking for especially rough places in the ice, and I quickly learned why we needed dogs. Wherever there was a jam-up of rough ice the snow had drifted heavily, and all the seal dens and breathing holes were well hidden under such drifts. I certainly couldn't spot any of them, and apart from the experienced old-timers like Angulaalik, there wasn't a hunter in the group who could function without the help of the dogs. Whenever a dog picked up the seal scent, he was anchored in the snow out of the way while the hunter went forward to check out the spot. We soon found several seal holes this way, but at each, when Angulaalik poked down through the snow with a special snow probe, he found the seal hole too thickly frozen over. 'No seal there.' He explained to me, 'If there were a seal using that hole, there wouldn't be any ice formed over it, or at least the ice would be very thin.'

The Eskimos know the seal as well as another seal might. They know that the seal has to come up to breathe about every five minutes when it is feeding under the ice, that it has to make a number of breathing holes in the ice, beginning when the ice begins to form on the sea and yet is still thin enough for the seal to break through. The seal keeps each hole open by repeatedly breaking through and scratching at it with its flippers as the surrounding ice thickens. The Eskimos know that the only way a seal can be killed in the winter is by catching it as it comes up for air at one of these holes, or when it is in its den under the snow alongside the breathing hole.

It is wholly because of his thorough practical knowledge of how the seal lives, and because of the special techniques and weapons developed over the centuries to hunt the seal under these winter conditions, that the Eskimo has been able to survive in the Arctic.

Finally Angulaalik found an open hole. 'Ah, a seal has been here,' he told me. 'There is no ice over the hole at all.' He showed me how to locate the centre of the seal hole under the snow and gave me a special little instrument called a *kaiptaq* (seal indicator) to insert through the snow down into the hole. When the seal came up for air at that hole again, it would cause this indicator to jiggle and alert me, serving, too, as a guide for my harpoon thrust. Then Angulaalik smoothed and repacked the snow where we had disturbed it, so that the seal wouldn't find any change in the light pattern above it when surfacing. 'The seal is smart,' Angulaalik explained. 'If the light is different when he comes up, he knows right away there is a bear or a man waiting for him there. Then you can sit by the seal hole all day and never see him.'

We cut a snowblock to sit on, and fixed the harpoon on a little stand made of two Y-shaped sticks so I could grab it up in a second. Angulaalik told me again to keep my eyes glued to the little black muskox-horn button on top of my *kaiptaq*, and to remember to jab straight down alongside it with my harpoon. This would ensure that the harpoon would go directly into the centre of the hole and into my target. Having set me up in business, Angulaalik disappeared over the ice to get on with his own hunting.

I sat there with the harpoon alongside me and my feet on the now-empty *tutiriaq* for warmth, and waited. It was a grand way to develop patience. Self-conscious and tense, but determined to be ready if that *kaiptaq* button started to move, I resisted all temptation to shift about or even to scratch. I had already tamped the snow under my *tutiriaq* so that no creaking would betray me to the seal when I stood up to go into action. The razor-sharp steel head had been attached to the harpoon shaft, and all I had to do was rise silently and quickly when the *kaiptaq* moved, then plunge the harpoon straight down in the snow. Even though I wouldn't be able to see the seal, I knew that if I hit truly along the *kaiptaq*, which marked the exact centre of the seal hole, I would smash the cutting edge of the harpoon right into the seal's head, or at worst its shoulder. It seemed ridiculously easy.

After Angulaalik left, I took a quick bearing on the sun and one on the camp, because we were several miles away from the camp and couldn't see it. None of us had travelled with sleds that morning; we had just walked—and walked and walked— with the seal dogs. I wasn't sure that I would see any of the others before returning to camp, and if I had to return alone I certainly didn't intend to get lost.

I sat all day and never had a seal. I just sat and burned in the sun and reviewed the lessons I had been taught that day: how to use the snow probe to test whether or not the seal was using a particular breathing hole, how to use the breathing hole gauge to find the exact centre of a hole that couldn't be seen under the snow, and how to use the *kaiptaq* to make the seal itself give warning of its presence. I knew the harpoon line would hold any seal I speared with it, because the detachable head of that remarkably efficient and ingenious weapon would bury itself in the animal, then, because it was made of a piece of diabolically curved metal, the head would twist inside its victim and form a sort of crossbar so that it would hold tight and not pull out as any ordinary spear would do. I knew that if the seal wasn't killed by my first thrust, I should brace against it by quickly wrapping the thong around my left foot, then disengage the heavy shaft of the harpoon and use it to bash in the skull. Not much to it as long as an overly excited hunter didn't miss the seal with his first thrust. One chance was all one got.

Comparing notes as we walked back to camp that night we found that only one man had killed a seal, and although this seemed disappointing to me, the others figured it to be about normal. They told me I mustn't expect to get too many seals. In an average week there, with ten hunters out every single day from morning to night, we never had more than nine seals in a week. It makes one think how difficult it must have been in the old days; nine seals provided barely enough meat for ourselves and the dogs.

Every evening after we had eaten, we sat around in warm snowhouses and smoked and talked. Angulaalik and old Matummiaq liked to talk of the hardships of living on the sea ice in previous years, how difficult it had been to go out every day in temperatures down to sixty degrees below zero and hunt seal.

'Every day you froze—you froze your face, your nose, your chin, and quite often you froze your heels.' It was one thing, they said, to go out in the balmy springtime as we were doing now when the temperature was barely below zero, and quite another to go out day after day in the murderously frigid temperatures of mid-winter in the Arctic. But in the old days, they had no choice. The seal hunt was the only thing between a man's family, his dogs and starvation through the long winter months.

On the fourth day, still having had no luck, I went back to my first seal hole. Several others came in closer to that area. Angulaalik had found a hole fairly close to mine, about four hundred yards away, and Amirairniq was about half a mile away to my left. All of them were just sitting and watching, like stone figures on the landscape.

I was daydreaming, my mind off in Scotland. All of a sudden the indicator began to move, and I leapt up in a panic. When the indicator shot up because the seal had struck it with its head, I plunged with my harpoon—and missed completely! I not only missed the seal but the breathing hole as well, for my harpoon head went right into the ice alongside the opening of the breathing hole.

What a fool I felt! The seal had actually surfaced under the snow, and gave a sort of grunt with the breath exploding out of its lungs. I heard a deep whoosh of breath as the seal exhaled. Then it realized I was there with my harpoon, whacking down on the ice close by its head. I heard a splash of water as the seal dived back down and was gone.

During our after-supper review of the day's activities, I told the others of my fiasco. I really hadn't much relish for admitting my folly, and as I expected, the Eskimos had a good laugh at my expense; but it was understanding laughter and I finally joined in.

Angulaalik said, 'Well, don't let it bother you. We're all the same. When I first went seal hunting I did exactly the same thing. I became so nervous and shaky that I too missed the seal.' He grinned at me and added, 'I didn't strike the ice, mind you, but I did miss the seal.'

So the next day, with my humour and my confidence both restored, I went back to the same seal hole. I had been there only about an hour, still early in the morning, when the indicator began to turn again. I rose to my feet as the seal rose and pushed up the indicator. I put all my strength into plunging my harpoon right down alongside the indicator, and I felt the solid shock all the way up my arm when the harpoon bashed into the head of the seal. My whole arm shook, and I felt a fierce joy. This was my first seal and I knew I had it good and proper!

With my harpoon in it, it fought, pulling and wriggling underneath the snow covering of the breathing hole. I wrapped the line around my left foot just as Angulaalik had taught me, and grabbed on the line to pull the seal up, all the while shouting to catch Angulaalik's attention. I couldn't seem to get the seal properly because it was jumping back and forward too much for me. It was simply because of lack of experience on my part, and I got too excited.

Shoving the shaft of the harpoon into the snow, I shouted to Angulaalik. Before he reached me I was using the shaft of my harpoon again. The seal was tiring rapidly. I could hear it under the snow grunting and spluttering trying to breathe; then it would come out of the water again, and I would pull it farther up with the hand line. I finally managed to use the shaft of the harpoon to finish the kill.

Seeing this, Angulaalik cried excitedly, '*Quanarunaqtuq!* Well done! *Inuinnangnguqtutit, inuinnangnguqpiaqtutit!* You're a real Eskimo, a real Eskimo!'

Now this was a very important moment in my life; this was the first time I had killed a seal with a harpoon. It is one of the milestones in an Eskimo's life. Normally, of course, it takes place at a much earlier age than I was—an Eskimo boy is usually fourteen or fifteen when he kills his first seal. But no Eskimo lad could have been more thrilled than this transplanted Scot in his early twenties! Now I could call the Arctic *Nunaga*: my land, my country.

After Angulaalik had congratulated me, he said, 'Now wait, we'll open up this breathing hole.' He was as excited as I was. He looked upon me as his son in this hunt and was as jubilant about my triumph as he would have been for a real son. We cleared the snow away and could see that it was a good-sized jar seal. We chiselled the ice away around the neck of the breathing hole and started pulling the seal up. Angulaalik said, 'Wait, wait! Don't rush it now. This is your first seal and we have to do things in the right manner. First, lie back.'

He pushed at me with one hand. 'Lie on your back in the snow, right here beside the hole, and spread your legs. You don't know about this, but we've got to do it. It's what people always do when they kill their first seal.'

So I lay back, totally uncomprehending, with my feet just about straddling the opening of the breathing hole. Angulaalik pulled the seal up, soaking wet, dripping with blood, and pulled it right over my body as I lay prone in the snow on my back. He pulled it over my body and my face.

'Now, get up.'

So I dutifully got on my feet.

'Now we've got to wrestle.'

I still hadn't the slightest idea what he was doing. 'What for?' Angulaalik was brusque: 'Don't ask questions, you'll offend the seal. Just wrestle with me.' He added, 'Just make it look good, but let me win.'

So we got up alongside the seal, and we wrestled around, and finally Angulaalik threw me on top of the seal, and he cried out to the seal, 'There, now you should feel happy!'

As we got up, the other hunters came running in, for once the word got round, everyone was hallooing and hollering. A man's first seal will bring the others to help the hunter celebrate properly. I felt about ten feet tall.

But Angulaalik took me by the arm and off to one side and scolded me. 'Don't smile too much,' he said. 'Look humble. It's bad manners if you look too proud of killing a seal.'

So then, in the Eskimo style, I began to explain to the other hunters how hopeless I was. I said it was purely luck; that if I had been a better hunter, I'd have got a much bigger seal, and look at the size of this poor little seal. Angulaalik looked pleased. An Eskimo must let his father or his nearest relative do the bragging for him; I myself couldn't boast.

One of the men ran off back to his seal hole where he had a sled. We were in high spirits, all of us laughing and enjoying ourselves as we put the seal onto the sled. We piled onto the sled and away we went; no more hunting for anyone that day, so that everyone could take part in the appropriate celebrations.

Back at the camp, the seal was taken into Angulaalik's snow-house where Irvana stood proudly awaiting us. The first thing she did was to wipe the blood away from around its head. Then she took some water out of a thermos flask and held the seal's head up, forced its mouth open, and poured in the fresh water. She said this was the ancient custom; after a man's first seal has been killed, it must have a drink of fresh water, because since seals live in salt water the taste of fresh water is a special treat.

Then she took a little coil of the birch bark frequently found as driftwood, set fire to it and used it to burn the seal's whiskers. After that she took an *atqut*, a pencil-sized piece of bone used to adjust the flame in a blubber lamp, and stabbed at the seal several times with each hand. She couldn't tell me why; she just said, 'It is what you always do.'

Ordinarily a man's first seal is butchered outside by the seal hole, but because I was an orphan, which the Eskimos knew, my seal was butchered inside the snowhouse by the wife of my 'nearest relative', Angulaalik. So it was up to Irvana to butcher my seal for me. As soon as she had finished flensing it, skinning and removing the layer of blubber, Angulaalik said, 'It's now time to get your partners.' Again I didn't know what he meant.

Angulaalik explained: 'When a man first kills a seal, he divides the seal up with his partners.' There are many different portions to a carcass, I discovered, about sixteen or seventeen of them, and these portions are given to the hunter's seal partners. Angulaalik himself was my heart partner, my *uummatiqatiga,* which meant that when the heart was cut out of my seal, I had to give it to Angulaalik as a present. Another man, Tupilliqqut, served as my lung partner, and got the lungs of my seal. And this went on right through the parts of my seal. A place was made for me as a new hunter, even though all these men already had long-standing partnerships.

Every time I killed a seal from then on, I would share with all my partners: Angulaalik the heart, Tupilliqqut the lungs, Amirairniq the ribs, and so on. Anyone who kills a seal will get only a few parts of it for himself, but nearly everyone shares in his good fortune. If a hunter has bad luck and doesn't kill a seal at all, the chances are good that if his partners are doing well, he will still get almost a full seal in the course of the hunt; he will be given these predetermined portions from his partners' seals.

This is the practice only when a man has killed a seal with the harpoon. We never shared when we shot seals in the summer, and there was no such sharing of caribou; it applied only to seals.

Another thing I learned about these seal partnerships: they are hereditary. If Angulaalik and I exchanged the hearts of our seals, and if Angulaalik had a son and I had a son, our two sons would automatically become heart partners. Among all the numerous real and acquired relationships among Eskimos, this was the only hereditary relationship I found.

Right off the bat I not only had friends among this group—I also had seventeen partners with an active interest in me; I had established a real relationship with seventeen families. With the wife exchange and the seal partner relationships, I was one of the people, not just an outsider, no longer even a whiteman.

After that first seal, I didn't get another for about three weeks. The record holder was a man who killed five—five seals in one day at the same hole! We celebrated the event with a drum dance.

We were in that seal camp about six weeks altogether, hunting with the harpoon, going out every day. When we had good luck and brought in some seals, they were dumped at the side of the porch or at the side of the house where the women butchered them. The entrails went to the dogs, which at that time of the year were fed blubber and entrails, never solid meat. The women usually kept some of the seal guts, especially the long intestine. They took it by one end and with their hands squeezed it right to the other end, pressing out a greyish-looking fluid with a foul taste. After they had squeezed out all they possibly could, they cut out long strips of blubber and braided the intestine and blubber strips together into a rope about three or four feet long. This they rolled up and tossed into a pot. It was very tasty.

In good weather the women brought the sealskins outside, and after using the *ulu*, a knife with a fan-shaped blade to flense the skin, would take up a special scraping knife to remove the epidermis from the sealskin. The skin was then staked out to stretch and dry in the sun, and some of the youngest children were designated to keep an eye on the dogs, in case any of them got loose and tried to chew up the skins.

The older boys, those from around ten or twelve, went out with their fathers to the seal holes, learning by watching what the hunters did. Girls stayed back at the camp and helped their mothers with the flensing of the seals and the cooking.

Generally by the time we got back from the day's hunting, the women were inside the snowhouses, the lamps were burning and the evening meal was cooking. Every house had a blubber lamp, a big soapstone lamp—some of them three to four feet long—which not only gave off a soft light but also a very soft, low heat, which took hours to boil up anything.

The hollowed-out bowl of the lamp was fed oil from a raised platform where little pieces of seal blubber were laid. These blubber pieces were broken down and the oil released by tapping them with a blubber-pounder made of muskox horn. The Perry Island Eskimos took seeds of cotton grass, gathered during the summer and saved for this purpose, and put them along the rim of the lamp where they absorbed the oil and could be ignited. Then the *atqut* was used to poke the seeds about; this adjusted the flame and kept it from smoking excessively.

Above the lamp there hung a pot, usually with seal meat in it. Quite often the pot might contain nothing but seal flippers. It was held above the lamp by a string looped over a stick that projected from the snowhouse wall. Not all the women cooked every night, just one or two on whom they had decided for the day. When the food was ready they called in all the hunters and we ate together in one house. They might have assigned just one woman as the cook for the day. But sometimes there were two or three: one woman might have cooked up seal flippers, another the braided intestines-and-blubber dish. When we men had eaten all the flippers we wanted in one house, we would move to the next and try the braided guts.

Boiled meat, like boiled seal (or caribou), was actually almost raw. Taken out of the pot, the pieces would still be dripping blood. The meat was barely touched by the heat at all. The best part was the gravy. The women gave each of us a plate—they had tin plates from the trading post—and they just ladled it out. When they put the meat on the plate they dumped a little pile of salt alongside it, and we dipped the meat into the salt.

Dinner, then, consisted of a barely warm piece of meat. If it was seal flippers, they still had the hair on them. Each diner had his own knife, usually just a pocket knife, and rather than cutting meat on the plate, would take the whole piece of meat into his mouth, grip it with his teeth and cut off a bite.

It was superbly comfortable in the *nallaqtaq*, the snowhouse, when we hunters came in and got out of our outer gear and filled our bellies. It was warm and cosy; we brought out our tobacco and rolled a cigarette or pulled out a pipe. Often the Eskimos had pipes bought from the trading posts, but always a few of the older men had pipes with soapstone bowls they had carved themselves, with a piece of willow for the stem. The evenings were spent in story-telling and re-enactments of the day's kill. Sometimes, if a hunter had sat out on the ice all day long without getting a seal, he composed a song, singing that night the words he thought of while waiting for the seal that didn't come. While the men ate and sat around afterwards smoking and talking in the snowhouse, the children of the camp played on the caribou blankets on the sleeping platform, often romping around naked because it was quite warm from the soapstone lamp and the body heat of so many of us in the house.

As spring came on, the sun began to get warmer and higher in the sky. When the hunt had begun, the seals were still hidden under the snow. But now the snow was melting, and it was warm on the surface of the sea ice. The seals crawled out on top of the ice. They were then referred to as 'basking seals,' which, of course, were no longer hunted with a harpoon.

At this stage, we took a team of dogs and scouted all over the sea ice area with an empty sled, maybe just a little grub box with some hardtack in it and a thermos of tea. When a seal was spotted, it was shot and loaded onto the sled—an easy matter when they were basking on the ice. But not so long ago the hunters had to creep quietly up on them with great patience, and get close enough to shoot them with bow and arrow.

This form of hunting continued a few more weeks, until the warmer weather forced us off the ice. It had begun to melt and would refreeze thinly at night, so that often we had to stalk through water topped by fresh ice. Sloshing through water is too noisy; the seals hear the hunter and get away. Then followed summer seal hunting, a different affair altogether. At Perry Island we did this often, hunting by canoe.

When I first arrived at Perry, we paid five dollars for a large sealskin in good condition. One year all traders got a wire in code from the Company instructing us to pay twenty-eight dollars for a seal. I doubt if any of the traders throughout the western Arctic believed their eyes when they read this; it was just too remarkable a jump. I sent a wire right away asking the Company to verify the price. Back came the confirmation—twenty-eight dollars.

I remember Paniuyaq was the first Eskimo to come in to the post that summer with sealskins, bringing two for which he expected to get ten dollars. They were both prime pelts so I casually said, 'Well, that's fifty-six dollars.' Poor Paniuyaq thought I was joking with him, and I had to explain that I was serious, that the Company had indeed changed the price.

The Eskimos went wild! Paniuyaq spread the word, and soon the entire settlement was out on the sea in canoes. In nice calm weather they would stay out all day. We never went seal hunting if the sea was very choppy; shooting from a bobbing canoe was a waste of ammunition. But on a good day that summer, canoes were everywhere, all over the sea. Some of the Eskimos put their transistor radios in the bottom of the canoe and played them at top volume. This, surprisingly, drew in the seals. They would hear the noise, and bit by bit work in towards it until they were close enough to give the hunter an easy shot.

When the chores were light at the post, I took off with my canoe myself. Just as the Eskimos did, I based my technique on taking advantage of the insatiable curiosity of the seals, though I didn't use a transistor radio. My method was an older one; I simply picked up my paddle and rapped against the side of the canoe, very sharply. The noise carries under the water, and this pulls in seals from a long way off. In due course I would see a seal, maybe two or three hundred yards away. As soon as I spotted him I would rap on the canoe again, not so loudly this time, and the seal would dive and invariably surface about a hundred yards closer. With my .22 rifle now ready, I would rap again, but very quietly, and keeping my head down. The seal would dive again and I never knew which side of the canoe it might surface, but I knew it would be within twenty or thirty yards. Then up it would come, floating upright, looking for the source of the noise. As soon as I spotted it, I would take aim with my rifle and then whistle sharply. When it heard the whistle, it would raise its head to look for the sound, and I would shoot it in the throat.

We tried not to shoot them in the head. At that time of year, immediately after breakup, a shot in a seal's head kills it instantly; unfortunately it sinks instantly too. There seem to be two reasons for this. The seals don't have enough blubber at that time of the year to keep them afloat; and during that part of the early summer, the rivers are pouring their fresh water runoff into the sea, and the water doesn't have its usual salinity to help float the seal.

Inevitably a lot of seals are lost at this time of the year. Very fast action with the canoe is required to get it alongside the sinking seal to put a gaff or harpoon into the body. At this season at least five out of ten seals killed are lost, perhaps even eight out of ten. Seals shot in the throat take a minute or two to die and sink, and by that time a good canoe man can reach the seal and haul it in. Either a head or throat shot is best for the pelt. Neither damages the skin like a body shot, which halves the price paid for the pelt.

Everyone hunted seal that summer the price sky-rocketed, and I never did learn what vagary of fashion or economy was responsible for the jump. Unfortunately for the Eskimos, the remarkable price bonanza didn't last.

The following year brought an uproar over the whitemen clubbing baby seals and skinning them alive off Newfoundland. In the Arctic we never killed baby seals. First of all, we were dealing with a different species. In the Arctic the ring or jar seal is not really migratory, whereas the harp seal, which is the type found off Newfoundland, is a migratory animal and very gregarious. They travel in schools or pods, gathering by the thousands, but one rarely finds even two jar seals together. Secondly, we killed seals either by harpooning them at their holes under the snow, or by shooting them on top of the ice or in the open sea. But the harp seals that congregate off Newfoundland clamber right up on the ice to have their pups out in the open; the sealers simply scramble ashore and club them to death. I have never really believed there have ever been many cases of skinning them alive. A seal skull is very thin and the animal can actually be killed by one good blow of the fist; a club isn't even necessary. I can't see any point in skinning a seal alive. If it is alive to wriggle around, it will be harder to skin and a mess will probably be made of the pelt. It would be much simpler to use the butt of a knife to give the seal pup a good hard rap and kill it.

Exaggerated or not, the hubbub knocked the price of seal in the Arctic from twenty-eight dollars down to two dollars overnight. Naturally, the pragmatic Eskimos simply stopped hunting seal. The price was not worth the effort.

Although skinning out seals is relatively easy and considered women's work by Eskimo men, it is a time-consuming process. The carcass has to be cut open, care being taken to slice around the flippers. Blubber and hide are pulled off together, then all the blubber and any bits of flesh carefully cut away and the flipper holes sewn up. The skin must be stretched on a frame or rack for drying, and finally a sort of black inner epidermis has to be scraped off—a task that takes four or five hours in itself. Under the new circumstances, the Eskimos simply shrugged and gave more time to their other hunting. What seal they did bring in were used primarily to feed the dogs, and they didn't waste time trading for them any longer at the post.

The Eskimos have always used some sealskin for the soles of boots and for a certain type of boot worn in spring when water-proof footwear is needed. And good strong thong can be made by cutting the skin in a continuous spiral and then stretching it between two rocks.

Coats or jackets of sealskin sell briskly on the southern market, but in the Arctic, Eskimos rarely wear sealskin parkas or clothes. There is just no comparison at all with caribou skin, which is very warm. Making a parka out of seal would be like making one out of an old sheet, compared to a caribou parka. But whitemen like the look of seal parkas, and three or four skins make a parka that sells for two or three hundred dollars. During the summer, when sealskins cost merely the price of the ammunition to shoot them, the return is pretty fair.

There has been a gradual small revival of seal hunting, but no one hunts the old way with harpoon any longer in Canada. The Perry Island hunters, and those of perhaps one or two other places like Bathurst Inlet, followed the ancient way up to a few years ago. But to be successful, many hunters have to work together so that all the breathing holes can be watched; I doubt that anyone hunts that way now, anywhere in the world. It has become a lost art.

15
❄ Nanuq—
The Polar Bear

One year at Perry Island the seal hunt proved discouragingly unproductive for those who went out on the sea ice after the fox season was over. After two weeks in the hunting camp, thirteen experienced hunters had only two seals to show for their efforts. Some of the men talked about a polar bear hunt. They knew they could get a good price for the bear skins. The decision was made. Four of them and I prepared to make a trip up to the north end of Victoria Island and see if we could get some bear. We asked Angulaalik to come along with us, but he declined. He had better things to do, he said, than chase off across the country with a bunch of wild young men.

We were certainly as enthusiastic as a bunch of kids. First we went back to the trading post to stock up; this would be a long trip, almost a thousand miles there and back, and we needed dogfood and camping gear. We left with our sleds piled high, each of us driving his own dogs, and unaccompanied by the women. We were all using good-sized teams; one of the Eskimos had seventeen dogs in his team. I was running thirteen; I had had to borrow three of them from another man because some of my dogs were sick.

We travelled north over the sea ice, cutting across Queen Maud Gulf to strike up the east side of Victoria Island, stopping first at a place called Uummannaq Island, where there was a small DEW line station. It made a handy place to rest the dogs and ourselves, but the real enticement there was the entertainment—a stock of popular movies.

We estimated it would take about ten sleeps to reach the bear country if everything went normally, though it was always necessary to be prepared for delays through bad weather in that part of the country. After a few days we hit the coastline of Victoria Island and followed the coast up northeast, cutting right across any bays. Only one of the men, Tupilliqqut, had been in that area before; none of the rest had been that far north on Victoria Island. Fortunately the landmarks were plentiful and easy to pick out, and each of us memorized the lay of the land as we went north, fixing the major landmarks in our minds just in case we decided to split up on the hunt and had to make our way back separately.

The party travelled on, making good time but not pushing the dogs too hard. That time of year, around the first of May, we had to stop quite often; the soft spring snow packs between the dogs' toes and turns into balls of ice, making their feet very sore. At intervals we paused long enough to pick these snowballs off the dogs' feet or let the dogs themselves chew off the snow, while we had a mug-up.

The weather conditions also made it difficult to find good snowhouse snow, and out on the sea ice we had to do without a snowhouse several times. The sleds were then flipped up on their sides, four of them together to form a sort of makeshift camp. Sled covers served as a sloping roof from the sleds down to the ground and were banked with snow. It wasn't very comfortable, but it was better than being out in the open.

We followed the coastline for about a week, steadily pushing north. We had been out nine days when we came across the first tracks of polar bear. We debated whether to follow the trail, but Tupilliqqut suggested that if we went farther north we should come into really good bear country, and that we shouldn't waste time chasing around here.

So we pushed on, and when we turned the curve at the top of Victoria Island and started to head west we really hit polar bear country, just as Tupilliqqut had promised. We were crossing as many as seven or eight individual bear trails a day, so when we found good snow for snowhouses, we set up a base camp. After our camp was in order, we had ourselves a good dinner of raw, frozen caribou and held a council of war on how to conduct the hunt. We decided to hunt light, with just our rifles and a grub box and a couple of thermos flasks each. Tupilliqqut was sure we could go out in any direction from our camp, find bear and get back to camp each night. In any case it would be better, when we sighted bear, if the dogs were not hauling a heavily laden sled.

Next morning, we all headed out together, moving out from shore a good twenty miles, until we could no longer see the coastal land, although we could see the reflection in the sky of the land beneath and always knew where to head to return.

Although I had never taken part in a polar bear hunt like this, I had killed or helped kill them before when we had stumbled across them by accident. My first such experience had been on one of the first trips I made by dog between Spence Bay and Gjoa Haven with Takolik, good polar bear country. It was one of those times when the moon wasn't out and we had just the stars reflecting off the snow to light our way for us. We were travelling along as usual, when without warning the dogs swung around, picking up a scent. At first we thought it was a seal, since there were seal holes all over the sea ice, but the dogs headed straight for a big mound of snow. Takolik shouted, '*Nanuq, nanuq!* Polar bear!' We both jumped off the sled and snatched up our rifles.

Takolik went up to the mound, took out his snowknife, and walked around to have a look. 'Be careful,' he warned, 'it's probably a female with cubs.'

That time of year—it was February—only the females would be denned up like that. They don't hibernate; they just den up to give birth to the cubs, born about December, and come out about March or April when the snow begins to thaw.

Takolik was studying the situation, and I was hopping with excitement. I walked over the mound. We could hear the bear grunting about down below; she obviously knew we were there. Takolik said, 'Stand back. I'm going to open up the den now. She might try to grab a leg or take a bite or something.'

He took his snowknife and cut a block of snow out of the mound. The stink that came out was overwhelming! A smell of bear crap and urine, so bad that Takolik had to retreat a bit and let the air rush out before he could look into this birthing den, what the Eskimos call *apittiq*.

'Right,' he said, as he peered into the hole, 'it's a female, and she has two cubs.'

We waited while the fetid air cleared out. The female bear

poked her head up and was thundering and growling at us with a deep belly growl, not as deep as a grizzly's but just as mean-sounding. As she stuck her head up higher Takolik took aim at the head and finished her off with one bullet. With our snow shovels we dug the den out and discovered the cubs. We debated whether or not we should keep them, but Takolik said, 'No, they are too much trouble.' We shot both of them.

That first polar bear encounter hadn't been nearly as frightening as I had assumed such a thing would be. My main worry had been that the roof of the den might fall through under our weight, and the female's growling and carrying on hardly sounded a friendly invitation to drop in on her.

I knew the kind of hunting we were now beginning on the northern coast of Victoria Island would be very different and much more exciting. We came across the fresh track of a bear shortly after we had got well out from the coastal land, but it was in very rough ice, jumbled-up, polar-pack ice with large ridges and raised slabs. We proceeded with some caution because if there were bears around, they could virtually ambush us. We weren't worried about male bears—they very rarely attack a sled—but female bears, when they have cubs with them, sometimes take right after you.

Nasarlulik took my binoculars, went up on top of a high hummock of ice piled up by a pressure ridge, and looked carefully round the country. Quite soon he spotted a bear off in another direction from the one whose trail we had all been following. Nasarlulik and I decided to go for that bear; now we had caught sight of it, we expected little trouble. The only hunt more exciting in the Arctic is for the grizzly bear, but para-doxically, there is very little real danger in hunting the polar bear or even the erratic and unpredictable grizzly if you have no bad luck. The rifle, properly handled, makes man the most powerful animal on earth. No animal, no matter how cunning or strong, can do anything against a rifle.

Of course, handling a rifle in the extreme low temperatures of the Arctic calls for a bit more care than the normal. The gun is prepared beforehand by cleaning all the oil and grease off any moving parts. This keeps the gun from freezing up and jamming. Greenhorns in the Arctic sometimes make the mistake of throwing their mitts off and grabbing the rifle with bare hands, only to discover to their horror that the skin of their fingers has frozen tightly to the barrel. The trick the Eskimo uses is simply to stick his hand into a snow bank until it has cooled so that his skin doesn't freeze to the gun. In the excitement of the hunt, however, even a wise Eskimo will sometimes forget to protect his fingers, and that usually costs him a patch of skin.

Rifle or no, there is plenty of excitement, for the polar bear is a potentially dangerous animal, and a mother bear defending her cubs will certainly be fierce. I have known hunters, Eskimos in Gjoa Haven, who have killed polar bears with hand axes. And in the old days, and not many years ago, Eskimos killed polar bears with a knife tied securely to the end of a harpoon handle or a shaft of driftwood, a weapon they called a *pana*. The use of the *pana* certainly took some courage. They would move in close to the bear, wait until the bear reared up on its hind legs, and then run right in front of the bear, shoving the butt of the *pana* into the snow and tempting the polar bear to lunge towards them. The bear's weight impaled it on the *pana*. This way they used the bear's own weight and the ferocity of its charge to make the kill, rather than trying to thrust the weapon into the bear with the puny strength of man.

Soon Nasarlulik and I crossed the tracks of the bear we had seen. It had left a clear track and from the way the trail wandered around we guessed this bear was a male, searching for seal breathing holes in the ice. Polar bears eat nothing but seals, just the blubber, never the meat unless they are really starving. We just kept moving, watching for that bear. As soon as we had hit its tracks, of course, the dogs had become excited, and with an almost empty sled, they were galloping along. Thirteen dogs can pick up a fair speed when following a scent.

We spotted our bear in the distance and sure enough it was standing with its head down a seal hole, as we had anticipated. I knew from my experiences at Spence Bay that this is a common seal-hunting position for a bear. The bear stands with its hind quarters right up in the air, its head and front paws right down the seal hole, so that its body blocks off any change in the pattern of light at the hole; when the seal surfaces to breathe, it can't tell that the bear is there. As the seal comes up, the bear hits it with a paw, crushing its skull, then pulls it out. It takes enormous strength to pull the seal up through the narrow bottleneck opening of its hole, and the process tears the seal open. The guts hang out, most bones are crushed, and the bear's meal is served up ready to eat.

The sound of the dogs barking and howling startled our bear out of its hole. It yanked up its head and started running like a bat out of hell with the dogs, the sled and ourselves in hot pursuit.

Finally, about three or four hundred yards behind the bear, we came into some more rough ice; the anchor on the sled caught and stopped the dogs. Lunging in their traces, yelping with excitement, they tried to get loose to go after the bear, which had no anchor and kept right on travelling. We cast off some of the dogs to let them round up the bear for us, and they took off like a pack of wolves. By the time they caught up with the bear, they were eight or nine hundred yards ahead of us, out of effective rifle range. They began to attack, dashing in and nipping the bear from behind.

Normally dogs are too agile for a bear and they are careful to avoid being pawed. As we watched, I saw one of my dogs dart in too close. The bear caught the poor animal bang-on with one swat and knocked the big husky at least twenty feet into the air. The dog was dead before we could catch up.

Once cornered by the dogs, the chase is over for the bear. I walked up and put a bullet into its head.

This was a large bear, a ten or eleven footer, and approximately six years old. The age is determined by examining the claws. A light band is followed by a dark band, then a light band again, and so on. A count of these bands will give the age of the bear quite accurately up to about nine years. Beyond that the method isn't reliable because the claws become worn with use.

We skinned out our bear—tough work because it had to be cut every inch of the way. The work took several hours. This was a prime pelt, in first class condition, so we were careful. We chopped up the carcass for dogfood, but we were careful to bury the liver, literally poison to the dogs.

By then it was getting late, and while the sun did not dip below the horizon at that time of year, we started back to camp.

Tupilliqqut and the other men came in a bit after our return. They had had tremendous luck; they brought back seven bears. We now had plenty of meat for dogfood and decided to stay at that camp for another week.

The only dangerous incident of the entire hunt came two or three days later, when we spotted two females with two cubs apiece, all within sight of each other. As we started chasing them, the bears turned toward each other, and then both doubled back on the sleds. Nasarlulik had left his dogs in camp that day, because their feet were badly cut up by the bad ice, and had come along on my sled. We stopped to cast off some dogs to round up the closest bear. Since losing one of my best dogs with our first bear, we always loosed the wheel dogs, the two closest to the sled, always the poorest dogs in the team.

This mother bear was desperately trying to protect her cubs. She was raging mad, far more dangerous than any male ever is. The two dogs stopped the bear for a moment, but before either Nasarlulik or I could get in a shot, the dogs were diverted by one of the cubs. The cub was just a little thing, about two or three feet long, and the dogs mistakenly took it for easy prey. But the cub turned around and belted the nearest of its tormentors in the chops. Surprised, the dog backed off in a hurry, and then both dogs ganged up, barking ever so bravely at that one game little cub.

Like a white bulldozer, one of the mother bears came charging in, bowling over the dogs on the way, and dived right at our sled. Nasarlulik and I moved like lightning. With a thousand pounds of white-coated fury coming straight for us, I lunged headfirst right over the top of the sled to get something, anything, between me and that mad bear, but Nasarlulik, turning to make a dive in the other direction, got his feet caught in the dog harness and flopped flat on his face right in the animal's path. My hunting partner frantically scrambled to his feet in the midst of what looked like a whirlpool of dogs and bear. I shall never forget the expression of terror on his face. He went flying over the sled with the bear half on top of him and the dogs going absolutely wild. The bear was lashing out right, left and centre with Nasarlulik dodging every which way, the dogs and harness all tangled around him. Fortunately, they were all too cramped and at close quarters for the bear to get in a really good, effective blow, or she would have taken off a head or two. Miraculously, beyond a few scratches that went unnoticed until later, Nasarlulik was not hurt at all. He managed to get his feet under him, jumped aside, and to my astonishment started laughing. It was dangerous enough; his life had been in the balance for a perilous few moments. Yet the scene was so chaotic, such a mixup of man, bear, dogs and sled all in a pile rolling around, that he had to laugh! Between spasms of laughter he was yelling at me, 'Shoot her! Shoot her, Takaq! I can't shoot. I can't shoot!' When he had fallen the barrel of his rifle had gone plunk into the snow and filled up with soft snow. He didn't dare shoot, because he knew the rifle might blow up in his face with the barrel plugged that way. He had a spare rifle, but it was lashed on the sled, and inaccessible in the tangle. I couldn't get a shot in myself because the bear was jumping all over the place, the dogs were after the bear and Nasarlulik was too close to the fray. I didn't want to bag one of my dogs or my hunting partner. At last Nasarlulik managed to get his spare rifle off the sled. He dashed nimbly out to one side, completely clear of the mêlée, turned just as the bear charged after him, and coolly shot her right in the eye, dropping her dead on the spot.

We still had a mess on our hands. Some of the dogs were badly beaten up, yelping with pain, others were trying to get up, their legs caught in the traces. The harness was tangled and torn up. We had to shoot the two cubs before the dogs would calm down enough for us to straighten out the bedlam. It had been a close thing; it could easily have been a tragedy. Luckily Nasarlulik, for all his comedy of errors, had moved pretty fast.

We stopped a moment to catch our breath, stuck our rifles butt-first in the snow, and set about trying to untangle the dogs and get the team in shape again. Suddenly Nasarlulik tapped me on the arm and pointed to the other female bear with her two cubs, sitting just several hundred yards away, calmly watching the whole show. In all the excitement we had entirely forgotten about her. I don't know why she hadn't taken off; perhaps she found the scene too entertaining to miss. We flopped down in the snow with our elbows propped on our knees in good stance for a long shot and sighted it on the bear. We brought her down with two shots.

This was the last straw for the dogs. They took off on their own, dragging the sled with them. Nasarlulik and I were left sitting there in the snow helpless to prevent them. Happily for us, they stopped to worry the body of the second bear, and we caught up with them while they were pawing and snapping at our latest victim.

Meanwhile this bear's cubs, which were quite a bit bigger than the first pair we had killed, were running helter-skelter over the ice. We decided to get them too, but that turned out to be more work than we had bargained for. The little devils got into rough ice and dashed and dodged all around it while we kept getting our sled jammed and caught. We had to laugh at our own awkwardness and the way those cubs took every advantage of the terrain to tangle us up. We were having a lot of fun but not getting any more bears, even though we twisted around and chased the cubs all over the place for what seemed like hours. Finally Nasarlulik bagged one with a lucky snap shot and the other seemed to vanish. It must have gone under an ice pan or something; we never saw it again; nor could the dogs sniff it out. However, our total kill for the day was the two big females and the three cubs, so we were quite pleased.

After hunting bears for ten or eleven days, we wound up with a total of twenty-six bears, counting the cubs; twenty-six bears for five men—pretty good hunting. We had more meat, of course, than we could use or even transport for dogfood. Most of the grown bears weighed a thousand pounds or more, and we had only five sleds. We butchered out the meaty parts, the hind quarters and legs and the shoulders, not bothering with ribs. We loaded up as much as it made sense to try to take back on the sleds on the return trip and just cached the rest of it, several thousand pounds of meat. We thought, because the hunting was so good, we might come back up that way or some other Perry Islanders, when they saw how well we had done, might want to come up there. If they did, we would tell them about those caches and how to find them, and they could use the meat.

We had all the skins to carry home too. Twenty-six hides make a good load, even though we had scraped them most carefully to take off as much weight as possible. We frost-dried the pelts, one of the simplest and handiest ways of preparing skins. Blocks of snow are set up together to build a sort of rack with air space underneath; the polar bear skins are laid over the racks with the hair side out and left in the cold and the sun and the wind. After about a week of that, if they have been properly cleaned and scraped, the hides turn a nice creamy white. They are stiff, of course, frozen as rigid as a board, but freeze-drying draws most of the moisture out and is an excellent way to preserve the pelts.

On the way back to Perry we stopped off at the DEW line post again and peddled a good many of the skins to the men working there. We could get far better prices from them than from anyone else. Some workers there bought three and four skins each. They must have planned to take them south to the United States when they finished their tour of duty and sell them at a good price, but we didn't care what they did with them as long as they were willing to pay what we asked. We knew very well that not all those skins were prime, certainly not good enough to command premium prices at the trading post, but the DEW line men didn't know that. They couldn't tell a good bear from a bad bear; they judged simply by size— the bigger it was the more they were happy, almost eager, it seemed to us, to pay for it. A polar bear skin traded to the Hudson's Bay Company in those days brought no more than about $125. Those DEW-liners were happy to pay $300 and better for even a mediocre pelt. They made good money up there at those isolated radar sites and had nothing to spend it on.

We kept some skins for bedding and sled padding and the like. The Eskimos in Greenland make pants out of polar bear skin, but as far as most Canadian Eskimos are concerned, such pants are too heavy, too bulky, and no warmer than the lighter and more convenient caribouskin pants. However, the great bear pelts make marvellous bedding on the sleeping platform, one pelt with the hair down and the next with the hair up. And they last a life time while caribouskins wear out every couple of years. So a couple of good-sized bear skins are well worth keeping for bedding rather than trading, regardless of the going price.

We headed back to Perry in high spirits. We had been gone almost a month, travelled about a thousand miles, and bagged a good catch. We came back just covered in glory, and had a wonderful time telling tales about our polar bear hunt. Because bears around Perry Island were pretty scarce, not many of the Perry Islanders ever had much chance to hunt the big beasts. And as a matter of fact we never had another bear hunt like that ourselves.

16
❄ Travelling
with Dogs

If you actually said 'Mush!' to an Eskimo dogteam, any Eskimos who heard you would roll in the snow and hold their sides. Eskimos appreciate a good joke. 'Mush!' has been getting the job done in the movies for years, but it wouldn't budge a dog an inch in the Arctic.

The words or sounds used as dog commands vary greatly in different parts of the North, and they vary from man to man, each training his own team to react to his individual orders. Generally the command to start or go is not so much a word as a harsh, explosive expulsion of breath from the throat, something like an excessively loud and rude clearing of the throat, something like a bark. This will start a team nearly anywhere, or at least make it pretty excited.

There was a time when a man without dogs in the Arctic was as helpless as a Plains Indian with no horse, or urban man today with no automobile. He couldn't keep up with the caribou migration; he couldn't make a trip to haul in seal meat; and he couldn't make the rounds of his trapline. He was almost entirely dependent upon having a good team of dogs. That is all changing with the coming of the power toboggan. The day of the working dog is coming to a close. The Eskimos themselves are more than willing to switch from dogs to snowmobile. A man with a powered toboggan can run in one day a trapline that took him a week to cover with dogs. To circumvent the danger of a breakdown, most trappers now work in pairs or teams. Less and less do Eskimos make the long trips, almost migrations, that used to be necessary; if they do, they find the money to buy a seat on a plane. And on long trips it makes sense to use a machine with which two or three hundred miles a day can be covered rather than a dogteam, that might make sixty but is more likely to make thirty. Nor does the Eskimo have to spend half his time working like a slave trying to kill or catch enough food for his dogs.

There are obvious advantages and disadvantages to either dogs or machines. As an old 'dog' man, who has travelled thousands of miles in the Arctic with a dogteam, and admittedly feels sentimental about that mode of travel, I would not like to trust my life to a machine that might not start in the sixty-below weather when it is needed the most. And as one Eskimo said, 'When the worst comes to the worst, have you ever tried eating a carburettor?'

For centuries Eskimos used dogs as beasts of burden in the Arctic, and as hunting companions, to help find seal or to bring the great white bear to bay. Before the coming of the whiteman, all Eskimo hunters might have had three or four dogs, no more. That was enough to pull a small sled with whatever gear one wanted to take along, and it wasn't too many to feed. When the whiteman came with his demands for fur, the Eskimo was transformed from a completely nomadic hunter to a comparatively sedentary trapper. With his rifle, which made it so much easier to get food, the trapping Eskimo found he needed larger and larger teams to haul his traps, food and other supplies, as well as the skins he took. In the past fifty years or so an Eskimo trapping family would keep fifteen or twenty dogs and use them all to haul the big sleds.

During my years in the Arctic, the dogteam was the only means of transportation during the long snowbound winter months in much of the North, and only if he owned a good dogteam could an Eskimo trapper hope to be productive. Indeed, a good team often meant the difference between life and death.

Anyone new to the Arctic would find the average team fierce, if not menacingly wild. And in fact he would do well to stay clear of the tie-in chain to which the dogs are secured, big dogs, many of them well over a hundred pounds, broad in the chest and heavy through the shoulders. Eskimos do not make pets of their working dogs. They treat them well generally and take as good care of them as circumstances permit because it makes good sense to do so, and Eskimos are an eminently sensible people. They know the value of the animals and they take care of them, but they handle them quite firmly. Few Eskimos beat a dog just for the hell of it, but if a dog steps out of line it will get a beating immediately. No nonsense is or can be tolerated.

Now and then, for various reasons, an individual dog or an entire team may be treated badly. Such a dog or team will grow up with a mean streak in it, because it has learned to be frightened of people. When a dog is frightened, it is likely to be dangerous and may even attack anyone getting too close. Sometimes a team may not be fed properly and will go for almost anything in its path, including its owner.

My own lead dog, Qaqquq, weighed a hefty one hundred and twenty pounds, and didn't look much like Hollywood's idea of an Eskimo husky. He was white with orange patches but he was a fine lead dog and a real killer. By this I don't mean he attacked people, but he was aggressive and very dangerous to other dogs. He loved to fight, and over the seven years I had him he must have killed thirty or thirty-five dogs. On the other hand, he was an intelligent animal, very affectionate and gentle with people. I've seen kids crawling all over Qaqquq, pulling his tail, sitting on his back, crawling all over him just as if he were a pet housedog. He would never harm a human being; he would just rub up against them and be friendly, and he really liked being petted.

I had driven other people's teams for years, travelled thousands of miles by dogteam, had learned all the ins and outs of handling a team either with the fan hitch favoured in the eastern Arctic or the tandem method used in the west, by the time I got to Perry Island. But I had never had a team of my own. Once settled in I began to think about putting together a team for myself.

At that time a good pup was worth about one white fox fur, and the going price for fox pelts was around $20. A trained adult dog would cost more of course. I started looking around, picking out the dogs I wanted and bargaining for them. Naturally, if an Eskimo had a really good dog the chances were he would want to keep that one, and would drive a hard bargain, so some cost me a good deal more than one pelt.

Eventually I built my team up to nine and then later to thirteen dogs, which was the standard size team for that part of the Arctic. I had been lucky in getting a good pup to develop into my lead dog.

Qaqquq was only a pup, five months old, when I got him, but he already weighed over a hundred pounds and showed signs of intelligence and aggressiveness. There is no sure way to tell that a pup will make a good lead dog or even a good dog. A buyer just has to watch for signs of the traits he will want.

Anyone putting together a new team or breaking pups into a team will take animals like Qaqquq and let them run loose alongside an experienced team at first, perhaps on a four- or five-day trip. This builds up their wind and endurance. After a few such trips, the pups are put into harness. The first time, a dog will be nervous and excited, and ignorant too. He will pull against the harness and bolt at the wrong times, but most dogs soon settle down. The owner can quickly gauge what kind of working dog the pup is likely to make. When pups are first put into harness they aren't pressured and generally just run along without actually pulling, but gradually the driver will apply pressure, touching them lightly with the whip or a stick, shouting at them to frighten them into running forward against the harness. Eventually the action becomes habitual for them, and as soon as they are harnessed in with the team they pull automatically. Some dogs, however, are natural loafers, like some people. Dogs like that don't last long in the North. As soon as a driver finds a good puller to take his place, the lazy one is off the team and is shot.

The two key dogs of any team are the lead dog and the boss dog. Sometimes, but not usually, the lead dog will turn out to be the boss dog too. If the lead dog is not a good animal, then the team will be a poor team. Even a team of good pullers will go bad with a poor leader. That is the reason I worked so hard with Qaqquq to train him properly. I used a small light sled like a hand sled and took Qaqquq out by himself. I would put him in harness and on the end of a trace, then shout the command to turn left, 'Haw! haw! haw!' and as soon as I shouted the command, I would throw a stick or a snowball to hit the snow alongside Qaqquq, just to his right, so that the noise or threat of the stick near his right flank would make him sheer to the left. In the eastern Arctic with a fan hitch, I should have

Above: An overnight snowhouse or *iglusuugyuk* under construction. The third row of snow blocks are put into place, each leaning slightly inward and fitted tightly to the one before. Spaces between the blocks on the outer wall will be chinked with snow

A Perry Island hunter, seated on a block of snow, waits patiently over a seal breathing hole for the animal to surface. The harpoon rests on two supports on either side of the hole, and the hunter grasps the hand line that will release his weapon

Left: Anangaip and her husband Uqsina, from Bathurst Inlet

Below left: An Eskimo boy at Bathurst Inlet, well bundled against
the winter chill. He wears a deerskin parka and pants and
his boots are made from the soft belly fur of the caribou

Below: Iksik poses with his kill on a hunting expedition at
Bathurst Inlet. Taken during the northward migration,
these caribou will feed the dogs on the return trip

Far right: Unable to find the proper snow with which to build shelter, our hunting party is forced to keep moving, though night is falling. Iksik, out in front, is testing for the distinctive creaking sound that indicates good snowhouse snow

Right: Neniruaq stops on the trail to ice his runners with lukewarm water, a procedure that may be necessary two or three times a day. The bumps will be smoothed out with his snowknife

Below: A mug-up on the trail. The dogs are played out after a hard day's travel on the soft snow of Bathurst Inlet

Right: Two polar bears, largest of the bear family yet the least aggressive, on sea ice

Below: Caribou at Bathurst Inlet

Above: A bull muskox stands guard over his herd on Bathurst Island

Left: Amid the summer grasses and lichens of Coronation Gulf, I discover the ruins of an Eskimo stone house

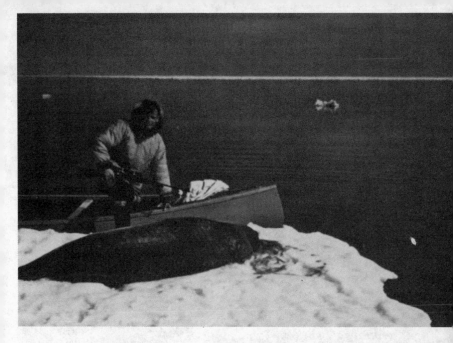

Above: A large bearded seal, the 'square-flipper', weighing close to eight hundred pounds

Right: Making camp in an inlet of Coronation Gulf: the gear and grub boxes are unloaded at a natural dock

used a thirty foot long sealskin whip, flicking it just to the right of Qaqquq to turn him left, but with the Nome or tandem hitch used in the west, in which the dogs are positioned two by two in front of the sled with a leader out in front alone, the whip is of little use except perhaps a short one to prod the wheel dogs, those closest to the sled in the harness.

Training a dog as I trained Qaqquq is just a matter of conditioning the animal to do what is required of it. By shouting 'haw' and throwing something, the dog is taught to turn left. After a bit, a smart dog like Qaqquq turns when he hears the command, and it is no longer necessary to throw anything. The same procedure conditions the dog to turn right when so commanded. From then on if the lead dog is bright, he soon picks up the little bits of the job he needs to know. For example, he will turn left on command, and if the 'haw' is shouted again he will keep turning until he finishes a complete circle, and on a long radius so that he doesn't turn back on his own team, which would allow the traces and towline to become slack. If the lead dog turns too short, the swing dogs just behind will overtake him, and there will be a fight. A smart lead dog always keeps the towline taut.

When a potential lead dog responds well to training, and learns to run with an always taut trace, there is not too much concern whether he is also a good puller or not. As long as the lead dog keeps the others going and responds well to all commands, then he is a good lead. I was lucky in Qaqquq. He was both a good leader and a puller. He would put his shoulder into the harness and really work. His only major fault was that he would never pass another team. I had a very fast team, but with Qaqquq I should never have won any races. He simply refused to pass. He would pull up alongside smartly enough, then just hold that position.

Because he was a killer and liked to fight, Qaqquq was also my boss dog, the one that keeps order on a team. There is a real pecking order on every team. The boss dog is the top dog, the one that can whip every other dog. He controls the team.

Gradually my team shaped up, but it takes two or three years to build up an outstanding team. I owned a good breeding female and most of the other dogs on my team were offspring from the bitch mated to Qaqquq. I rarely had more than the one female on my team; I preferred the bigger, stronger males.

At about one year, a dog begins to do a good job of pulling, but the best dogs are two or three years old. They are fully developed, strong and tough by then, with enough experience to know the job, used to working in a team, and not as flighty and prone to horsing around as the younger dogs are.

The RCMP, which used to maintain some of the best teams in the North, always claimed that they spent half their time working for the dogs. By that they meant finding food for the dogs. I believe the RCMP may have understated the case. A driver with thirteen working animals has to feed them well to keep them in top shape to do the work he wants of them. I would even say that the owner of a team might spend three quarters of his time 'fuelling' his dogs. All summer long he will fish for them and in the fall when he shoots caribou, he knows that the dogs will eat the bulk of whatever he can kill. Having thirteen dogs is like having thirteen people to feed. A dog will eat as much as a human being, and of course has to eat whether it is working or not. The average husky will eat four or five pounds of caribou or seal or fish every day, whether pulling a heavy-laden sled on a trip or sitting on his butt and howling at the moon in camp.

A driver can grow very attached to a team of dogs when he has a good bunch and is working them every day. Individual dogs are just like individual human beings. They have their own idiosyncrasies. After a time, the driver learns that a certain two dogs work well together, so they are placed side by side in the team. Two dogs may dislike one another; the wise driver learns this quickly and never puts them alongside each other. It takes a great deal of shifting the dogs around in a team to find the best combination.

When I was building my team, I would breed my lone female to Qaqquq, and if there resulted a litter of six or seven pups, I would kill all except two. The chosen two pups received plenty of milk and grew fat and strong. When the new pups were ready, I would break them in at the wheel position and chuck out one of the loafers. The loafer was always shot; it is simply too expensive to keep a dog that doesn't work in the Arctic.

A driver should always dominate his team. If the dogs do get into a fight, and there are thirteen or more dogs scrambling and biting and mauling each other, he should be able to wade right into the middle of the team with just a stick in his hand and break the fighters apart. When two dogs are working on each other, the best method is to grab up a stick or snowknife and smack the dogs hard on the snout. It's painful and quickly breaks them loose from each other.

When a new dog is introduced into a team, he has to be put in harness alongside each of the dogs in the team, one by one, so that the dog can find out just where he stands in the team pecking order. He is teamed up with the weakest dog first and then worked up the line. Often the strange dog and the dog from the established team won't actually fight. One or the other will sense that his opponent is stronger, and when the aggressive one comes up, the dog that doubts his own strength will lie on his back—the sign of submission.

I once bought a huge dog, thinking he would make a good alternative leader when I wanted to rest Qaqquq. I had paid a good price for the new dog, a top-grade fox skin worth about $30. The new dog had plenty of confidence. He and Qaqquq walked stiff-legged around each other, hair bristling, tails straight out, no signs of friendliness, no tailwagging, and no indication of surrender. I expected them to fight but not for long. The fur around a husky's neck is so thick that usually when they attack each other they never get a good grip; they grab a paw or snout and after a few seconds of pain the dog in trouble will give up and the fight is over. This new dog jumped at Qaqquq; Qaqquq got him by the neck and just ripped his throat out. I could see his windpipe sticking out and blood all over the place. In a few minutes the new dog was dead. I was mad, and gave Qaqquq a good licking; but that was the way he was.

A good working dog will last five or six years in the Arctic. When it gets to be about six or seven, and too old for the job, it is shot, even though it may have served well for several years and the owner may be very fond of it. Since there is no point in wasting either the meat or the skin when a dog is killed, it is usually skinned out; the other dogs won't eat a dog from their own team when the skin is still on it—they presumably recognize the scent. The carcass is allowed to freeze, which also helps to reduce the familiar scent, then it can be chopped up and fed to its surviving mates. The skin is good for trimming around the hood of a parka, or for mitts. That way its owner can keep a memento of a dog he has liked—he wears it on his hands or around his face.

Many people seem to think that Eskimo dogs are part wolf. That must be the influence of the movies again. There is no wolf in them to my knowledge. I have never heard of an instance of a wolf mating with an Eskimo dog under normal conditions. I have heard of dog-breeders who have bred wolves to dogs, so I know it is genetically possible, but I have never known it to be done in the Arctic. I knew an Eskimo who caught two young wolves and tried using them in his team. But when the mating season came along the wolves went crazy, and he had to shoot them. Furthermore the wolves didn't prove to be much good on the team and weren't nearly as good pullers as the dogs. Another Eskimo told me that he and some friends caught a couple of adult wolves and worked them into a team, but they said this proved dangerous, because although the wolves became friendly with the dogs, they were unpredictable to handle and never seemed to fit in as part of the team. Most people think that because wolves are bigger—an adult wolf may weigh up to two hundred pounds in the Arctic—they should make better working dogs than the dogs themselves, but size isn't everything. For one thing a wolf has a very narrow chest and small shoulder compared to a dog. Wolves simply don't have the pulling power.

Rabies is a common disease in the North, almost endemic, and dreaded by the Eskimos. It seems to start with foxes and wolves. The afflicted animals, half crazed with the disease, will fearlessly descend into camp or settlement, attacking dogs and people alike. One winter at Perry Island we killed seventeen rabid foxes at the trading post itself; we clubbed or kicked them to death, but the damage had already been done. The dogs were infected, and we lost eighty-three out of a total of around two hundred and fifty, a good third of the dogs. That hit the economy of the post pretty hard. Men who lost all their dogs couldn't trap unless they were able to join camps with luckier men who had healthy teams. They had to wait for a new crop of pups before they could build up a new team.

Fortunately, none of the people at Perry got rabies. I think probably it was their loose caribouskin clothing that saved many from being bitten. The fox or dog found itself with a mouthful of caribou hair and never touched the intended victim.

As my team improved I began to range farther and farther away from the trading post by myself. At first I would go out for only a few hours and then turn back. That way one quickly begins to learn the landmarks that serve as guideposts in the Arctic. Travelling alone, one must study the country and learn the landmarks very quickly or soon become hopelessly lost. Even the Eskimos get lost in the trackless wastes of the Arctic.

It isn't necessary to learn every little turn in a creek or every tiny little island or hump of land. What the traveller does is memorize two or three major landmarks in a day's journey. They might be large islands or an outcropping or a cliff with red rocks, any natural feature which is large and easily identifiable from many miles away. When a landmark is spotted, the traveller knows he has only to keep headed in a certain direction and he will find the next landmark, which might be four or five hours away. Over a period of time he will build up a knowledge of such natural guideposts and always know where he is. By the time I had had my team a year or so, I was travelling hundreds of miles along the coast on my own and quite confidently.

It was quite otherwise with my first dogteam trip with Naigo back at Baker Lake. I was determined to become as much like an Eskimo as was possible for a skinny Scottish ex-sailor. So in November, at the start of the trapping season when Naigo prepared to go out to lay his trapline, I dressed up in my new deerskins and took off with him.

Naigo planned to put his traps out about seventy miles from the post, so we made a good start at six o'clock one morning so as to travel as far as possible the first day. I dressed just like Naigo, head to foot in deerskins, but that was the only similarity. He knew the country like the back of his hand, and I was a complete greenhorn.

Naigo was running a team of fourteen dogs in a fan hitch. With a fan hitch each dog in the team is at the end of a different trace, which might run up to thirty feet out from the sled, all the traces being united at one shackle at the bow of the sled. Each trace is of a different length. The sled Naigo loaded up was a normal sled for that kind of work, big enough to carry a lot of gear, his traps and two men. The runners were made of heavy timbers he had bought from the post for about $48 each, good hard wood about twenty-two feet long, four inches thick and a foot high. Crossbars to hold the runners properly apart were lashed to the runners with sealskin thongs every three or four feet; lashing them individually gave the sled a flexibility it would not have had with bolts or nails holding the crossbars more rigidly. The flexibility was very necessary for running over rough ice. The bow had a steep upturn on it. We piled a good load on this big *komatik*.

There was a good deal of snow on the ground by then, and it was cold. I didn't know the first thing about harnessing the dogs or loading up the sled and Naigo had to do it all. But I was excited at my first trip. My head was full of romantic notions, and I carefully watched everything Naigo did.

We were carrying sleeping bags and two grub boxes, one with kettles and pots and stoves. We had rifles, of course, the traps, and a good load of caribou meat, and a supply of fish for the dogs. We had mud for the sled runners, packages of rolled oats for porridge or to augment the mud for the runners if need be, four or five boxes of hardtack biscuits, tea and sugar and some lard. We didn't pack a tent because Naigo intended to build snowhouses for our overnight stops. The load stacked up two and a half feet above the crossbars of the sled and Naigo even had to show me how to ride on it. A rider never straddles a sled like this; he sits side on. Naigo told me to get on and hold on, because when he yanked up the snow anchor the fourteen dogs would take off at a tremendous pace. They were all excited, too; this was their first trip of the winter after being chained up all summer, so they were anxious to cut loose and run.

The sled anchor is a heavy, steel, two-pronged hook like a grapnel, with an eye at one end for the rope that fastens it to the sled. The twin hooks dig into the snow to hold the dogs until the driver is ready. Naigo told me to stand on the anchor because as he harnessed the excited dogs they were lunging back and forth in the harnesses. Every now and then he had to snap out his sealskin whip to flick one of the dogs and quiet it down. Naigo could pick a black fly off the left ear of his lead dog thirty feet away with his whip and never touch the dog's ear.

We were ready. Naigo gave the word, and I threw the anchor on the sled and jumped aboard. Those dogs really gave us a run. We raced out four or five miles at a gallop, out over the ice on Baker Lake, bouncing along and hanging on for dear life. Then the dogs got the excitement out of their systems and settled down to a trot, a fast standard pace that they keep up hour after hour, day after day. On smooth ice or snow a team can cover forty miles a day with no difficulty at that pace.

By then we were well chilled, racing along in the cold fall air. Once in a while we got off and ran along behind the sled to warm up. An experienced man knows the trick of running into a brisk wind without freezing his face. The face must be kept averted, turned to one side or the other, the parka hood pulled around to protect the exposed flesh from the cutting wind.

After a while it occurred to me that my first romantic trip by dogteam was actually pretty boring and monotonous. I couldn't talk to Naigo because I didn't know enough Eskimo words yet to carry on much of a conversation. He spent a lot of time steering the sled around chipped ice or chunks of ice, and every time one of the dogs left something behind, Naigo deftly steered the sled around so that it wouldn't stick like a lump to the runner and slow us up.

We had been out about three or four hours and the wind was blowing very hard. There was quite a ground drift—it was almost as if the ground were smoking. Drifting snow, tossed about by the wind, would rise a few feet off the ground. It was cold, but with that kind of ground drift, very common in the Arctic, the sled really glides. It is the best of times for sled travel, because the snow has been frozen and whipped into pellet shapes and the little granules make the sled roll along almost as though it were on ball-bearings.

Naigo shouted the dogs to a stop, and we had a mug-up there on the trail. The wind was blowing so strongly that we pulled the sled side on to the wind and anchored it. The dogs flopped down where they stood and curled up against the wind, their snouts tucked into their front paws.

We had a terrible time lighting the primus stove for the tea because the wind kept blowing it out. Finally Naigo went out and cut some snowblocks and built a wind break, and we crouched behind that. We were so cold that I couldn't take my hands out of my mitts to hold a mug of tea. When I did, the cold wind numbed my fingers even more. So I sat there on my block of snow and Naigo had to do all the work. He got the primus going and made the tea and gave me some hardtack biscuits to chew. I felt like excess baggage and wanted to help, but knew that if I tried I should just be in the way. I sat there and froze, and was thoroughly miserable. 'If this is adventure in the Arctic,' I thought, 'they can keep it!'

I had no idea which way we were headed. There was no sun to guide us since the sky was completely overcast. Naigo knew the landmarks, but I didn't even realize there were any, and couldn't figure out how he could head out so confidently.

The tea warmed me up a bit and after a while we turned inland off the lake, following a creek. It was tough going for a while because we hit some soft deep snow and the dogs floundered. We had to help pull and push the sled to get out of the creek bottom up over a hill. In the far North, no one wears snowshoes because there is seldom any use for them on the wind-packed snow. They are useful in the soft snow of the brush country to the south, but just get in the way in the Arctic proper. However, we could have used them getting up out of that gulley. We were sinking to our hips in the soft drifts. My thighs ached, I thought my feet and hands would never warm up again, and I was certain my nose was frozen. By that time we had covered about twenty miles.

Naigo might have gone farther if he had been on his own, but he took pity on me and stopped to build our snowhouse. He searched on foot for the proper type of snow, and finding it, shouted back at me to bring the team. I lifted up the snow anchor. The dogs took off with such a rush that I was yanked off my feet and into the snow. Naigo was a good hundred yards away. There we were, the dogs galloping away with our sled and all our provisions and me flat on my face in the snow. I jumped up and raced madly after them, finally catching up with them.

Then we began building the snowhouse, or rather Naigo did, and I tried to be useful. It didn't take Naigo long, but I was not to enjoy its warmth just yet.

Naigo started unloading the sled, pulling all the gear off, and he threw out the tie-out chain for the dogs. This was a long chain, about a hundred and twenty feet long, that he carried in a box. He turned the sled over, shoved the peaked bow down into the snow to anchor it, and fastened the long chain with a clasp to a shackle on the bow of the sled. He walked out from the sled pulling the chain with him until he had it stretched out full length. Attached to the long tie-out chain were individual chains each three or four feet long with little snaps to hook into a dog's harness. When Naigo got to the end of the long chain, he cut down into the snow and made a slit trench at right angles to the chain. At the end of the chain was a ring with a wooden stake. I knew there was no way he could drive that stake into the frozen ground to anchor the dogs, so I watched closely to see how he would do it. First he placed the stake flat down in the slot he had scraped out in the snow; then he cut another slot at right angles to the stake and along the line of the tie-out chain. Then with soft snow he packed both the chain and the anchor stake in tight and stamped on them. In no time they were frozen in rock-hard, strong enough to hold any team of dogs.

Next he began to unharness the dogs. I didn't know the dogs nor the proper way to handle them, and dogs as big as they were, jumping around because they were excited and knew they were about to be fed, were a real handful. It took us about half an hour to get all the dogs tied out.

Then we went back to the snowhouse and took all the deerskins inside. I passed them in through the little low entrance and Naigo took a snow beater, a piece of wood about a foot and a half long and all smoothed off, and used that for knocking the snow out of the skins. The first skin went on the snow floor hair side down, the next hair side up, and so on, skin to skin, and ending with the hair up on the top one. If the snow wasn't carefully and thoroughly beaten off it would melt on the skin when the snowhouse warmed up. Then, when the stove was turned off for the night, the skins would freeze up and be of no use. Eight or nine such bedding skins covered about two thirds of the floor of the snowhouse. Bit by bit we brought in all the gear, carefully knocking the loose snow off everything, We lit candles, and soon it looked like a scene out of a fairy tale—light and warm-looking and bright, while outside a blizzard was blowing up.

Chopping up three or four pounds of frozen trout and whitefish for each dog took half an hour. And were they eager! They would grab their chunk of fish and place it between their paws and tear into it, gnawing off bites which were almost as hard as rock. It gave me a new appreciation of the power of their jaws.

With the chores all done, we re-entered the snowhouse and Naigo drew in the final block of snow to close in the doorway. Just as we had done with the bedding skins, we beat the snow out of our outer parkas and pants and *kamiks* before Naigo lit the primus stove. The place warmed up surprisingly fast. Naigo cut up some blocks of snow to melt down for our tea and in no time we were snug and warm. I could feel myself beginning to feel like a human being again. I took my mitts off, and Naigo showed me how to turn them inside out and put them on the drying rack, a crisscrossed framework of willow sticks with some twine netting. When he turned my mitts inside out, Naigo scraped off the frost—sweat at the wrists had frosted up quickly —with his snowknife, and then when he had them on the drying frame, he stuck the ends of the frame in the snow wall just above the stove. We took off our boots and did the same thing, scraping the frost and snow crusting off the inside, and stuck them up on drying racks too. We kept on our inside pants and parkas and slippers.

There was one more thing to do before eating, I discovered; we had a pile of harness to mend. That was one of those never-ending chores, something that had to be done nearly every night, because the dogs chewed up or broke some every day. At least I felt at home with seaman's twine and an old sailmaker's needle.

So there we were. I had warmed up nicely, but I was so tired and hungry that I was ready to fall asleep right there and then, and so was Naigo. Instead of cooking anything, he just carved off a chunk of caribou meat for me, about the size of my hand, a chunk of raw, frozen caribou. He laid out some hardtack biscuits, hard as buttered rocks, and that was our two-course meal. I gnawed on the biscuits a while and then worked on a piece of raw meat. I felt like one of the dogs. I wanted to enjoy the caribou, but I was psychologically repulsed at the idea of eating raw meat. I went to bed hungry that night.

Next morning when we woke up in our sleeping bags, it must have been thirty below. We had had no heat in the snowhouse all night. Reaching out from his sleeping bag without having to get up in the cold, Naigo got the little stove going and the kettle full of snow to start the water for our tea. The snowhouse quickly warmed up, and we crawled out of our sacks. Breakfast was another batch of hardtack biscuits and plenty of tea.

When we went outside, Naigo showed me that the sled runners had a coating of frozen mud and ice on them, and how to scrape and smooth it off and ice the runners up again so that they would glide easily over the snow and ice. Mud has a special importance to anyone in the North who wants to run a dogteam. In the fall the Eskimos all gather up mud of a particular consistency; there are about ten different kinds of mud with different qualities for use on a sled. The mud is necessary because the wooden runners of the sleds are sheathed with a strip of steel on the bottom to keep them from wearing out quickly. In the bitter cold of winter the steel freezes tight to the ice and snow, and the dogs can't budge the sled. A stop of seconds is enough to freeze the bare steel to the ice and snow. Steel shoeing is particularly necessary in spring-time when the snow is thawing.

When it gets cold, the Eskimos flip the sled over upside down and mix the mud with water to make mud balls about the size of a baseball. The mud ball is slapped on the steel runner and pressed down tight. More mud balls are added all along the runner, covering it completely. The mud is then worked up and down the length of the runner so that it is four or five inches deep, and is plastered right down around the edges of the runner too, to help it grip. Handling a mixture of mud and water is certainly cold work in below-zero weather. The mud runner is allowed to freeze until it sets almost like concrete. Then an ordinary jackplane is used to plane the frozen mud smooth, just as though it were wood. When it is as smooth as possible, a pad of bear skin is dipped in water and brushed continuously along the mud runner. If this is done in a fluid smooth manner, the water it deposits freezes instantly on the mud, building up a layer of ice. This is kept up until the ice is half an inch thick. The sled is ready to go, and there is no way to get a slicker runner. The only problem is keeping the artificial mud and ice runner intact. Running the sled over bare ground will quickly wear it off, and so will bouncing over choppy, chunky ice. Chunks of the artificial layer broken away, of course, have to be patched. Runners sometimes have to be re-iced two or three times a day, and in bad travel conditions more often.

In mild weather flaps of skin or hide are hung along the sides of the sled to keep the runners shaded and prevent the mud from softening. In the spring, loose snow can be kicked up against the sled, piling it up along the runners so that the direct rays of the sun won't thaw it out.

Naturally a dogteam driver will always try to have a box of

mud with him to patch up his runners when a chunk is knocked off. There are many substitutes and oddly enough one of the best is rolled oats. Yet even rolled oats has its disadvantages. On one of my solo trips, I had lost a lot of mudding and had to patch, but had run out of mud. I used the Eskimo technique of boiling up some oats as for porridge, and when it is nice and thick slapping it on in place of mud. It might have worked well had not one of my dogs broken loose that night. Next morning I discovered that most of my new porridge runner had been eaten. I thought there must have been a bit of Scot in that dog.

Our second day was as bad as the first, travelling with a nasty ground blow all day, with a full blizzard by afternoon. We simply couldn't see where we were going any longer. I hadn't been able to see the lead dog for a couple of hours, and not even Naigo could find any landmarks. It was uncanny how he kept going so long, cutting along the banks of a frozen creek. He just seemed to sense his way along, but finally it was too much even for him. It took a little longer than last time to get a good camp set up in that blow, but we made it pretty snug, and it was a good thing we did. We were stuck there for four days.

I have never been so bored in my life. We just lay there in our sleeping bags, emerging once or twice a day to check on the dogs. When we went outside the wind buffeted us unmercifully. We couldn't see the dogs or the sled, but both were within nine or ten feet of the snowhouse. Naigo would get out and walk over to the drifts and poke around a bit. He would presently reach down into what looked just like another drift to me, yank on the chain, and the first dog would appear, groaning miserably and complaining at being disturbed in its warm den under the snow. Naigo would work his way down the line, yanking each of the dogs out, making sure they didn't get so badly drifted over that they smothered. When dogs get entirely drifted over, sometimes it happens that the body heat of the dog will put a film of ice around the inside of the natural cave of snow that the animal has hollowed out, and when such ice forms the dog may smother. Once a day we fed the dogs and ourselves, and the remainder of the time we spent in our sleeping bags.

From Naigo I learned two fundamental northern traits— patience and acceptance. When one is caught in a blow in the Arctic, the best thing to do is just to hole up in a snow- house or any possible kind of shelter and sit it out. 'It will always end eventually,' Naigo told me.

After the blow ended we pushed on to the area where Naigo wanted to put out his traps. He was after white fox and had about two hundred traps. They were scarcely bigger than the ones used for muskrat, with about a three-inch trigger pad, the type that can be opened with one hand by pressing down on the spring.

To me it looked as if Naigo was just setting the traps out in the middle of nowhere, on a vast, featureless plain. There was no sign of fox that I could see, yet he seemed to be placing the traps with purpose and precision.

Naigo paid little attention to my questions. To set a trap, he used his snowknife to cut down about a foot deep into the packed snow, making a little circular cut so that he could lift out a neat little cylinder of snow. Next he put the bait in the bottom of the hole he had cut in the snow, with just a few drops of perfume from a cheap vial—sometimes he used rotten fish or rancid seal oil—then he put the trap down into the hole on top of the perfume. The trap was attached by a chain to a wooden crossbar. He did the same thing he had done with the dogs' tie-out chain, just made two slots in the snow at right angles, put the crossbar in one and lay the chain along the other, and stamped them down with soft snow. The more a trapped fox pulled against that the more it would jam the crossbar tightly under the snow. To make it doubly certain, when Naigo had the chain and crossbar packed in he would take a leak on it. That froze everything. At last it became clear to me why we had drunk so many mugs of tea. Once the trap was set and anchored, Naigo picked up the cylinder of snow he had removed earlier, and with his knife whittled it down to fit exactly over the open edge of the hole, so that it made just the thinnest of covering to hide the trap.

We put out a number of traps like that, all over the area, some a hundred yards apart, some a mile, some down in deep snow, and some up among the rocks where the wind had swept the frozen tundra clear. At each trap Naigo cut a second cylindrical block of snow and stood it on end for a guide. I noticed he always slanted the block so that it leaned in a particular way directly towards the trap, and always roughly three paces away, so that he could spot the block and know immediately where the trap should be.

Finally we got all two hundred traps out and headed back for the post. We stopped overnight at a little settlement Naigo knew, and I enjoyed the experience, including an eye-popping look at a 'topless' Eskimo girl. On the way back we ran across some caribou, and Naigo shot a couple of them. That was my first sight of caribou out in the open, and I was thrilled. We had surprised a small herd as we came over a little hill, and though they made off immediately Naigo, old experienced hunter that he was, had reacted with surprising speed in grabbing up his rifle and getting two of them.

The trip back was just as cold and wretched as the trip out. It had truly been a miserable first brush with reality in the Arctic, and made me wonder if I was really cut out to be an Arctic man. But by making a trip like that I was learning the things that a man had to learn to live like an Eskimo: how to handle a snowknife, how to build a trail house, how to handle the dogs, how to find landmarks and travel alone hundreds of miles by dogteam.

It seemed to me that learning to live in the Arctic was like learning a trade. I had been a seaman. No one had expected me to become a seaman overnight. I first had to be an apprentice to learn about ropes and sails and engines, each in turn, step by step. Tackling the trade step by step meant that I would not be overwhelmed by the mass of experience needed to become a well-rounded seaman. Anyone with determination and patience can learn how to live in the Arctic if he is willing to learn a step at a time, how to read the snow, how to follow a trail, how to trap a fox. And nowhere could he find more willing or patient teachers than the Eskimos themselves.

A couple of years later, when I finally put together my own dogteam at Perry Island, I knew a great deal more than I had when I started my lessons with Naigo, and yet I had a great deal still to learn. Testing myself, I travelled farther and farther. Sometimes I headed down the coast to the east, almost to Gjoa Haven. Sometimes I would head west and inland, up the Perry River to McAlpine Lake, which was only about seventy miles inland. I was very interested in this lake, because the Eskimos said a huge monster called Iqaluaqpak lived there, the Loch Ness monster of the Canadian Arctic. No Eskimo would paddle a canoe or a kayak on McAlpine because it was well known that Iqaluaqpak swallowed such unwary visitors whole, kayak and all.

On these exploratory trips I would carry along some caribou meat, and fish for the dogs, along with some hardtack biscuits, tea, sugar and such, and if I expected to be out long, maybe a fifty-pound sack of flour and some baking powder, salt, and lard to make bannock. One handy food mix that I often took was a sort of home-made instant stew. Before leaving I would set out thirty tins with the bottoms greased lightly, mix up a hash or stew out of whatever happened to be handy, corned beef, macaroni, beans and what not, fill all the pie plates and let the mixture freeze solid. Then I would empty those quick-frozen, precooked slabs—they looked like huge pancakes—into an empty flour sack and bash them up with a hammer until they were a coarse powder. On the trail, when it was time for an evening meal, all I had to do was dump some of the powder in a pot of hot water, and in a couple of minutes—instant stew.

Sometimes, because of its lightness, I would carry commercial dog food in pellet form instead of fish. A twenty-five pound bag of this dried dog food will do a team for several days, but since each dog eats between four and five pounds of fish in a day, if I had no commercial dog food I would need several hundred pounds of fish on the same sort of trip. Sometimes late in the year we might be running out of fish or caribou and the dried dog food would be all we had, so it came to be quite common in our part of the Arctic to buy commercial dog food.

I would take along a two burner and a single burner Coleman stove on my trips. These dependable stoves had pretty well replaced the old primus stove, which was compact and handy but sometimes terribly difficult to light in cold weather. When I made camp, my first move would be to light the two burner stove and put a ten gallon keg on it full of snow. I let the snow melt, then added more until I had a keg about three-quarters full of warming water. Then I added the dog food and let it start warming. While that was cooking I would start to build the snowhouse. That might take anything from half an hour to three hours depending upon the snow quality. By the time the snowhouse was finished, the dog food was usually ready. The temperature of the food had to be just right, lukewarm. Too hot and it wasn't good for the dogs, but too cold and it just froze when it hit the snow.

In the movies the sled that is always used is the little western Arctic basket type, the kind used in Alaska, or around the Mackenzie Delta. They always show a man holding onto two handlebars at the back and standing on the sled all the time as the dogs scurry along. The trouble with that sort of sled in the Canadian Arctic is that it is too puny to haul the things a sled is needed for, and the poor driver would freeze to death standing there all the time holding those handlebars.

The Eskimo *komatik* (the term is a corruption of the actual Eskimo word *qamutik*) generally measured twenty or twenty-two feet long and a foot high. On top of the crossbars was spread a tarp or canvas sled cover, or if none was available heavy skins, caribou or bear. The sleeping skins for the snowhouse would be stacked on next to help serve as a cushion for the load, which could take quite a jostling sometimes as the sled bounced over rough ice or hard-packed, ridged Arctic snow. Arctic snow is nothing like the soft stuff of the south; the constant winds in the Arctic pack the snow nearly as hard as pavement. With the skins down to form a bed on the sled, the grub boxes went on next, in the bow, then the sleeping bags, rifles and other gear. A sled cover would be folded over that and lashed down with a continuous diamond lashing back and forth, over and back, and fastened with thongs stretched between the sides. The sled could take a load as high as four or five feet above ground, and the driver or passengers would sit on top of that, feet to either side. Much of the time, of course, they would be running alongside the sled to keep warm. But the dogs could pull the whole load and never mind another man or two riding along. A man with thirteen dogs had a fairly powerful engine for his sled. When the driver did ride, he sat near the boss of the sled where he could jump off quickly and steer the sled around any large bumps, chunks of ice or inevitable dog droppings.

The dogs had to be watched all the time, particularly in caribou country. They became quite adept at slipping the collar over their heads and getting free of the dog chain when at rest. Then they were likely to wander around the camp for a while looking for scraps of food, but often just took off on their own, chasing after caribou. Almost all dogs that escaped died of starvation. I once lost Qaqquq, and he was gone almost ten days. He joined another team belonging to a friend. The Eskimo recognized him as my lead dog and brought him back to me, but Qaqquq must have lost forty pounds by that time. A dog is taken care of and is not used to hunting on his own like a wolf. He is not fast enough to catch a caribou and doesn't know the tricks a wolf uses to bring one down.

For the driver, dog travel is far from boring. He is always talking to the dogs, watching to see they don't get their feet tangled in the harness, checking to make sure their feet are not balled up with ice, always watching for rough ice and at the same time keeping an eye out for caribou or seal. The driver out on the sea-ice has to remember to pass downwind of any island so that the dogs can scent any caribou there, and he has to find the landmarks that tell him where he is. The driver has plenty to do, but for a passenger it can be a long and dull trip. Sometimes, when all the conditions are just right, the dogs pulling smoothly and steadily, no distracting caribou around, the ice or snow smooth and the course straight, a driver can just lie back on the sled in a mild sun and daydream. The Eskimos say that is the best time to compose drum dance songs and poetry.

In recent years in the North, particularly in the larger settlements such as Cambridge Bay, there has been a startling change in the appearance of dogteams. It would be impossible today to find teams that look anything like the teams oldtimers in the area remember, matched teams of big, fine-looking huskies. People who have come to such northern places as Cambridge Bay have brought their pets with them, and of course these funny-looking southern dogs have mated with the local Eskimo dogs to produce some even funnier-looking offspring.

Inevitably the newcomers have discovered that virtually any dog can be trained to pull a sled. The result is that some of the dogteams in the big settlements are composed of the weirdest assortment of animals ever to be seen outside Dr Seuss. I remember one team that had a dog with a shaggy white coat looking something like a huge sheep dog as the lead, then a couple of dogs that looked as if they had started out to be poodles and lost interest along the way, and then an enormous black dog that looked for all the world like a stunted muskox.

I even saw someone hitching a pair of dachshunds to a little sled. I didn't wait to see the result. Perhaps it is just as well that the powered toboggans are taking over.

17
❋ Tuktu—
The Caribou

Early one summer morning when we had been camped in the fishing settlement on the Perry River for several days, one of the young Eskimos who had set his nets about a mile downstream came paddling back furiously and shouting, '*Tukturaaluit, tukturaaluit!*—Lots of caribou!'

A mist had come down, shrouding the river and the tents of our camp, and we could hear young Aivuuq shouting in the still, moist air even before we could see his canoe thrusting back upstream. We all ran down to the sandbar to meet him. He was still shouting excitedly: 'Tuktu!' As soon as we beached his canoe, he exclaimed that he had seen a great herd of caribou by the river.

We grabbed our rifles and piled into canoes and headed down the river after our exultant young guide. It was always grand to get a chance of caribou meat after a winter of nothing but seal and fish.

When we reached the spot where Aivuuq had seen the herd, there wasn't an animal in sight, but we could read the signs and decided the herd had moved inland a bit. We pulled the canoes up on the bank and followed the trail. Four of us went to the left and five to the right; we hoped to encircle the herd in a valley where we expected to find the animals grazing. After some three hours scouting, we breasted a hill, carefully stopping just before reaching the crest—a hunter never exposes more of his body above the horizon than he has to in order to get a careful look—and there below us in a huge narrow valley was the herd Aivuuq had seen. There were easily five thousand animals.

There were five of us looking down into the valley where the caribou were quietly grazing, moving slowly along as they cropped the moss. We didn't know where the other party of four hunters had got to, so we made our own plans. First we sent one man around to the end of the valley where there was a kind of ravine that the caribou would use as a natural exit. I moved to another little valley, and Angulaalik took a ravine just left of our hill. Thus we placed all our men to seal off the herd in the valley and frighten and confuse the animals no matter which way they ran when the shooting started. We checked each other with our binoculars and were just getting ready to start firing when we heard the sound of shots at the other end of the valley. It was the other four men, who had come over the hill at the far end of the valley and were now in perfect position to drive the caribou straight towards us. We all began shooting then.

A herd that size doesn't scare easily. When there are only ten or twenty caribou in a bunch, they will take off like the wind at the first sign of hunters or sound of guns, but in a big herd, the animals will only become confused and mill around. We simply sat in our hiding places and picked off the targets we wanted.

We picked the biggest, fattest cows, because we knew that most of the females in the herd would be pregnant during such a migration. When a hunter kills a pregnant cow, he also gets the foetus, prized as a delicacy. The unborn calf provides the tenderest, most succulent morsel of meat anyone could desire, soft like lamb and wonderfully tasty.

With the frightened and bewildered caribou stampeding around, it was difficult to pick out a single animal to shoot. In the old days when bullets were scarce, a good Eskimo hunter would have carefully lined up two animals for each shot, so that a bullet going through one body would strike a second. After holding my fire for some time I began to select the cows I wanted. After I had dropped a couple in their tracks with nice, clean heart shots, Angulaalik came running over, scolding me as he came.

'Don't kill them, don't kill them!' he shouted. Nasarlulik, the hunter on my other side, came over too. He and Angulaalik were shooting Eskimo-style, shooting to cripple the animals, not to kill. Angulaalik, seeing how confused I was, explained:

'There are so many caribou, you can take your time. Just aim at the rear leg.'

I protested. I thought this was really cruel.

Nasarlulik explained, 'Just use your head a minute. We've got to carry all the dead ones back to the river. Just shatter a leg and the caribou can be driven back to the river on his three good legs, but he can't run fast enough to get away. We can kill them when we reach the river.'

I stared dumbfounded at my two companions. This had never occurred to me.

'Use your head,' Nasarlulik repeated. 'Would you rather carry them back or drive them back?'

By then the shooting had almost stopped. There was no sense in taking more than we could handle. Even so, nine of us had shot fifty-nine caribou in the few minutes before the panicked herd was able to flee over the hills. It was a good hunt. These animals would give us meat for many weeks and provide badly needed hides. We could have slaughtered many more, but the meat would have been wasted. We should never have been able to get it all dressed out before the heat of the sun rotted the carcasses.

Several caribou were down, shot in the leg and crippled. One of these close to me jumped up and tried to run, but flopped over almost immediately from the pain. My natural impulse was to go up and put a bullet through its head to put the suffering creature out of its misery. But Nasarlulik held out a restraining arm, 'Don't waste bullets,' he counselled. 'We'll kill them when we get back to the river.' And he and Angulaalik booted the poor animal in the rump and got it going again in the direction they wanted. Actually I could see that this was good reasoning. Each animal weighed about a hundred and fifty pounds—a lot of weight to try to carry across the tundra even a few miles.

The dead caribou were skinned out and backpacks made. The wounded animals were driven ahead of us as we trekked back toward our canoes. They would hobble about a hundred yards, then flop down. We would come up and boot them or prod them with our guns until they got up and staggered a few more yards.

It was hard walking with the backpacks of up to a hundred and fifty pounds each, so the men who were herding the cripples changed with the men toting the meat now and then. We had skinned the animals carefully, because the Eskimos at Perry Island never had access to all the caribou they needed. They could use all the hides we could bring in. As for the carcasses, we cut off each hindquarters section and slipped it over our shoulders. The ribs and shoulders went on top, all of it tied in place with the hide.

When we reached the river, we finished off the crippled animals and loaded as much as we could into the canoes and paddled up to camp. On a second trip downstream some of the women came along to help skin out the remaining caribou and butcher them. As we brought the meat into camp other women there got out their *ulus* and cut the meat into thin strips and spread it out over the rocks and poles and on lines to let the sun cure it. That method, the old Eskimo method, requires no salt, nothing. The sun cures the strips perfectly, and they will keep for over a year. The kids around the camp were assigned to watch the dogs and make certain no foxes sneaked into camp to steal a feast.

We could hardly wait to finish the work and have a really big feast. We cooked up a great batch of bannock, and put some caribou heads with the eyes still in and the hair still on in a pot and boiled them up for soup. We made blood soup and caribou stew, and in another pot boiled up some leg bones to be shattered later for the *patiq* (marrow). As we had butchered each animal, we were careful to save the contents of the stomach, a semi-digested moss-lichen mixture which the Eskimos call *nirukkaq*. The *nirukkaq* was spread out on rocks to dry and then gathered up to be eaten with the meat. This version of Eskimo salad tastes remarkably like a green salad. A meal was enjoyed that night that is not eaten every day.

We never again saw such a big herd that near Perry Island. Usually the most we could expect was ten or twelve animals, and by the time a couple had been killed the others had fled right away. The feast was not the last of that hunt, though. The skins had to be prepared carefully for clothing and a myriad other uses.

Watching the women work expertly on the hides jogged my memory back to my first winter in the Arctic at Baker Lake when for the first time I saw Eskimos actually dressed in 'deerskins', the skins of the caribou. I had been at Baker Lake with Sandy Lunan only a few days when a family came in from one of the fur trapping camps. I was rearranging shelves in the store when I heard dogs outside. A team had pulled up in front of the post, and three Eskimos came in, wearing full winter clothing. To me the Arctic became real at that moment.

The three men looked enormously bulky in their deerskins— they were short of stature but seemed as wide as the door, in their big double parkas. (Later I was to discover that there were distinctive differences in the cut and style of parkas in different parts of the Arctic.) In true winter travel dress, these men were wearing both inner and outer caribouskin parkas, the inner one with the hair next to their bodies and the outer one with the hair on the outside. The Baker Lake people and most of the inland Eskimos had their parkas slit up the side to just above the waist and all fringed. They wore a fringe about six inches long down the front part of the apron in front and over the tail flap, like a long jacket with side vents. The front of the parka came down to about mid-thigh, but the rear was down almost to the back of their knees. The idea of this was to provide an insulating flap to sit on. The parkas favoured in this part of the country didn't have the distinctive wolf ruffs around the hoods, like those worn by Eskimos in the western Arctic. The Baker Lake people wore eastern-Arctic-style pants, big, wide, floppy-legged trousers that came down to just above the knee. Underneath the pants were leggings, usually duffle cloth obtained at the trading post, going right up their thighs all the way from the ankles, and a long stocking of soft skin or wool. A caribou slipper, low-cut and soft, was covered by two pairs of caribou *kamiks* or boots, the first with the hair turned in and the second with the hair side out. The hair was left on the sole, too, so that layers of caribou hair insulated their feet against the snow and cold. Parkas in that part of the north always had a carefully worked design on the back, insets made of the white belly fur of the caribou, which stands out nicely against the dark skin.

The Eskimo-made caribou parkas and pants are lighter and warmer than anything yet devised for Arctic weather by the whiteman. The armed forces of many nations have been testing materials for years and have yet to come up with anything as good. The caribou hair is hollow, which makes the skins both warm and lightweight. A complete outfit of inner and outer caribou garments might weigh no more than four or five pounds if made from the proper skins; a parka which would give the equivalent warmth made of any other material would be much heavier.

My three visitors had brought in some caribou skins for trading. At that time I was still learning how to grade the hides. The animals may be killed at any time of the year, but the prime hides, the only skins really good for clothing, are those taken in the late fall or early winter. By then the warble flies have gone and the skin has healed from the larvae infestations of the summer, and is free of holes and scars. The hair is deep enough by then to be warm but not as deep as it gets later on, when it actually becomes too heavy for best use as clothing. The summer pelt is as thin as paper and not good for anything much other than underwear. Prime clothing skins, the early winter hides, were worth two dollars each at the post in those days. The heavier, later skins, useful as sleeping skins, mattresses or blankets, were worth a dollar each.

Every part of the deerskin has a different function. The leg skin, being much tougher than that from other parts of the body, is used for mitts and footwear. The back and sides, of course, are used to make parkas and pants and inner boots where toughness is not so necessary. The belly fur (*pukiq*) is used to make fringes and fancy insets for decoration and sometimes children's clothing.

One of my first moves at Baker Lake was to acquire a complete outfit of caribou, so that I could travel with the Eskimos. To the inland Eskimos the caribou used to be a staple in the same way the buffalo was to the Plains Indians. The caribou provided food; tools were made from antlers and bones; and the skins went for everything from underwear to bedding for the platform in the snowhouse, tents in the summer, and clothing the year round. Today most Eskimos buy canvas or nylon tents from the Bay stores, but one of the advantages of the caribouskin tent was that it stayed dark in the interior, which kept the mosquitos out. Open the flap on an ordinary white-man's tent and in ten minutes it is full of mosquitos.

All Eskimos were anxious to find caribou. Not only were they a welcome change in diet for coastal Eskimos, but when the caribou were scarce, the people either had to trade for hides or make do with other skins, all of which were inferior for the many necessary uses. When an Eskimo was travelling by dogteam he automatically kept one eye cocked for caribou. It was as natural as driving on the right side of the street for the Eskimo out on the ice to pass an island downwind rather than upwind.

In the wintertime, given some daylight, any large group of caribou can be spotted a long way off, even before they can be seen with the naked eye or scented by the dogs. Above a herd there is always a cloud bank. The warm breath of the animals and their body heat combine and condense in the cold air, causing a fogbank over the herd, a give-away for miles.

However, the same cold air that helps give the animals away also protects them. In the very cold, still air of the Arctic, sound carries tremendous distances. The best time in the winter to hunt is when there is a ground drift blowing. The howling of the wind masks the noise of the hunter's approach from even the unusually acute ears of the caribou. On top of that, the animals instinctively stand with their backs into such a ground blizzard, making it easier for the hunter to sneak up close behind them.

Before the whiteman's rifle was available to the people of the North, crude spears, bows and arrows, and the guile learned for survival, were the only weapons Eskimos used to take caribou. But in the winter the bow was no good. It nearly always snapped in the frigid air. So the inland or Caribou Eskimos developed a unique pitfall method. Picking a section of land which they knew from experience the migrating herds would probably cross, they would dig a series of pitfalls in the hard, crusted snow, each pitfall being about as wide as a man's shoulders, deep into the drifts, side by side right across the selected valley. Then, jumping and shouting and waving skins to frighten the herd, they would drive the caribou down through the valley. The animals would fall or be pushed into the pitfalls, so narrow that the caribou would become jammed in them, trapped there helpless while the hunter came up with his spear to make the kill. That type of pitfall was called a *qalgitaq* and was a technique that worked very well under the right conditions. It had to be done in snow, however, as the permafrost made it impossible to dig pits deep enough in the summer. If there were not enough Eskimos around to herd the animals toward the prepared pits, the Eskimos used the urine of old women as bait. Urine from young women or men didn't work, it seems. The Eskimos said that the caribou were able to tell the difference. Poured in puddles around the pits, this odd bait was apparently almost irresistible to the animals.

Before the rifle changed the entire pattern of Eskimo life, the coastal Eskimos depended upon the seal and sea life and only moved off the sea ice for the caribou hunt in late spring and summertime. In late April or May hunters would trek to those valleys through which the age-old migration routes lay. So long had the hunters used some valleys that many generations of Eskimos had built up rock cairns (called *insuksuk*) made to resemble man in general outline all along the tops of the hills, about fifty or a hundred feet apart. In between the *insuksuk* they placed caribou antlers or sticks of some sort with pieces of caribouskin flapping, or bones tied together loosely, anything that would flutter or rattle in the wind and distract and frighten the caribou. The long, V-shaped valley they picked for the kill would be outlined with these *insuksuk* and noise-making devices. When the caribou entered the valley they would see the cairns and flapping objects up on the ridges all along the horizon of the valley, and they would be effectively herded right up the valley, not daring to try to break out over the hills. At the apex of the valley the hunters lay in wait.

There they built low blinds, called *talu*, by setting up small semi-circles of rock and earth, seldom over a foot and a half or two feet high. (In the Copper Eskimo dialect, the Arctic settlement of Spence Bay, which lies on the migration route, was known as *taluryuat*, which is a plural term meaning 'big blinds'.) The hunters crouched low behind the *talu* with their bows and arrows. Sometimes if the caribou failed to enter the proper valley where all was in readiness for them, the women and children would be sent around the valley to come up behind the herd and frighten the animals in the proper direction. When the caribou passed by the *talu* the hunters would leap out with their primitive weapons and get as many caribou as they could. They had to be in close, because the Eskimo bow and arrow never had a killing range of more than forty or fifty yards.

Another summer-time killing technique wasn't much easier. Just as the hunters knew the migration routes and which valleys to choose, they also knew the water crossing points where the herd had to cross a river or the neck of a lake. There the hunters would gather with their kayaks and await the coming of the herds. Once the caribou were well into the water the hunters, paddling furiously, would sweep down on them in their little skin crafts. On the foredeck of the kayak the hunter carried two long caribou spears, each tipped by a very sharp caribou antler. Manoeuvring up alongside the frantically swimming caribou, the hunter would brace his paddle in a special attachment on the kayak so that the paddle served as a kind of outrigger to give him balance when he thrust at the caribou. The most effective kill was made by spearing the caribou from behind, close to the backbone, so that the point of the spear drove up and into the heart or lungs. A good hunter could kill eight or nine caribou out of an average size herd at such a crossing. Then he would hook each carcass to a towline on his kayak and pull them to shore where the women would be waiting to butcher them.

When the rifle arrived in the Arctic, however, the old ways were superseded. Bows and arrows were discarded in favour of the new weapon, which the Eskimos were quick to adopt.

Often in mid-summer caribou can be spotted along the ridges. They are up there hoping to catch enough breeze to free them for a few blessed moments from the warble flies, the nostril flies, and the ubiquitous mosquitos, which in swarming millions make life hell for man and beast alike down in the swampy tundra areas for a few weeks each year. Sometimes caribou can be seen madly racing back and forth at top speed. Clouds of mosquitos are driving them literally berserk. The jumpy animals are often made nervous by the loud buzzing that tells them the dread warble fly is at hand again. The warble flies come out about the same time as the mosquitos, and while they don't bite human beings, they swarm all over the poor caribou, boring holes in the skin, depositing their eggs on the animal's back. The larvae grow and penetrate the hide so that a caribou skin taken in that season looks like an old Swiss cheese. The blow flies so infest any exposed meat that they sometimes ruin a winter's supply.

The only good thing about warble flies seems to be that they provide the Eskimos with 'candy.' Caribou skins taken in the late summer or early fall will be covered with the warble larvae, now grown to the size of large marbles. Eskimos comb the infested hides, popping warble larvae into their mouths with great delight. Actually, while some white people might shudder at the thought, the warble grubs taste much like a watery jam, not bad at all if one likes that sort of thing.

In some respects the nostril flies are a more bothersome pest. These flies, buzzing in incredible numbers for a few days, land in the animal's nostrils and walk up through the nasal passages to deposit their eggs in the throat of the host animal. Many times, skinning out a caribou, one will find the throat absolutely packed with the larvae of this pest. The Eskimos call them *tagiuq*, which is the stem of the word 'to sneeze.' It would appear that the larvae in the throat and nostrils of the animal cause it to make its characteristic wheezing, sneezing sound.

White hunters, especially greenhorns in the Arctic, try to take advantage of the insect-tormented animals, which are easily spotted on the high ridges. But these caribou have the advantage of high ground and almost always spot the hunter in time to race away. The greenhorn gives up, but the old Eskimo hunter knows that the animals seldom run far. They nearly always stop just out of sight over the next ridge. When they don't see anyone any more and can't hear or smell a wary hunter creeping up on them downwind, they think they are safe. An experienced hunter will follow and get his caribou in the next valley every time. Sometimes when a hunter mounts a ridge, he will spot a lone caribou in the valley, motionless and head down, sides heaving. The hunter knows that he is seeing an animal that has truly had it. There it stands, overcome, dazed by the heat, pestered into insensibility by the insects, head drooping, unseeing, unhearing, uncaring. Even in the old days a hunter with a bow had no trouble getting close enough to such an animal to drive an arrow through it.

One spring a hunter named Palvik from Bathurst Inlet and I decided to take my dogteam and make a trip down the inlet looking for caribou. Normally in that area the migration came in March, and since we had already seen a few caribou around the inlet, we thought we might find some badly needed fresh meat.

Off we went to camp about thirty miles south of the trading post on the west coast of the inlet. We built a tight snowhouse there and spent a couple of days working out of that base, picking up the odd caribou sign here and there, but never actually seeing a herd. As occasionally happens, we just couldn't locate them at that particular time.

Then one day we were sitting outside the snowhouse in the sun, warming and resting, when suddenly all the dogs began to perk up. We watched the dogs one at a time sit up suddenly in the snow, their ears pricked, listening, until they were all up and alert. We couldn't hear a thing; we had no idea what had caught the dogs' attention.

Our camp was on the edge of the inlet, right on the sea; behind our snowhouse a small hill blocked our view inland. We climbed the back of the hill just to look around, but still couldn't see a thing. We came back to the camp convinced our dogs had gone strange, but kept an eye on them. They still acted as though they knew something we didn't.

Almost three hours later, just as Palvik and I were ready to turn in, we heard a kind of rumbling noise. The dogs were all on their feet again, their noses in the air sniffing. It always pays to investigate behaviour out of the norm in the Arctic, so back up the hill we went, and this time, away off in the distance, we could see what appeared to be a greyish-brown flood moving slowly over the land. We knew immediately that we were seeing an immense herd of caribou.

At that distance we couldn't distinguish individual animals. As far north as we could look and as far south, we saw the flood of animals moving east. Then we caught the drumming of their hooves on the frozen tundra, and the clicking noise made by their hooves hitting together. We were right in the path of the most tremendous herd of caribou either of us had ever seen. We wondered momentarily if we should hitch up the dogs and move off in one direction or another before they overran us. We were pretty excited, each in our own way. As the animals came nearer I cried out, 'What an amazing sight!' Palvik replied, '*Niqiraaluit!*' ('What a lot of food!') Two cultures!

The upshot of our hasty conference was an eminently northern decision. We decided, since the caribou were still many miles away, that we would just go back to camp and have a mug-up and then come back up the hill and keep an eye on them. We returned to our snowhouse for half an hour, long enough to have our tea. By then we could hear the click-clack of thousands of hooves and the drumming noise much more clearly. We climbed the hill once more. The gigantic herd was much closer and still coming right for us.

Palvik suggested, 'We'd better go back and move the dog-team around in between the hill and the snowhouse and make certain they are securely chained before they become too excited to handle.' The dogs were all on their feet, howling and yipping and lunging against the restraining chain. We pulled the entire team around and rechained them so they would be between the advancing herd and our snowhouse.

We didn't as yet have any really accurate idea of how many caribou there were. At our angle we could see only the first twenty or thirty rows. We knew there were a good number. I thought maybe seven or eight thousand. As we watched from the hilltop they came closer and closer, and through the binoculars we could see that what looked to the naked eye like one undulating wave of animals actually consisted of countless scores of herds of about fifty to sixty animals each.

We were still discussing what we should do. The churning mass of caribou was advancing directly upon us, tearing up the tundra as they came. I was uneasy, wondering if they might not simply by force and pressure of numbers just run right over us. I thought it might be smarter to leave while we could. But Palvik couldn't see beyond all that meat. He wanted to stand his ground and kill a lot of caribou, enough for an entire winter's supply.

We grabbed up our rifles and went back up the hill, for about the tenth time, it seemed, and stayed up there until the vanguard of the herd actually began coming up the slope of the hill straight towards us. Then we could see more clearly the immensity of the advancing herd. We could see over the animals leading the migration all the way back to the horizon; as far as vision was possible, to left, right, everywhere, the whole land just flowed and moved like a brown tide pouring over the snow. It seemed to me then that we were seeing millions of caribou.

When the first of the caribou breasted the hill, we retreated toward the snowhouse, keeping carefully between the dogs and the caribou. The dogs were going absolutely crackers. It was fortunate we had fastened them tightly. Finally we could back up no more, so we carefully shot down two of the leaders and then several more right behind them. Just as we hoped, the herd split to go around the fallen animals, the flow going to either side and around the dogs and our snowhouse. This was dramatic evidence of Palvik's common sense and his practical knowledge of the lay of the land and the reaction of the caribou. By placing the dogs between the snowhouse and the advancing herd, and by holding our fire until we did, we probably saved the snowhouse and all our gear from being trampled into the ground.

As it was we sat there on our sled and watched the caribou come within fifteen feet on either side of us. Everywhere we looked there were caribou, caribou, and more caribou. The stench of the animals was overpowering. And the din of hooves clicking and drumming combined with the hysterical yelping of the dogs was completely deafening. We kept checking the dog chain to make certain the dogs didn't get loose. As it was, half the dogs lunged toward the caribou passing on the right, the other half at those on the left, so the dogs helped to keep the caribou herd split.

Seeing those caribou at such close range, and in such astonishing numbers, remains the most amazing sight I have ever seen in my life. We just sat there on the hill and watched in wonder. It was hopeless to even try to get any sort of count. Now and then the pressure of the herd coming on behind would push animals so close to us that we could almost reach out and touch them. From where we stood we could see right down the inlet past our snowhouse; by now caribou everywhere were crossing the inlet. We were a tiny island in a great flood of heaving brown backs, tossing antlers, and pounding hooves.

The migrating caribou kept coming until darkness fell. Then suddenly, they stopped and began to graze. All night long we could smell the strong stench of the animals and hear the clicking of their feet and the whoofing-grunting noise they made as they grazed. Finally, still awed, we went into the snowhouse and fell asleep with the sound and smell of caribou all around us. When we woke up in the morning the caribou migration was continuing. I would estimate that the herd was moving at the rate of about two miles an hour. The animals weren't in any hurry; they simply walked along. This time Palvik and I decided to watch in comfort. We cut a couple of snowblocks for seats and sat right outside our house and watched the caribou go by. Every now and then we would pick out an especially fat cow, obviously pregnant, and shoot it.

The majority of animals in this migration were females. A

migration like this comes in two waves, about a week or two apart. The big one is the first: the cows, with only the yearling bulls accompanying them. The old bull caribou come in the next wave.

We shot only four or five caribou that day. Some of the first ones we killed were trampled and the meat ruined, so we took a rope from the sled and fashioned a kind of lasso, and whenever we made a kill we tossed the lasso over the antlers and dragged our victim out of the path of the migration. We didn't worry much about the hides, since at that time of year the animals were shedding and the skin wasn't good for much. We butchered out the good cuts of meat and sliced some of it into strips to dry. It was still cold enough to have no worries about the meat spoiling, and much too cold for the warble flies, but we soon discovered that we had a problem. There was simply nowhere to hang up or spread out the strips we cut for drying. The caribou were still pressing in against us and coming so thick and fast that we couldn't even go up the hill to see where the end of the herd was.

About noon the second day the herd stopped again to browse. The thousands upon thousands of pounding hooves literally dug up craters on the hills and the ridges and down the slopes where they pawed away snow and dirt to get at the moss.

Palvik and I didn't know what to do. We didn't see any sense in killing more caribou as long as we had no space to dry the meat. So we decided to hold up any more killing until the tag-end of the herd came by so we could take care of the meat without wasting it.

We had to wait there nine full, unbelievable days, all that time with caribou in every direction as far as we could see. The stench no longer bothered us. Either we had grown immune or smelled like caribou ourselves by now. Again, it seemed to me that if I had to make an estimate I would still put my count at no less than a million. This was the sort of spectacle related by thunderstruck early explorers and fur traders, speaking in awe of millions of caribou. I suppose that if the herd had remained constantly on the move instead of stopping twice a day to feed, the migration would have passed us in three days, certainly no less.

When the caribou finally began to thin out a bit, we were able to start shooting again, and shot our entire year's supply in about half a day, carefully picking only the finest animals.

When the Game Branch people came up that summer to run a game census on the herds, we sent them to look on a huge plain beyond the hills about thirty miles east of the inlet. There they found 93,000 animals in one herd and estimated that there were at least a quarter of a million caribou in the area. Specialists with the branch said that a safe kill of the animals would run at about ten percent, so that meant that in the Bathurst Inlet area, hunters could take up to 25,000 caribou without endangering the herd. At that time there were only about eighteen or nineteen adult hunters in the region, and normally they wouldn't kill more than two or three thousand caribou a year. It followed that the herds in that area must be increasing by leaps and bounds every year within the limitation of graze.

There seems little doubt that herds such as this could be marketed commercially without in any way endangering the species, and in fact, proper game control of the animals with sensible harvesting would help preserve the grazing area and be good conservation for the herds. Meat could be shipped to nearby Cambridge Bay and to other Arctic settlements and sold to the Eskimos instead of meat they buy at the Bay post now for prices boosted skyward by high freight rates.

The only time the Canadian government tried to domesticate reindeer (almost identical to caribou), in the Mackenzie Delta area, the experiment was a complete failure. I don't think the Eskimos really liked working as herders, even though experienced Laplanders were brought in to teach them the trade. But the herds around Bathurst could be exploited without any nonsense over domesticating them. If just excess population were killed off each year, there would be plenty of meat for export. Eskimo hunters could count on getting around $20 per animal. A reasonably large caribou will provide 150 or more pounds of meat, which means that the meat wouldn't cost more than a few cents a pound. And it is marvellous eating. It could even be shipped as far as Edmonton and marketed as cheap meat in spite of the high cost of freighting it out. At fifty cents a pound it would be much cheaper than even low-grade beef. And as for the market for warble fly larvae as a gourmet speciality!

18

❄ The Move to Bathurst Inlet

In July 1965, after I had been at Perry Island several years, the Hudson's Bay Company asked me to transfer to Bathurst Inlet, a couple of hundred miles or so west. Like the Perry Island post, it was very isolated. Problems had developed at the old Bathurst Inlet post, which was near the closed end of the 120-mile inlet, and the Company wanted to re-establish it in a new location, somewhere to the north near the mouth of the inlet. In effect, it would be the same as establishing a new post, and while I enjoyed life at Perry Island and didn't particularly want to leave the people there, I felt it an honour that the Company had asked me to set up a new post. I agreed.

I flew into the old Bathurst Inlet post aboard the Company inspection plane and met the manager there, John Stanners, a near-legendary trader who had spent thirty years in the North and was now retiring. Typically his post and his accounts were absolutely shipshape, and his wife Lorna had kept their home properly tidied. It was a pleasure to take over from him. Once we had checked the inventory, he and Lorna were able to take off in the same plane that had brought me in.

I hired two Eskimos to start taking the old warehouses apart; we would use the lumber at the new site. There were Eskimo camps all around the inlet, and the people had heard a new manager was coming in, so many of them had come to the post to look me over. It was well-known that I spoke Eskimo, something that was very important to the people, and I received a very warm welcome.

Three days later, I went to check a site the Eskimos called Umingmaktuuq (the place of many muskox), taking just a tent and a sleeping bag and a few odds and ends of supplies. I found that the bay (known as Baychimo to the whiteman) enclosed quite an extensive, well-protected harbour. At one side of the bay there was a flat, level plain with a creek about fifteen feet wide and deep enough, it appeared, to float a small barge. I took my canoe right up the creek and pitched my tent on the shallow plain.

Just across the harbour from me, close enough for an easy rifle shot, a herd of six or seven hundred caribou watched me curiously, and some of them even trotted down to the creek across from me to see what I was up to. Eight or nine wolves were sitting there watching the caribou. We all quietly kept an eye on each other.

I knew well the criteria for establishing a new post. First, its location must be central to the Eskimo hunting and trapping camps. In canoeing up the inlet, some eighty miles from the old post, I had spotted a dozen or more such camps, and Stanners had told me there were twenty or more families living around the inlet. It would be just as easy if not easier for them to come to this place as to the old post.

Secondly, a good building site is a must: level or slightly sloping ground with good drainage for the post and its auxiliary buildings. The little plain by the creek seemed to be just the right spot.

Thirdly, no site has any value without a safe supply of fresh water nearby. I hiked up the creek and found it draining from a couple of good-sized lakes about two miles inland, so that matter seemed settled.

A fourth need was sheltered anchorage for the annual supply ship and a deep enough channel or good sandy beach for the docking of the supply barge. The ship came only once a year, but when it came, all the supplies—fuel oil, gasoline, flour, trade goods for an entire year, had to come in on it. If the ship couldn't anchor off the post, there would be no point in setting up there at all. Right at the foot of the harbour there was a hill, so I climbed to the top and examined the water from there. The dark blue of the sea showed me that there was plenty of deep anchorage for the ship. Then I had to determine how badly the creek had silted up the harbour. If the barges from the ship could come right up the creek to the site I had selected for the actual post buildings, it would simplify the problem greatly.

The siltage was pretty bad, but the creek seemed swift enough to keep a fairly good channel scoured out. A tide of a foot or two, which was average for the Arctic coast in that area, would help if the water was low in the fall. I went back down the hill and explored the mouth of the creek in my canoe and marked a channel so that boats bringing the lumber in for the new post could push right up to the bank where my tent was. I was satisfied that the location offered everything needed.

Since I had to wait for the Eskimos to bring up the first load of lumber I passed a couple of leisurely days loafing in the late summer sun. It was glorious. I put in a lot of time watching the caribou and wolves. I didn't even have to use my binoculars. A lone man didn't seem to bother them one bit, and on some occasions they were less than a hundred feet from me, just across the creek. On the plain behind me, where the land began its climb up into the hills, there were hundreds of fat little ground squirrels, sitting bolt upright in front of their burrows going '*chk-chk-chk-chk*' at me. I shot one or two to give myself a change of diet. They were fat and tasty, not unlike chicken.

For the first time in a long while I was free to soak up the startling beauty of an Arctic summer. For some reason the Baychimo Harbour area seemed to be eight to ten degrees warmer than Cambridge Bay or the Perry Island region, and accordingly had a much richer vegetation and more wild life. It was too far north for trees, of course, but some of the willow bushes along the creek were six to seven feet high and quite dense right to the mouth of the creek. The grass growing back from the river across the alluvial areas was far more lush than anywhere I had seen in the Arctic. Bees buzzed everywhere, and butterflies, six or eight different species, big yellow ones, smaller white ones, some black ones with vivid markings, and even some huge moths were all about. And something I could hardly believe, something I have never seen anywhere else in the Arctic—grasshoppers. Walking through the grass I heard the harsh sound of their rear legs rubbing together and doubted my ears until I managed to catch a few.

Heather, a blanket of fragrant whiteness spread low all over the ground and climbing part way up the hills behind the harbour, put me right back in Scotland. Flowers were everywhere of every colour—bright red, brilliant yellow, gay little Arctic poppies nodding in the breeze, a blue alpine blossom of some sort, the masses of white cotton flowers, tiny blooms smaller than a man's little finger nail, but in great profusion. The Arctic in summer bloom is really exceedingly colourful. Farther up the hills and back in the swampy fingers of the creek's small delta there were many different berries: crow berry, bear berry, five or six different ones, mingling with alder, remarkable so far north, and dwarf birch, more creeping shrub than tree, spread out across the rocks and ground no more than a foot or two high but with the circumference of a large tent.

The skies remained a vibrant blue, seldom touched by cloud on those late August days, and were full of birds—and mosquitos, black flies, gnats, midges, dung flies, and the monstrous bluebottle flies. The variety of birdlife astonished me. Robins hopped boldly near my feet, and there were many other small birds, the grey-cheeked thrush with its clear call, the shy little willow ptarmigan, sandpipers, and even tree sparrows making do on the higher willow shoots. There were bigger birds too, the Arctic tern, the rough-legged hawk and the gyrfalcon and the marvellously swift peregrine falcon, even a pair of majestic golden eagles called *qupanuaqpak* by the Eskimos. At night I heard the haunting cry of *ukpik*, the great snowy owl, but never caught a glimpse of that most impressive and beautiful creature.

The very lie of the land was not at all what I had come to think of as Arctic topography. Steep cliffs running three and four hundred feet high and slicing right down into the inlet were separated by narrow channels from the razor-back islands. Above the cliffs where I explored and on the uplands behind my campsite there were long plains and plateaus spotted with lakes in a great diversity of colours. Mineralization in the area painted the lakes green and blue and yellow-brown, even red. It occurred to me that the area looked more like Scandinavian fjord country than the Canadian Arctic coast.

The air was bright and sparkly clean; there was no more pollution than what I could make by puffing on a cigarette, and everything glistened as though just created for my enjoyment.

After a few idyllic days the first Eskimo canoe arrived with the old lumber, and it was back to work. We used the first load to build a small dock in front of my tent so that the following loads could be dumped where they would be handiest.

I went back to the old post with the canoes to load up more lumber. When we returned we discovered a Hudson's Bay charter plane had arrived with three carpenters to help build the new post, and a young fellow named Ian Copland, whom I had already met in Ottawa. His father had spent eighteen years in the North with the Company and wanted his son to have the kind of training available only at isolated posts. The Company had agreed to take him on as an apprentice although he was barely sixteen years old. He was a likeable kid, shy and a real greenhorn, even worse than I had been when I arrived from Scotland.

We continued with the dismantling of the old buildings and shuttling the lumber up to Baychimo. The carpenters went up to make a start on the foundations. The first building I wanted up was the main warehouse. We expected the supply ship in shortly with more lumber and our portable powerhouse, as well as our supplies for the coming year, so storage areas were needed as soon as possible. We didn't even start on the main post and house until the warehouse walls were up.

It had been decided to bring the supply ship in to the old post first to pick up all the remaining inventory from there and to get directions to Baychimo. When the ship arrived at the old post, we were ready and added to the cargo a sixty-foot flagstaff that had been the mast of a whaling ship. We wanted to put it up at the new site.

Normal procedure was for the traders to send in their orders for the following year in January after taking a careful inventory of the goods on hand and estimating just how much food and the type of goods that should be carried the next year. Then to that estimate the prudent and Arctic-wise trader added one year's supply of basic stock plus his own personal needs. The annual supply ship would deliver late in the summer after the ice went out, but some years the ice never went out, and then the wisdom of having a surplus year's supplies on hand paid off.

It is different today, as nearly everything can be ordered by radio and shipped by air. In the old days, the worst thing that could happen to an Arctic man was to have his yearly supply of personal liquor fail to make it through. There are few settlements now where it would take longer than a week to rectify such a disaster.

At Baychimo we were quick to unload and store the supplies in the newly completed warehouses. Fall was upon us and the weather was becoming nippier every day. The carpenters had been living in tents like me, but now we all moved into the warehouses and began racing against time to get the store and house up before freeze-up. Winter was imminent, and the carpenters, all southerners, were scared half to death they would get caught in the Arctic during freeze-up and not get out for months. I wanted the store up and functional so I could take care of the Eskimos who wanted to come in and get their supplies for the winter trapping season.

By this time all the inland lakes were frozen over, and the seas were icing up, but the swift waters of the creek kept a pool open in front of the post. While the carpenters chafed, it blew or rained or snowed for about three weeks and they were beginning to worry in earnest.

Finally we managed to hook the power up and decided to erect our sixty-foot mast for a flagpole. The ground was frozen solid, so we had to hack out a shallow hole for the butt with spades and axes and then pour a little kerosene and fuel oil in and set it alight. That melted a few more inches of permafrost, and we dug that out and started another fire. We kept that up until we had literally burned out a hole four feet deep for the base of the pole; then we set up a jury-rigged block and tackle and with everyone in the settlement plus a bunch of dogs hitched up, all hauling away with all our strength, we raised the pole and ran up the Hudson's Bay Company flag.

That night I got on the radio and advised the Company by wire that the new post of Baychimo was established and in operation.

The poor carpenters had almost given up hope when finally out of the blue a small plane landed in the rapidly diminishing pool in front of the post and took them out, leaving Ian and myself the only whitemen within a couple of hundred miles.

To Ian, sharing in the establishment of a new post was a great adventure. In a different way it was an adventure for me too. I had never had an apprentice before, and I set about teaching the lad all the things I thought he should know to become a fur trader himself one day: how to handle the dogs, how to grade fur, how to keep the accounts, how to learn the country. As fast as he mastered something I would turn over that bit of responsibility to him and let him gain the experience. He was eager and turned out to be a good hand. About the only thing he couldn't pick up was the language. He just didn't seem to have an ear for Eskimo.

When I taught Ian how to trade with the Eskimos, I followed the same barter system I had learned in Baker Lake under Sandy Lunan and used later at places like Spence Bay, Gjoa Haven and Perry Island. From the beginning the Company had used aluminium coins or tokens to get around the rather haphazard way Eskimos had of counting. For example, almost any Eskimo would correctly count up to three caribou, but any more frequently just became 'many'. An Eskimo might say, 'I saw a bunch of caribou and killed some.' Ask him how many were 'some', and if it had been more than three he would probably say 'many'.

A square token represented one white fox. The round token, about an inch in diameter with an HBC 'one' stamped in the middle (to represent one dollar) was followed in size by smaller tokens representing smaller amounts. The tokens provided a visual form of counting for the Eskimos that they quickly understood.

For example, if a hunter brought in ten white fox pelts, the prime economic unit in the furtrading world of the North, we would lay out one square token for each white fox. Suppose that that year the price of fox was twenty dollars each; we would take up one square token and replace it with twenty round one-dollar tokens. Whenever an Eskimo bought something, the tokens representing the value of his purchase were removed and the change was made in smaller tokens. The biggest trouble with these thin aluminium tokens was that all our trading was done in an unheated store, and the tokens were too thin to pick up without the trader taking off his mitts. When fingers were bared, the tokens froze nicely to the skin.

Sure enough, just as Sandy had so long ago promised, there were frozen fingers. Even though few Eskimos could read or write English in those days, every sale was written out on a counter-slip and the Eskimos were given the carbon copy. Most of the time, for all our trouble, they just threw them away, but if an Eskimo so desired he could show those slips to a missionary or a mountie, just to make certain that everything was fair and square.

Of course, Ian soon learned, as I had learned from Sandy, that numb hands in the trading room made a good excuse to head for the native room and a mug-up every forty-five minutes or so. Every post, and ours at Bathurst was no exception, had a 'native room' in it, a kind of social room. When the Eskimos were in the settlement, they would come over to this heated room, where we had a few old sofas, some chairs and a table, and usually some magazines, maybe a checkers board—the Eskimos liked checkers and played well—or a jigsaw puzzle or two. They could loaf around there and we kept it warm. Normally there would be few Eskimos around the post at Bathurst. They would be out on the land hunting or trapping except when they came in to trade.

When an Eskimo came in, we never tried to rush him in the store. That would have been considered a frightful breach of manners. I taught Ian to go and sit with the people in the native room and let them get warmed up. I impressed it on Ian that these were not just customers but real friends, people the trader got to know, often for many years. They enjoyed sitting around, talking, finding out who else had been in to trade recently, who had had a baby or got married, how the trapping was in this place or that, whether caribou had been seen and so on. It was truly a social occasion when a family came in to trade. A family might stay at the post three or four days, and fifty percent of that time would be spent in the native room.

The last thing to be brought up was business itself. Not until a man and his wife were ready to go into the store would his trapping be mentioned. Then the trader might casually say, 'Well, did you get lots of deerskins?' or 'Did you trap lots of foxes?'

The man would answer, in the old Eskimo manner, always belittling himself and his own efforts. 'Well, I've only got a few skins—really poor—hardly worth bothering to show the trader,' and then as likely as not he would bring out some of the loveliest hides you could wish to see.

The Eskimos really enjoyed the trading. A man and his wife might come in with ten white foxes worth $200. Ian and I would lay the tokens out and start trading, and we would know we were in for a long session in that frigid room. They would look all around the store as if they had never seen it before, and they would wander around—not that we minded, but all the time we would be getting colder and colder even though we were dressed like the Eskimos, in a full set of skins.

The trading Eskimo might have ten of those square tokens for his fox pelts, then he would trade each of the square tokens for twenty of the round dollar tokens, so there he would be with 200 tokens representing $200. But for some reason he would nearly always start off by deciding he wanted some small item— a package of needles or something like that. We would break into one of the dollar tokens and give him the needles and his change. It was always the man who did the trading; he would do all the talking, but they both, the man and the wife, knew exactly what they wanted, right down to the smallest item. The woman would stand quietly off to one side, but every now and then they would have a little whispered conference, then the man would turn around and say, 'It seems that I need a couple of yards of calico,' or 'My wife just reminded me that I need some twine.'

Sometimes we would trade all morning and afternoon, counting the trips to the native room to have a mug-up. It was a glorious experience for the Eskimos, especially if they had come from a far-away camp to the post. After they had spent hours buying all the small goods like pins and thread, they would move quickly into the big stuff: a hundred pounds of flour, several boxes of ammunition, kerosene for their primus stoves, and so on.

At Baker we could count on hundreds and hundreds of white foxes being turned in. Bathurst Inlet was nearly as good. While Ian and I were at Bathurst, the average price for foxes was $20. Instead of grading each skin and paying accordingly, we just took them all in and paid $20 for good and bad alike. They pretty well averaged out. If there was a tear in a skin or if the trapper brought in the whole carcass, we would knock some off. I had been fooled when I first started trading at Baker Lake, and I warned Ian about this. The foxes aren't very big, not much larger than Arctic hares, and the first time I bought a bunch of foxes, I discovered I had bought two hares along with them. Sandy had a good laugh at that, and some Eskimo went away hugging himself.

Sandy had taught me that it wasn't good for business or the trapper to have the Eskimos hanging around the post, for the obvious reason that they were not productive unless they were out on the land. Ian would get a kick out of the way I hustled the Eskimos back out on the trapline after a few days at Bathurst, but I was never nearly as fierce about it as Sandy had been. He was a kind-hearted man, but he was firm too, and he saw no need for a man to hang around more than four or five days. I remember one Eskimo who came in and built his snow-house right in front of the post at Baker. After he had been there five days, Sandy became agitated, particularly as he could look right out through the front door and see the newcomer still squatting there. Finally Sandy got in a frenzy about it, and one morning he just picked up his snow shovel and went out and started shovelling the house in. The Eskimo came shooting out in his underwear, and he and Sandy began to argue. The next thing I saw, he was hitching up his dogs and taking off.

Over the years I have heard a good many people criticize the Hudson's Bay Company for 'exploiting' the Eskimos and Indians. In my experience the charge is nonsense. When I prepared their books, I saw myself that Gjoa Haven, Spence Bay, Perry River and Bathurst Inlet all operated at a loss. The Company may have felt that some of these outposts would develop into money-makers over the long run, but mainly they kept them open because of a sense of responsibility to the natives. When the posts were first opened thirty or forty years ago and the price of fur was much higher, they probably made a good profit, but in the past twenty years, with the price of white fox down, the Company has lost money accordingly.

Individually, all the traders I have known over my years in the north country were honest men, who gave the Indians or Eskimos in their region a fair break, and Company policy bent over backwards to treat the natives properly.

19

❄ *To the
Last Dog*

In January 1967, when still at Bathurst Inlet, I was seized by a sudden desire to go to Coppermine. It was just that I was restless. Two Eskimos, Iksik and Palvik, had far superior motivation. They wanted to find wives.

Iksik had been married, but while he was in an Edmonton hospital with tuberculosis, his wife had been stolen. Palvik was a husky, good-looking young man, only twenty at the time. He thought a nice Coppermine romance would be just what he needed.

I was still running thirteen dogs on my team, all big strong huskies and good workers. Palvik had twelve dogs. Iksik hadn't been able to maintain his own team, but was fit enough to help Palvik with his.

We started out on January 3 during the dark part of winter, with no light to guide us except what starlight filtered through broken clouds. It was definitely cold at forty-eight below zero with a wind from the northwest, the direction in which we were heading. It had been a queer winter, a factor that was to affect our trip. In the fall of the year, right after freeze-up, there had been a tremendous gale which had shattered the new sea ice in the inlet. This had been followed by another freeze-up. Surprisingly, the winds had been light all winter; the usual blizzards did not occur. The results made for poor travelling. First, there was virtually no snow on the glare ice of the sea; secondly, that ice had been broken up in great slabs, tossed around at all angles, frozen into contorted positions, broken up and slammed around some more, and refrozen to make the roughest tangle and jumble of ice I had ever seen.

We expected the trip to Coppermine to take seven sleeps. It could be done, given decent weather, in less, but we knew that it was wise at that time of year to allow extra time for storms. The distance from Bathurst Inlet to Coppermine is 220 air miles, about 320 by dogteam. We headed right out west from the inlet, expecting that we would have the usual rough coastal ice to contend with for a while. But the tortured jumble we saw in the pale starlight looked like a frozen moonscape, a white hell. Rough ice like that is murder on sled runners, knocking the mud and icing off, causing the sleds to drag heavily, putting an extra strain on the dogs. Sharp icy edges slice up the dogs' feet and slash their legs. It is the very toughest sort of sled travel.

To make it worse, we didn't dare jump off the sleds in the dark onto the dangerously uneven footing on the ice. In that mess it would have been all too easy to slip and go down with a broken ankle or banged-up leg. Yet we desperately needed to get off the sleds and run alongside to keep warm. We decided to continue out toward the sea, away from the coast for a while, because normally rough ice like that lies in a narrow strip along the shore, seldom extending out beyond two or three miles.

After travelling all day in the piercing cold and depressing darkness all of us had started to freeze up, sitting there on our sleds, our arms tucked underneath our parkas and our legs hugged together in vain effort to keep warm. Some twenty miles offshore we despaired of ever finding smooth ice, and the dogs were playing out, their feet cut and bleeding. In that sort of ice it seemed that every few feet the dogs' traces were caught on a snag or a sled became stuck in a crevice or jammed on a hummock. This meant continual scrambling about, chopping with a hand axe to free the sled and groping work with the dogs to keep them untangled.

The logical thing to do was make camp and rest, but to top off the day, there wasn't even enough snow to build a snowhouse. Since we had planned to use snowhouses at each stop, we carried no tent. There was nothing to do but head back toward the coast in the hope of finding some drifted snow with which to build our shelter.

The night was jet black, without even any starlight by now, and the run in to the coast was even more miserable than the ride out. We couldn't see to steer the sleds around chunks of ice, so it was crash, bang, bump all the way, and we knew we were losing the mud off our runners. It took a full night of travel to get back to the shore. We located a drift that would do for the snowhouse; exhausted and frozen, we didn't even eat, didn't even bother to light the primus stoves for a mug of tea, and a northern man has to be thoroughly beat to neglect that. But—did those sleeping bags feel good.

Next morning we walked to the top of a nearby hill to survey our route as best we could in the dark. Even with good binoculars, there was nothing to be seen but rough ice. The ground along the shoreline was bare, except in places in the gully where we had found our snowdrift. It meant going back out onto the rough ice again. Iksik, the experienced hand, pointed out that we might as well stick close to shore since then we should at least stand a better chance of finding snow for our shelter each night.

The ice remained treacherous, and the dogs were having a really tough time of it. Three more days of that saw us more beat up and battered every day. The weather never once let up on us. We were beginning to have serious trouble with the sleds. They were literally being knocked apart, bouncing up and down on chunks of ice and slabs that would hit between the runners, breaking up the crossbars. We spent hours repairing them, eventually having to unload the sleds completely and relash all the crossbars. With bare hands, in fifty-below weather.

We could tell by the landmarks that we were not making anything like the time we had expected to on this trip.

Then we came up against a pressure ridge on the ice, about fifteen feet high. We couldn't cross it, because it was sheer ice, huge blocks pressed into each other, welded together where two great beds of ice had jammed together as the sea was freezing over. We couldn't get over it, and we couldn't get through it. The only course was to follow along it until some break in the wall presented itself. Unfortunately, when a passage was discovered, I lost control of my sled as it slid down the other side of the ridge. It bounced off a hummock of ice way up into the air and came down with a terrible crash.

All the lashings on the crossbars snapped and both runners buckled down flat, spread out like skates on a kid with weak ankles.

We had just relashed that sled, and it had been a hellish job. And now a ground wind had sprung up and was blowing snow right in our faces.

There was nothing for it, when we had finished cursing the fates, but to unload and go to work on the lashings once again. At the rear of the sled sat a ten gallon keg of gasoline, our only fuel for the primus stoves for the trip. It was more than we needed, even estimating a profligate half gallon to the day, but it is better to be warm than sorry in such a case. I went back to take the keg off the sled, automatically bracing for the heavy lift. To my surprise, the keg lifted easily, light as a balloon. With sinking hearts we checked it and discovered that somewhere along the way, as the sled bounced around, a sharp pointed pinnacle of ice had jammed right through the sled cover and into the keg, puncturing it. All our precious fuel lay across the sea ice.

This was a genuine crisis. There we were in the middle of nowhere, ten tough days out of Bathurst with terrible ice behind us all the way to the Inlet, and as near as we could figure, about an equal distance yet to go to reach Coppermine. For us the loss of the gas meant a cold camp, no more fires for tea or food or warmth in the snowhouse. But we were less worried about ourselves than we were about the dogs. We had decided to carry the dry commercial dogfood on this trip because of its lightness, but the dogs wouldn't eat it dry and now we had no way to cook it up for them.

Iksik shrugged, '*Ayurnarmat*. It can't be helped.' Then he suggested the obvious: 'We've got to decide whether to turn back or go on and try to get to Coppermine.'

We talked it over and decided to go on. We knew for certain that there were ten bad days ahead of us if we turned back to Bathurst. For all we knew the bad ice might give out in a day or so ahead of us on the way to Coppermine, and we might find good sledding again. Better to push on than to retrace our route over the bad ice we had already travelled.

Since we had stopped anyhow to fix my sled, we decided to camp right there and give the dogs a rest. There was good snow along the pressure ridge for a snowhouse. Lashing up that sled again was even worse than the first time. By now we all had frostbitten fingers, which functioned clumsily. Even taking it in relays, our hands went numb in a few minutes. Our fingertips were black (the penultimate stage of frostbite, before the affected area becomes gangrenous); our faces had frozen too. For most of the way we had been running right into the wind, and it is impossible for a driver to steer the sled and keep his face averted from the wind all the time. Iksik's nose and cheekbones were already showing severe frostbite, and my nose was badly frozen. Palvik had a patch of frostbite on one cheek.

Just by being in out of the wind, we were a little warmer in the camp before setting out again the next day. Once underway, however, it was so cold that I had quit trying to steer the sled and was lying on top of it. I had started out sitting on it as usual, but the wind was so penetrating that, since I couldn't control the sled anyhow, I just lay back on the sled covers and let it bump along. The dogs were in bad shape with sore paws and empty bellies. All of a sudden as I was lying there on my back, looking up at the stars I noticed a star moving right across the sky. I was puzzled until I realized this must be a satellite, and behind it came another one. I stopped the sled to watch through the binoculars. How ironic it seemed that in the time that one of those satellites took to make a revolution around the world, we had travelled only a few miles.

When we camped at night, the exertion of building the snow-house, setting up our camp, and putting the dogs out on their chain caused us to sweat, but with no warming stove we couldn't dry out our mitts and boots and other clothing. We knew that if we took them off, damp as they were from our sweat, they would freeze up: we should never get them back on. Additionally, we discovered that the leaking gasoline had penetrated most of our meat supply, and all we had to eat was a small chunk of raw, frozen caribou, a few hardtack biscuits and some bannock.

We slept on top of our sleeping bags because, as with clothing, our perspiration would make them damp. Once we got out the next morning, they would freeze up too.

That night a wolf howled. It sounded several miles away but the howling echoed back and forth in the still, cold air, and immediately the dogs joined in. It was eerie to hear the dogs howl at different, spaced-out intervals, and yet after they all got going they would stop, all of them, instantly. It was a symphony of the North that lifted the short hairs on the back of my neck.

If we were not happy, neither were the dogs the next morning. They were cold and shivering and weakened because they had not been fed. Another blow had come up, and the dogs didn't like facing it one bit. With no food in their bellies they had no energy, but there was no choice but to hitch up and travel on. The dogs began to give us trouble that day. We had to hit them and force them to keep going. At a time like that a driver can't afford to be easy on his dogs; if they don't keep going, then everyone is in trouble.

A number of dogs on both teams would flop down every now and then, dropping in the harness from tiredness or weakness. We would stumble forward and pull them onto their feet again, give them a clout and chase them on. They would go twenty yards, catch a paw on a piece of ice and flop again.

One of my dogs, one I had always considered one of my best pullers, dropped in his tracks. He was dragged several yards in harness by the other dogs, knocking his head and body against the ice, before I could stop the sled and pull him back on his feet again. I went back to the sled, kicked the frozen runners loose, and barked the command to go. The dogs barely started; the wheel dogs stood there until they were dragged forward. This one dog flopped onto the ice again. I stood him on his feet once more, gave him a good cuff and told him to quit fooling around. But no sooner had we started off than the poor animal collapsed. I knew he was really in a bad way, and he had been only two days without food.

Unsnapping his harness, I let him out to come along with us with nothing to pull. He tried to stay up with us, walking along but very slowly, and every now and then stopping and staring after us. We were leaving him farther and farther behind. I really had liked that dog, so I called to him and he came walking on, wobbling and staggering. I went back, patted him and talked to him, and carried him up to the sled and put him on the sled right beside me where I could hold him. But he wasn't accustomed to riding, and it frightened him so that he struggled. I couldn't hold him and steer at the same time. He kept falling off and hurting himself all the more. For a while I just held him and let the sled hit whatever bumps it was going to, thinking maybe the rest would perk him up, but he kept struggling feebly and falling off. Finally I got tired of going back and picking him up. I was too tired and cold and miserable myself to be kind-hearted. Instead of riding as usual with my hands tucked down in my groin, the warmest part of my body, I had to keep that dog on the sled by holding my arm around him, and I could feel my hand freezing. My face was giving me some trouble with frostbite by this time, too. Bitter with the cold, and with what I had to do, I left that dog behind. I hoped when we made camp that night that he just might wander in; if not, well, too bad. It wouldn't be the first time I had lost a dog. We never saw him again.

We had another cold camp that night. When we started the next morning the dogs had run two full days without eating and were starting their third. When they stopped at night they just dropped. Normally a dog will dig down into the snow and curl up to protect itself from the cold, but now we had to build windbreaks around them to keep the wind off. My lead dog, Qaqquq, and one other kept up their strength, but the others were listless and beat. Iksik and Palvik were having a lot of trouble with their dogs, too. The animals simply couldn't keep going in the bitter cold without some fuel.

We pushed on through the day without losing any more dogs, but we knew it was just a question of time. We didn't make very many miles, and the dogs were visibly weakening. Palvik and Iksik were as worried as I was. That night we tried to feed the dogs the dry dogfood. We held their mouths open and pushed the stuff down their throats, but as soon as we let a dog go he just spat and coughed the stuff up. They just wouldn't take it dry. We even tried urinating on it to soften it and warm it, but they wouldn't take it. Their refusal to eat proved what really alarming shape they were in.

The next day was a nightmare. If anything, the weather had deteriorated. We were passing through quite steep country now, cliffs along the shoreline and a lot of steep islands. We went around some and then decided to climb one and see if we could sight Coppermine yet, if only for the needed psychological lift. But we couldn't see a sign of lights anywhere that would indicate a settlement. We looked at each other without a word. Once more there was nothing to do but keep going.

Eight dogs died that day. They dropped in their tracks, lay

there, and after a short while died. We took them out of the
harness, and we patted them and talked to them, but it didn't
help. They were freezing now that they were so weakened by
the lack of food. As we travelled along we noticed that a lot of
them were gnawing at their groins and rear legs where they
were getting frostbitten. Dogs can freeze in that kind of weather
just as human beings can. Where they froze their flesh just
seemed to split and become a raw wound; they would try to
bite at the pain or lick the frozen places because they hurt.

We were apprehensive by now, although confident that even
if all the dogs died we could still walk in to Coppermine ourselves. We had enough food for several days, and knew we must
be well over halfway there. That rough ice still dominated our
route.

Skinning out the dogs that had died, and allowing the
carcasses to freeze, thereby cutting down the familiar dog smell,
we fed them to the survivors, little by little.

It didn't surprise us that it was just as hard as ever to get the
dogs started the next morning. They were still very weak and
their legs looked bad. We had sat up most of the night in our
cold snowhouse discussing our situation. It had taken us a long
time to fall asleep with the cold. It was still blowing, and now
with a bit of wind again we had the ground drift to contend with.
So we sat there in that cold and knew the dogs weren't going to
last out the day if we didn't do something. As we sat there my
eyes fell on the punctured ten gallon tin we still carried along.
Suddenly an idea came.

I took the empty keg, which Iksik had decided to keep for
its $5 value at the trading post, and stood it on its end. Then I
unfastened the bung near the puncture hole. With the axe I
cut two square holes on the side of the drum, one small hole
behind, one larger at the front. I then rummaged through our
gear until I found a can of dried milk, emptied the contents and
knocked out the bottom. This bottomless can I wedged into
the small hole on the side of the keg, and laid the keg on its side.
Using pliers I bent up the rough edges of the hole to grip the
can.

By using other tins and the outer shells from several thermos
bottles, we soon fashioned a crude stove with a stovepipe. We
put it in the snowhouse on a platform of snowblocks, knocked a
hole in the wall for the stovepipe to fit through, and closed over

the gap with a piece of caribouskin, so that we wouldn't melt the snow wall when we got the fire going. Next we took the two battered sleds and with the best parts of each, made one good sled out of the two. The remaining pieces gave us quite a pile of wood, which we quickly chopped up and set ablaze. We stood there with our mitts off, coughing and choking on the soot and smoke, but enjoying the first warmth we had felt in days. Our hands were so numb that we could put them right on top of that hot stove, and even though our hands were practically sizzling, we couldn't feel it.

We were warm at last. To begin with it felt great, but soon we were in agony. Our hands and faces, our noses, cheeks and chins had all been frozen, and now they suddenly began to thaw out. Huge frost blisters burst out on our faces. I had a blister down one side of my nose, another across my chin, and blisters on both cheekbones. They expanded, and later burst, leaving my cheekbones exposed, surrounded by raw flesh.

We knew that the sudden warmth would cause trouble with our frostbite, but really had no option. Much dangerously misleading advice is given on how to take care of frostbite and similar cold weather problems—such notions as rubbing snow on the affected areas. I can't think of anything worse one could do in the Arctic. Snow in the high Arctic areas is composed almost entirely of hard little frost granules, gritty stuff like sand. It would tear the frostbitten skin and flesh away like sandpaper.

Eskimos say that the best way to fight frostbite is to put the affected part in cold water, but that was scarcely practical in our position—we had too many 'affected parts'.

Part of our problem was whiskers. The popular conception of a real Arctic man invariably pictures him with a bushy beard. The truth is that the only people who wear beards in the Arctic are either greenhorns, men who rarely spend time out of doors, or men in desperate trouble. Beards are a nuisance in cold climates. Every breath condenses and freezes in a man's beard, and he soon faces trouble. With no hot water, we had been unable to shave for some time, and the ice around our fledgling beards contributed seriously to our frostbitten condition.

But we were happy to get that stove going. The first thing we did as soon as we could stand moving around was to get the kettle out and melt some snow to make tea. The snowhouse filled up with smoke because the stove wasn't drawing properly. We finally had to kick a fairly substantial hole in the rear wall of the snowhouse in a line with the wind. Then, of course, we had condensation and the place fogged up, and we had to retreat outside until it cleared up. Our faces were so black with this soot that we looked like a bunch of chimney sweeps. But when we went back inside, we found that the stove was now drawing beautifully, throwing out a blast of heat that soon had the kettle going. We drank three or four mugs of steaming tea, dipped our hardtack biscuits in the tea and never enjoyed such a simple meal as much. We pulled out the frying pan and put some lard in it and some caribou backfat, and threw in some of the biscuits. We let them fry for a few minutes and flipped them over. They tasted like pastry, light and fluffy, and just melted in our mouths. This was a trick Iksik had learned years back travelling with an old Hudson's Bay manager along the Arctic coast.

Feeling full and warm ourselves, the next thing was to cook up some food for the dogs. As soon as it was ready we went out and fed them, doling out a little bit at a time until they could handle it. Were they glad to get it! We decided to stay there in camp for a day to rest the dogs, feed them and take care of their legs and feet, and get some rest ourselves.

The dogs were much improved a day later. We put the two teams together to pull the one good sled, with Qaqquq in the lead. We travelled a few more days over the rough ice, but had fewer worries now; the dogs were in reasonable shape again, and could cope with that rough ice that plagued us all the way to Coppermine.

We finally pulled into the settlement and stopped in front of the Hudson's Bay store. An Eskimo came out and was amazed to see us; we had taken twice the normal time to make this trip. He told us that the RCMP were just about to send out teams to look for us. They thought we had had a bad accident along the way.

We went into the post and realized what a sight we were. We were sore, black from the soot, blisters had broken out all over our faces. I was all bearded with whiskers growing out through the frostbite and blisters.

Recently I happened to be flying in a nice, warm twin-engine

Otter from Bathurst to Coppermine with Palvik, and he was shaving with a cordless electric razor while we flew along in comfort. I pointed down at the coast where we had spent such a bad time and said, 'Palvik, would you like to try it the old way again?' He just shook his head, smiled and waved his electric razor at me.

Incidentally, neither Palvik nor Iksik found a wife in Coppermine.

20

❋ *Fin and*
Feather

One summer at Baychimo, three families and I decided to go to the Honkytonk River together and set up a summer fish camp. There were seven adults and a dozen or more kids of varying ages. We put up four tents about sixty feet from the shore, at the mouth of the river. Beyond the plain where we pitched our tents, the hills rolled up to the tundra that stretched off to the horizon. I remember that summer as a time of laziness and plenty. The sun was hot and with us around the clock. The air was so clean that everything looked freshly washed. Acres of multi-coloured Arctic flowers covered the south slopes of the hills, their feathery heads bobbing in the slightest stir of wind. To the seaward, the ocean was dotted with razor-backed islands, brown teeth in a blue maw. On the opposite side of the river as well as on our side, river bottom plains gave way to hills covered with coarse grass and dotted with blooms. It has always been almost unbelievable to me how the Arctic lands burst into life, the flowers popping up in the long days of spring, grass transforming the bleak barren lands overnight. In the Honkytonk River area especially, the lushness of the country in the late spring made you pinch yourself to be sure it was the Arctic. Long plains, just like the prairies when they are fresh green with the early crops, stretched out behind our camp. On almost any day we could see caribou and wolves.

From the vantage point of a hillside the camp seemed to hum with activity. We had just come off the winter ice, and the women were busier than anyone because they had all the sealskins yet to scrape. They had shed their winter caribou and were dressed in calico garments looking like shapeless maxi-dresses with long sleeves, more to protect against mosquitos than for warmth. Some of them wore cheap print dresses from the post store.

Fires were usually going, fed with driftwood and pieces of dead willow shoots that had been winter-killed, and the red meat of the *iqalukpik* (arctic char) was drying on racks near the fires. Although we had only a few nets out yet and the run of the beautiful Arctic salmon-trout hadn't really started, a few of these marvellously tasty fish were soon taken. Split down the middle with the guts removed, the red flesh lay spread open to the fire and the sun for curing.

On a little sandy beach men would be working on canoes, hauled out of the water and placed upside down so that new canvas could be stretched over them. The men wore parkas with the hoods thrown back, and seal kamiks, like some of the women. Young boys would paddle about in the river and yell to their companions on the riverbank where the dogs were chained. Most of the dogs burrowed two or three feet into the bank for coolness and respite from the constant hordes of mosquitos. All three families had brought their teams, as I had mine; so there were at least fifty dogs there. They wouldn't work again until the snow came and the sea froze over.

Two of the three women were heavily pregnant, normal at that time of year, and waddled as they moved about the camp at their chores. After a while one of them would shout '*Tiituritti!*'—the call for a mug-up, or soup. The women cooked outside in the summer, and always had a big pot of caribou ribs boiling on stones around the fire. There would be a kettle of hot water for the tea sitting on a flat rock at the back of the fire. As it was still early in the summer, there might be still another pot, full of water and seal blood...blood soup.

When they heard the welcome '*Tiituritti*,' the men would leave their work and walk to the fire in front of the tents. Two of the families that year had white canvas tents from the trading post, like mine, and one family still used a caribouskin tent. The women would set out pie plates and big enamel mugs, and we each poured a little pile of salt on our plate to dip the meat in before each bite. After the men had eaten, the women took their plates and helped themselves and the kids would dart in to grab a rib and run off and eat it.

Some of the seven or eight-year-old girls carried babies on their backs—it was their job to look after their baby brothers and sisters. The women sent the girls out to pick crowberries and bearberries from the bushes along the riverbank, or scout along the esker looking for *masu* roots, a sort of licorice considered a delicacy at that time of the year.

The women, and the girls too, spent much of their time gathering fuel. They used a caribou antler sawn off to leave one prong, and pulled up willow and heather in great bundles with the hook. The dwarf birch and willow and heather could be yanked up almost like moss to be dried in the sun and used on the fires. There would always be a bit of driftwood around the sea coast, and the girls gathered that up. The boys would often be sent out into the tundra to hunt ptarmigan and Arctic hare.

Sometimes when the sun was really beating down, the temperature climbed to eighty degrees, right there on the Arctic Coast, but generally it was nearer sixty. When it was very hot the mosquitos were quiet; then it would turn humid, the prelude to summer rain, the wind picked up strongly and that swept the mosquitos away; then the clouds would break and everyone ran for the tents as the big, splashy raindrops began to fall. When everyone was inside, someone lit a primus stove, inevitable mugs of tea were passed around, and everyone just sat around talking and gossiping and enjoying life.

We men would go out on the river in the morning and again in the evening to check the nets; when we returned we threw the fish on the shore and the women would come down and clean them. Gutting the fish was considered women's work. They threw the guts into a ten gallon drum and later fed them to the dogs.

It was a lazy time of the year when it was a delight to be alive. Once in a while there would be a bit of excitement. Someone might sight caribou, and the men would decide to go after them. Or a grizzly might come shambling down from the esker along the river.

Another summer, when I had been at Perry Island, Angulaalik and eight or nine families decided to go up the Perry River for the summer's fishing. We took the remains of the seal we had harpooned and headed up river. The Perry at that time of year

—mid-June—was high and muddy and fast flowing. In a couple of weeks the spring run-off would be finished and the river would become quite placid. After crossing numerous little side valleys and ravines we came to the rapids, the foot of the Perry River waterfalls, and pitched our tents at the foot of the rapids. That would be our base for the summer.

We mended our nets and got them out in the water, stretched nearly across the river below the rapids. We didn't expect to net much that early. We were depending upon the remnants of seal meat we had brought along and on caribou and birds for food. We would be happy to get enough fish to keep the dogs going and one or two a day for us. Each net stretched out about 150 yards from the bank, and we would place one every 300 or 400 yards. We caught Arctic char, whitefish and flounder.

At that early part of the summer we could count on birds for food, too. The Perry River up inland, as I have already described, is one of the greatest nesting grounds in the world. Every day we saw geese flying overhead, snow-geese, brant, the big Canada honkers, white-fronted geese, and Ross's geese. Perry is the only breeding ground in the world for Ross's goose, the smallest goose known, a beautiful bird like a tiny snow-goose; it has a warty face around the beak and appears to be grinning all the time. There were a myriad other species there, too: sandhill cranes, one of the earliest harbingers of spring along the coast, ducks of all kinds, swans, loons; the country was alive and breathing with birds.

Each morning we sent one of the boys up the nearby hills with binoculars to watch for caribou, and we would check our nets and then sit around in the sun. The few fish we caught were brought in for the women to take care of. They would use the *ulu* to gut them out and hang the good meat over rocks or on lines to dry. As long as none of the dogs got loose, there was no problem. When the women were not working on the fish or gathering wood or shooting ground squirrels or cooking, or making bannock, they worked on the sealskins.

Then would come the time to catch the birds. By late summer the geese were flightless. They had hatched their young and were moulting. We would see them cruising about on the river, whole flocks of them with their goslings. We built a sort of keyhole-shaped corral along the bank with rocks, stakes, and bits of canvas and caribou hide. We left one funnel open and leading out into the water, another funnel running up along the bank. The two funnels narrowed and led into a circular pen. A couple of men went out in their canoes and herded the birds downstream until they came to the funnel on the water. The birds would swim along that into shore and then walk right up into the pen at the mouth of our corral, and we had them. We would catch them one at a time and wring their necks.

We rarely killed all the geese we caught, although they were a welcome change of diet. We never bothered plucking those we killed, but just yanked the skin off and boiled the birds. Now and then we managed to shoot a few swans. There were swarms of them in that country, and a real treat to eat at that time of year as they had quite a heavy layer of yellow fat and were exceedingly tender. Occasionally someone would find a loon caught and drowned in his net. The Eskimos boiled and ate them, but for me they were too tough and stringy. But the wings made good fans to keep the mosquitos off.

Sometimes it was warm enough for the kids to swim in a little pool just behind our tents. The water was only a few feet deep there and shallow enough for the sun to warm it. Sometimes it looked so refreshing that the men would strip off and fool around in the pool too.

Except for the Caribou Eskimos, who rarely ate fish at all, Eskimos welcomed the chance to get some fresh fish when spring came. When I was at Spence Bay I used to go out with the people when leads began to open up in the ice and use an Eskimo jigging rod to catch fish. Sometimes we attached a huge hook, about six inches long, like a small gaff, and jigged for tom cod. The idea was to jerk the rod up and down, flapping two little shanks of bone or ivory, to attract the cod. When the fish came over to investigate, one quick tug and it was hooked by the belly and yanked out onto the ice. We would get sizeable cod that way. On fresh water lakes a different type of hook was used to jig for trout, a much smaller hook with a little bit of carved ivory or bone at the shank to lure the fish.

In October in the spawning season I went up with the Eskimos to the little lakes around Bathurst Inlet and Perry Island. Most of these lakes are connected to the sea by small creeks or rivers, and they are the spawning area for the red Arctic char. Just after each lake had frozen over, with maybe three inches of ice on it, enough to hold a man's weight, we would walk along and look through the ice until we found one of the spawning beds where the female fish pushes small pebbles and gravel together to form a kind of raised bed, where she lays her eggs. When we found such a place, we would chisel a hole through the ice and stand there with a three-pronged fish harpoon called a leister. We could see the female char swimming around the bed. The male char is attracted to the spot, and comes to fertilize the eggs. The female char, which has a reddish tinge, stays close to the spawning bed all the time, but at this period the male char becomes quite distinctive, his body bright red like a spawning salmon, and his lower jaw extended out like an inverted beak. It is easy to tell the two apart, and we never speared the female. We would spear the male and toss him up onto the ice. The commotion would cause the female to shoot away, but she would come back in a few minutes, and then another male would be attracted. A diligent Eskimo could easily get fifteen or twenty char in a day, some up to twenty pounds. As long as he didn't touch the female he had a going business.

Sometimes in the fall we would build a *saputit* in the river, a sort of keyhole weir in a shallow section of the stream with the open end of the keyhole facing downstream so that the fish heading upstream on their annual spawning run would swim into it. Where the water was shallow, the Eskimos sometimes dammed off the entire river with a weir built of rocks piled on top of each other, but normally they built a kind of big round corral, piling up stones until they stuck up above the surface. Two arms or walls would be built out from the entrance of the corral to force the fish to swim into the trap, which might be a hundred yards in circumference. Once a number of fish were in the corral, a few rocks quickly closed off the gate, and we went in after the fish with leisters. We would splash around in that chilly water, sometimes up to our waists, spearing fish and throwing them out to the bank. The women often joined in; it was sport and pleasure as well as a way of starting up a fish supply for the dogs for the winter. I got a kick out of knowing that the same beautiful Arctic chars we were catching to feed our dogs were selling as a gourmet dish in the top restaurants of Canada and the United States.

Before the whiteman brought nets, the Eskimos did most of

their fishing by building *saputits* and nearly every well-known Arctic char stream in the North anywhere near a settlement has the remains of the stone weirs along its bed. Once the Eskimos had enough fish, they opened the corral at the upstream end so that the fish could go on up and spawn. Unlike the whitemen they never left a stream dammed up without providing a way for the fish to get through and spawn.

This sort of fishing was a pleasure, but there was plenty of hard, cold, serious fishing when we had to stock enough to last the dogs all winter. At Spence Bay we used to go some thirty miles up the Nattilik River by canoe and camp there for a month of fishing. We would draw out five or six nets and lift the fish. When we started there might be only twelve caught in a day, but when the run started, all of a sudden there might be as many as eighty of those big char in the nets. We would spend the day hauling the fish in, gutting them, and preparing them for dogfood.

As the weather turned cooler it was grim work lifting those nets twice a day, using bare hands, taking the mesh off the fish's gills, and the hands turned into numb raw pulp. Later, as the snows began to come and we could just toss the fish ashore and let them freeze, it wasn't quite as bad, but it was still hell on the hands. At Spence Bay we kept up two complete dogteams for the run to Gjoa Haven and back, and we figured we had to stock up about five thousand pounds of fish in the fall to run the dogs through the winter.

It was surprising the number of species of fish we had in the Bathurst Inlet area: just to name a few of them, the starry flounder, the Arctic flounder, the Arctic char, of course, the nine-spined stickleback, lake trout, tom cod, saffron cod, several varieties of sculp, including one called the short-horned sculp, capelin, whitefish, fackfish, greyling, and wolf fish.

The wolf fish is the most remarkable of all the species of fish in the Bathurst Inlet area; it seems to be found in no other part of Canada's Arctic. When I heard about this fish from the Eskimos I thought either they were putting me on, or it was a legendary fish. The Eskimos described it as a big fish, up to four or five feet long, with a massive head and the jaw, the lips and teeth of a human being. Then I caught my first one and found it was a real fish. After that I caught many in Baychimo Harbour, where they are numerous.

When they hit a fish net it was almost as bad as getting a seal in it; they literally tore it up. And they were very hard to kill — you had to be careful with them because of their powerful jaws; they would grab at anything. I remember tossing one into the bottom of my canoe, where I had a bunch of Arctic char and other fish I had just hauled in by net. That wolf fish snapped a big char in two with one crunch of its jaws. The teeth are very strong, square-looking molars like a man's back teeth, I discovered how strong when I cut one open and examined its stomach. It was full of crushed mussel shells.

The wolf fish has a tough skin, and in the old days the Eskimos skinned them whole and made quivers for their arrows from the fish. Oddly enough, it is one of the tastiest of all the northern species. The scientific name for the species is *Anarrhicas denticulatus*. I advised the National Museum of the presence of the wolf fish at Baychimo, and acquired some samples for them, marking the first place the wolf fish had ever been recorded in the Canadian Arctic. It is mainly found in the North Atlantic, ranging from Nova Scotia as far east and south as the coast of France.

The Eskimos would keep a lookout for the coming of the *angmagiaq*, which is a sardine-like fish about six inches in length. I had never seen them until I ran into an immense school of them, acres and acres, when I was travelling alone by canoe across a little bay. The sea was frothing and boiling with millions of these fish. The Eskimos say that they make a spawning run once a year, and when they hit the inlet they are only there at the most three days. They swim up with the high tide along the beaches, deposit their eggs, and go back out again. If there happens to be an onshore wind, thousands of them are cast up in windrows of fish, and the Eskimos get boxes and sacks, anything that will hold them, and shovel them up. They are very good eating, rich, fat, very tender. We always ate them raw, bones and all because the bones are soft. Some day perhaps the Eskimos will be able to exploit this resource commercially, as I understand the fishermen off Newfoundland do with a similar type of fish.

21

✳ *The*
Great
White Zoo

Before the Eskimo became a townsman, a sociological phenomenon of the past fifteen years, and the whiteman's ecologists began calling for a great white zoo of the North, the Eskimo, like primitive man anywhere, knew every beast and bird in his domain, everything that had fin, fur or feather. The caribou was life itself to him, and the seal had equal importance for those who dwelt along the coast.

The Eskimo knew the meaning of every track in the snow or the mud, read the signs left when a wolverine dragged a robbed trap aside and buried it, saw where the wingtips of the great snowy owl brushed the white tundra as it swooped low to put an abrupt end to the helter-skelter trail left by a hapless ground squirrel, knew from the sound of a splash whether it was made by fish or seal. He knew that the stomach of a wolf was more likely to be full of lemming than caribou, that the big hump-shouldered grizzly of the barren lands was more to be feared than the elegant polar bear of the ice floes.

It meant survival to the Eskimo to know these things, and I wanted to learn them.

One day Palvik and I were checking traps along a trapline we were running together down the south coast of Kent Peninsula, north and east of Baychimo Harbour, and we discovered that a wolverine was working our line. This wolverine had followed the sled tracks we had made on our first run down the line, and many traps we checked had been dug up by the sly spoiler and either sprung or exposed. In some cases we would find scraps of a fox in the trap to show that the wolverine had beaten us to the prize. A wolverine often seems to work a trapline not out of hunger, but just for fun. Sometimes it will simply take the fox out of the trap, drag it off thirty yards and bury it. Normally, however, it chews it up enough to ruin the pelt. A single wolverine could reduce our take of fur considerably.

But we had a few tricks of our own. We went back to our base camp for an old sawn-off shotgun Palvik had used before on wolverines. Back at the trapline we dug a little pit in the snow near one of the traps that the wolverine had not yet visited, and buried the gun in the snow so that about two inches of the muzzle stuck out. Then we attached a string to the trigger of the shotgun and to a chunk of raw caribou meat, which we thawed out long enough to wrap around the mouth of the shotgun, where it froze tight. When we came back on our reverse trip down the trapline, we had our wolverine, minus its head.

Wolverine fur is prized for parka trim in the Arctic, because it is supposed that moisture doesn't condense on it and freeze up as it will on most fur. This is important for a fur ruff around the face. But the truth of the matter is that wolverine is little better than wolf or any other fur.

One can live a lifetime in the North and seldom see a living wolverine. They are exceedingly wary animals. I don't think I've seen more than four in all my time in the Arctic. Once I was walking along with a couple of Eskimos looking for caribou when we saw a wolverine, and one of my companions raced after it. The wolverine dashed into a burrow with the Eskimo hot on its tail, and then surprisingly it sprang out again and raced between the man's legs and off over the tundra. We dug into the burrow and found a litter of wolverine cubs. Normally a wolverine, a vicious member of the weasel family with fearful jaws and teeth, utterly unafraid of anything, would have attacked.

Another time a smart wolverine had the best of us. Nasar-lulik, another Eskimo called Qurvik and I had killed some caribou, but couldn't get all the meat in our canoe to take back to the post. We decided to cache what was left. We skinned them out and put them on the ground, and gathered up a great pile of rocks to cover the carcasses. After the carcasses were well covered, we took a tea-pail and scooped up water, sloshing it all over the cache. Each pail of water froze, binding the rocks like cement. We were making certain that no wolves would get our caribou before we could return for it ourselves. The cache was frozen solid.

When we eventually got back to pick up that meat, we discovered that a clever wolverine had found a way to outwit us. Unable to tear the frozen rocks away, the cunning beast had lain on top of one rock until its body heat had melted the ice around it; it then plucked the rock out and did the same thing with the next rock, until it was able to pull enough rocks away to get at the caribou.

Wolves will sometimes work a trapline too, but they don't stick with it like the wolverine does. They will follow the scent of the trapper's dogs and hit his traps once or twice and then go off after something else.

The Eskimos would often use a forty-five gallon fuel oil keg to make a deadly trap for wolves. With an axe or handsaw they cut a star-shaped hole in the top, bending the points and sharp edges inward so as to make an opening slightly smaller than a wolf's head. Then they buried the drum in the snow and put a chunk of meat or fish in the bottom of it. When a wolf came along it scented the bait and shoved its head in through the star-shaped hole at the top of the keg to get the bait. The wolf could get in all right, but when it tried to withdraw its head, it was impaled on the sharp edges of the star shaped points. Each wolf was worth about $70 to an Eskimo—a $45 bounty and about $25 for the fur.

One viciously effective trap the Eskimos used with great success made use of a small seal bone or bone from a large fish. They would file the ends to a point, then bend the bone over, carefully tying the ends together with a piece of sinew, but not too tightly. Then they took a chunk of meat about the size of a man's fist and wrapped that around the bone and let it freeze. When a wolf found the piece of meat it gulped it down without chewing it, as wolves do. Inside its stomach the meat thawed out, pulling the sinews around the ends of the bone loose, and the bone would spring out and its ends pierce the wolf's stomach. The Eskimo often didn't find the body to claim his bounty, but the trick did bring about a horrible death for any wolf that might be robbing his traps.

Wolves have long been falsely painted as the villains in the decline of the caribou herds in the Arctic. At one time it was government policy to hire so-called predator control officers, who set out strychnine-packed baits to poison the wolves which invariably accompanied the caribou migrations. The poisoning programme worked extremely well, but has since been mercifully abandoned.

We used to go out caribou hunting at Bathurst Inlet when the herds were calving inland from the eastern side of the inlet. Always we would find many wolves tagging around the herd. It would be warm by that time of year, and it was not uncommon to spot wolves just lolling in the sun along with the caribou, not bothering them at all; nor did the caribou seem to worry much about the wolves.

A wolf pair, a male and female, before whelping time, will sit in the sun together and fool around like a couple of dogs. In spite of their reputation for ferocity, towards all kinds of animals and human beings, from what I have seen of wolves with my own eyes I would call them very tender and loving animals. Certainly both male and female are very tender towards each other.

One may see a wolf make a run at a knot of caribou, and if the caribou take off and there appears to be no wounded or sick animal among them to lag back, then the wolf immediately quits the chase. It seems to know there is no point in it. Usually the only time wolves make a real run for caribou is when one which is sick or crippled drops back and the wolves have a chance to bring it down. Often in the summer the caribou simply head for the nearest lake and plunge in; the wolves never follow them into the water. Healthy caribou seem to regard wolves more as a nuisance than a danger.

The only time a wolf can expect to bring down a healthy caribou is during the winter, when by sheer persistence the wolf finally wears the caribou down. I would suspect this seldom happens, for every wolf we ever killed in the winter was scrawny, thin and badly undernourished. In the summer wolves put on a lot of weight, and look fat and sleek, but when we cut them open and checked their stomachs, nine out of ten had not a scrap of caribou meat in them. Their stomachs were loaded with lemmings, the mouse-like Arctic rodent, and ground squirrels. Now and then we found ptarmigan feathers. In summer wolves are often to be seen leaping and pouncing in the grass catching lemmings. They are easier to handle than frisky caribou.

Yet we shot many wolves, not because we thought they were harmful to the caribou, but simply because of the $45 bounty on each skin (which included cubs).

Wolves den up in the eskers, those long sand and gravel banks left throughout the North by retreating ice age glaciers, or in any sandy soil they can find to dig in. The animals live widely scattered, each pair staking out a wide territory, and two families of wolves are seldom found living in close proximity. I have never seen more than seven wolves together, although when I was at Baker Lake there were reports of an immense pack of about sixty. No pack of that size would stay together long because it would be unable to find food to support itself. The usual pack consists of the adult pair and four or five cubs, which stay with them during the year it takes them to grow to adult size.

On one remarkable occasion I saw wolves in winter run a relay system to bring down a caribou. I was hunting with Iksik from Bathurst Inlet and we were on top of a ridge from which we watched a complete chase-and-kill sequence down in the valley. A single wolf opened the relay, chasing a cow caribou. There were caribou all over the valley, but the wolf ignored all but the one it had picked out. Caribou and wolf came racing down the valley towards us at top speed. A caribou can hit fifty miles per hour in short sprints when it is in a hurry—and this one was. The wolf couldn't sustain that speed as long as the caribou, so it dropped out and another wolf, which had obviously been lying in wait, sprang up and took over the chase. It seemed to be a family thing, as one wolf after another picked up the run, one at a time, until the last wolf chasing it leaped on it and brought it down by the shoulder.

Iksik was about to shoot, but I checked him. I wanted to see how long it took the wolf to complete the kill. So we watched, and the time from when that final wolf in the relay brought the caribou down until the caribou was dead was well over two hours. Curiously, the other wolves stayed back and left it to the single wolf to complete the kill. The caribou was down on its rump with its rear legs splayed at an awkward angle, and every time the wolf made a rush at it, the caribou would sweep at it with its antlers and knock it aside. The wolf tried to come in from behind but the caribou kept swivelling on its rump. Sometimes, when the caribou became too tired to use its antlers, it lashed out with its front hooves, and the wolf rapidly scrambled back. A caribou's hooves are sharp enough to kill. When the caribou was finally dead, the other wolves moved in and there was a shared feast.

The length of time taken by the wolf to complete this kill was most unusual. Normally the length of time between the incredibly fast killing-sprint of the wolf and the actual kill itself is no more than three or four minutes.

The technique of the kill itself, the bringing down of the caribou, is worth comment. I have often read that the wolf accomplishes this by 'hamstringing' the fleeing animal by severing the large tendon of a rear leg. I strongly doubt that this is the usual way of dropping a caribou. The only method I have observed has been for the wolf to race alongside the forequarters of the caribou and slash at the shoulders or neck, toppling the victim to the ground. The kill in these cases would be almost instant; only a few moments later one could see the wolf feeding on the soft belly parts and entrails of the unfortunate prey. Perhaps the caribou goes into shock when the blow is struck.

The average number of wolves killed in the Northwest Territories in any one year now that the poisoners have been called off is no more than four hundred. There are approximately 1,300,000 square miles of territory in the Northwest Territories, so it seems unlikely that the wolves are being driven into a corner yet. Every hunter and trapper in the North could have told the government that the wolves do not really deplete the caribou population, which was the excuse for the indiscriminate poisoning campaign. I would estimate that a wolf in the course of a year won't kill more than a dozen caribou. A man with a rifle in good deer country can better this total in a single day. Most government agencies now agree that wolves actually aid in the ecology of the caribou by picking off the weaklings, sick and crippled.

Curiously enough, while trapping was the backbone of the Hudson's Bay Company effort in the North, only a few Eskimos really ever took to trapping as a preferred way of life. In the old days, of course, the Eskimo was a nomadic hunter, who spent most of the year seal hunting by harpoon on the sea ice. He never trapped at all except for food. But when the whiteman came and offered items of trade which the Eskimo wanted, the only currency the Eskimo had to offer in exchange was fur. But who wants to live by trapping? Who wants to go out in forty below zero weather and run a string of traps? Many Eskimos half-heartedly set out twenty or thirty traps which they may check every three weeks or so. No one expects the take from that kind of trapping to amount to much. Traps drift over; they are exposed by the wind; wolverines or wolves or foxes eat the carcasses—the returns are inevitably minimal. When it comes down to it, some Eskimos prefer to live like some of their white brothers—on welfare. It beats trapping as a way of life and generally pays more. I don't know any whitemen who have given up welfare to go trapping.

In a very few places in the Arctic, and Sachs Harbour on Banks Island is the foremost, the Eskimos have become full-time trappers, however. To the Eskimos there, hunting has become secondary. They are trappers and proud of it; they only hunt as a side pursuit. They live on the food they buy and they feed their teams commercial dogfood.

These Eskimos are the professionals of the trapping world. They run eight or nine hundred traps each, with a trapline extending as much as two hundred and fifty miles. They work steadily at it all winter, all through the fur season—just like a regular job. They will go out and face fifty and sixty below weather because they are making good money. They accept the hardships as part of the job and some make $10,000 a year at it.

But to most Eskimos hunting has always been the best natural way of life. Hunting caribou, seals and bear is where the excitement and the romance is. There is no romance in trapping, which has to be done in the most miserable part of the year, during the coldest, darkest months of winter.

One fall, at the trading post at Baychimo, Palvik and I bagged a few caribou which we cached alongside the warehouse. We put down a couple of sheets of plywood, threw the carcasses onto them and piled some unused lumber on top. No extra precautions seemed called for; we didn't expect to have trouble with marauders right next to the post. Wolverines and wolves wouldn't dare come in so close.

A few nights later, as we passed the warehouse on some

errand, we heard a scurrying sound, and right in front of our eyes about twenty white foxes scattered in all directions. We decided to wait where we were; we knew those foxes would come back. After about fifteen minutes they did. There were two families, four adults and perhaps sixteen pups. The pups were only about a foot long, just bundles of fur. It was still too early in the season for their coats to be fully white—they were off-white, bluish-grey.

We decided we should catch one. I took the flashlight and when a little pup came close to my feet again I flashed the light in its eyes, temporarily blinding it. Palvik swooped down and grabbed it by the back of the neck. We took it into the trading post, and when we got into my living room Palvik turned it loose. It was scared to death, and scurried around before ducking underneath the chesterfield. We chased it out, and it then got behind the oil stove. The back of the stove had ventilation holes, and the pup popped through one of them into the stove where it was nice and dark. We banged on the stove and poked and prodded through the holes, and finally the pup popped out again. The little beast was covered from nose to tail tip with black soot, and it raced around the room, leaving everywhere it went a trail of black sooty tracks. I have never seen a room become so filthy in such a short time. We did our best to chase the tiny thing out of the house. Finally it ran into the hallway, and I shoved it along with a broom while Palvik opened the door. It made a dash past me to go back into the living room, but Palvik caught it with a perfect dropkick and lifted it right out into the yard, where it took off yipping.

We found on investigation that those two families of foxes had burrowed underneath the lumber in the warehouse and were chewing up our caribou meat at an alarming rate.

Now and then I went south to the old Bathurst Inlet post to observe the herd of muskox there. For some years there had been a herd of around a hundred animals that would come within a mile or two of the coast. The Eskimos didn't bother with them ordinarily because a muskox is much tougher meat than a caribou, the only tender part on an adult animal being the brisket.

But I wanted to observe this herd during the rutting season, so I headed off by myself in a canoe. I knew the herd wouldn't have wandered far. In the winter the males and females of all ages band together, but this was August and the mating season, and the old bulls were sure to have driven the young males away from their harem of cows.

I canoed across to Daniel Moore Bay and walked inland a few miles. In a small valley there I came across the herd. I was carrying my rifle, not that I expected to use it, but it was the prudent way to behave in that wild country. The muskox were scattered around the valley, with the young bulls, as I had expected, segregated off to one side in a little herd of their own.

I lay on the ridge all day and watched them through my binoculars and then went back to my canoe and pitched my tent, for I wanted to make closer observations. I counted 111 muskox in that herd, including fourteen calves.

While I was watching next day, one of the old bulls was challenged by a young hopeful. The big bull, and he really was ancient from the looks of him, interposed himself between the herd of females in a meadow and the ambitious young bull. The challenger was a husky animal although obviously quite young. Quick and agile, he ran back and forth about two hundred yards from the females, strutting with his stiff tail straight out, showing off and making the old bull madder and madder. But the old bull just stood his ground. Finally, the young bull turned and made a rush, galloping in at the old one, but this was just a feint to test the old bull's nerve. The youngster pulled up a good hundred feet short and went trotting away again, his long hair flying in the breeze, his tail arched and switching. I was sure he was thinking about how good he must look to the females down in the meadow.

Next time was for real. The young bull turned and pawed at the ground. I could see the smart old boss bull get ready, flexing his forelegs a bit and lowering his massive horns. He knew this was the moment. The young challenger came thundering in, tearing up the turf, and the two animals met head-on with a shocking crash. The fickle females looked up, mildly interested for a moment, then resumed grazing.

The young bull's momentum drove the old bull right back on his haunches. The challenger literally bounced off, flying back several feet. Then the old bull got up and shook his head, and the young bull walked around half-dazed for about five or ten minutes and wandered off a good half mile. But after a rest he came waltzing back in again for a second try. He followed the same routine, pacing back and forth, trotting determinedly towards the old bull and then veering off, doing his best to attract the cows, who barely looked up, and to intimidate his dignified antagonist, who merely stolidly stood his ground. The youngster mustered his courage for another go. In he charged as hard as he could and smacked the old bull right back on his haunches again. But the older head was harder. The young bull bounced back and fell half to one side, then got up and staggered off. This time he stayed away.

Eventually one of the young bulls will beat the old herd bull and drive him into exile. He becomes a *kisimngaaq*, which means 'the solitary one'. The defeated old bull becomes a rogue muskox, and wanders around by himself pretty sour on the world. The Eskimos say that a rogue bull must be treated with respect and watched closely because it is bad-tempered and always ready to pick a fight, and a muskox bull is big and strong enough to be really dangerous.

I had been watching from my vantage point for about a week without ever showing myself to the herd, and I wondered what would happen if I walked down the valley towards them. I expected that they would 'fort up', form the famous defensive circle with the calves in the centre of the circle and a solid ring of tough males and cows facing out with their horns down ready to defend themselves. I wanted to see that, so I took my gun and casually strolled down the valley, thinking that the little herds scattered along the valley floor would run together and form a big circle; but no such thing happened. Instead, the tough old bull came racing out to meet me. I had my gun and could have heart-shot the animal, but I didn't want to do that, so I turned on my heel and ran up the hill. He kept right after me, and I think could have caught me if he had wanted to, but he seemed content to make sure I simply stayed back from the herd.

After that I stayed on the ridge and watched with my glasses again. I eventually walked down to the other end of the valley, over another hill, and found a second herd. I thought that maybe the old bull that had chased me was just ugly because the young bulls were giving him a bad time, so I walked down the valley toward this new herd thinking they would form up in the defensive ring I wanted to see. But no, this herd just took off, and while they were scooting up the valley the herd bull charged right at me and chased me back up the hill just as the other one had done. Then he trotted back and forth between me and the herd, as if to say, 'Okay, just as long as you keep your distance.'

Hunting muskox has been prohibited since 1917 to both whites and Eskimos. The Eskimos have continued to kill a few, but the herds have been thriving to the point of over-population, and limited hunting may be allowed again soon.

The *qiviuq* (undercoat) of the muskox, the inner fur, is a very fine wool. *Qiviuq* is a term the Eskimos use for the underfur of any Arctic animal, but the *qiviuq* of the muskox is especially fine and would make marvellous garments, lighter and warmer than cashmere. Perhaps some day the herds in the Arctic might be successfully domesticated and a business based on that lovely wool.

One summer a museum asked me to obtain some samples of ground squirrel skins taken from different areas of Bathurst Inlet. They wanted samples from all around the inlet and all through the summer.

These small animals are common throughout Bathurst, and I headed off to some specific locations. At the mouth of the Hiukitak River, I tied my canoe to a rock and hiked inland with nothing but a game bag and my .22 rifle. I was concentrating on getting the required ground squirrel samples and enjoying the scenery. It was a nice warm day, and I quickly shot two or three specimens. I was walking along, my rifle strapped flat on my back, in the Eskimo style which leaves both arms free. About three miles inland I came to a big esker. At the end of this esker was a huge boulder, about three times the size of a house. I was half-daydreaming as I walked around the big rock, and I found myself practically eyeball to eyeball with a grizzly bear. The suddenness of the encounter took my breath away and made my testicles arch with fright.

The Bathurst country is well known as the home of the big Barren Ground grizzlies. I stood about seven feet from this one. It flashed through my mind that the Eskimos say a grizzly is about ten times more dangerous than a polar bear.

The grizzly was as surprised as I was. It jumped backwards and let out an almighty growl, and when a grizzly growls, it rumbles deep from the stomach, a horrible sound that I can't describe and have no desire to hear again. I stood petrified.

What I wanted to do was to run like hell, but I decided that the best thing I could do was not to make any motion at all. I knew that bear could catch me in about six bounds, so I just stood there, dead still, trying my best not to shake. I even kept my hands in just the position they were when I had come around the boulder. I could feel the flow of adrenalin.

The grizzly recovered quickly from its surprise, got to its feet, and began swaying its huge head from side to side as it fastened its beady eyes on me. Then it started clawing up the gravel, and I watched intently, trying to figure which paw this grizzly would hit me with. Grizzlies, like polar bears, favour one paw over the other when hitting. Knowing which one a particular animal used was a definite advantage in the days when Eskimos had no rifles and had to kill a bear with a knife or *pana*. Knowing which way the bear will strike, one can move to the offside so that the bear must turn before lashing out.

This bear was a right-hander, as I could tell from the paw it used to claw at the gravel. It wasn't actually a very big bear, probably no more than nine feet, but its head was monstrous and the characteristic hump on the shoulders appeared huge at such close range. I had always heard from the Eskimos that while grizzlies are notoriously unpredictable, one thing you could count on was that a surprised bear usually attacked. I stood looking a surprised one right in the teeth.

I just had that little .22 with me and it was strapped to my back. Even if I had been able to swing it off and pump a shell into the chamber, a .22 bullet wouldn't do more than sting that bear and make it mad. All I could think was: 'I'm going to be killed right here and no one will ever know how it happened.'

The monster growled again and swung its head and my eyes swivelled with it. It growled some more and rose up on its hind feet for a moment like a circus bear, then dropped back to all fours and walked off to one side about fifteen feet, sniffing, trying to decide what I was and what kind of threat. There wasn't much breeze, but I was wondering if my scent was carrying to the bear or being carried away from it.

I stood my ground, afraid to move a muscle, and the bear sniffed at me again, then lifted its head and began to make a queer chomping noise with its back teeth, clacking them together, not a sound that gave me much comfort. Then it ambled off to one side about thirty feet further away, turned and walked away from me. The second it turned its back, I scrambled up the boulder. When I got to the top I saw that it had turned and was charging. I jumped down the other side and started running as fast as I could, running like mad across the tundra, heading for the coast in the most direct line possible. I yanked the gun off my back on the run and levered a shell into the chamber, but knew I wouldn't use it except as a last desperate resort.

My big friend came around the rock instead of over it, saw me running and took chase. I was running with my head turned back so that I could watch it and I stumbled from tussock to tussock. To my relief, after its initial charge, the bear settled down to an easy lope. For the first time since I rounded that rock, it looked as if there was a chance.

I ran the whole three miles back to the coast with that bear following after about fifty yards behind me. I sprinted over a little rise and saw my canoe on the beach and raced over the rocks to launch it. I threw myself into it and let it float out into the inlet. I thought my heart was going to pack up with the strain. I was lying flat on the bottom of the canoe, collapsed, panting and trying to catch my wind. I had a powerful rifle in the canoe, and could have loaded it up and finished the bear, but I didn't have the strength. It had stopped at the top of the rise and was squatting on its haunches. When I had time to think about it I decided that it was lucky for me the bear apparently was neither hungry nor in a bad mood, or I should have been killed for sure.

Eskimos avoid hunting grizzlies. The hides are no good, too heavy for clothing and in the summer they are in terrible shape, all scraggly. Grizzlies den up during the winter, the season when the coats on other Arctic animals thicken up and become valuable. Eskimos never tangle with them if they can help it, but the animals are numerous along the inlet.

In the fall, about the time of the first snow, the big bears hibernate for the winter. Once Iksik and I found the entrance to a den up one of the eskers. We scouted around and made sure the female and her cub were off on a trip, and while Iksik kept his eyes on the place, I crawled in to investigate the den. The entrance channel was about three feet high and went back into the bank about ten feet. Then it opened up into quite a wide room and the top was close to the surface of the ground. The bears usually wait until the ground is slightly frozen before excavating the den, so that it won't cave in on them, and the last thing they do is dig a ventilation hole through the ceiling to the open air.

The floor of the den and all the way in through the entrance channel I found lined about a foot deep with the ground roots of dwarf birch. In the main chamber there was a deep bed, almost two feet deep, of the same roots. I came back out, and we watched from a distance until the bear returned. She was gathering up more birch. She had a great armful of the stuff, and walked backwards hauling it into her den.

Then it started to snow, and the old bear came out, gathered up a final armful of roots and dragged them into the entrance. Then from the inside she scooped up dirt and snow and blocked up the opening, sealing the den up for the winter.

The Eskimos regard the grizzly as the most dangerous animal in the Arctic—with good reason, since there are many cases of people being attacked by these bears. On one such occasion a grizzly ambled into a hunting camp near Baychimo and made for a little child who was playing outside. The child's mother saw the bear and screamed. Her husband ran out with a rifle, got between the grizzly and his son, and desperately began firing. The grizzly charged after the first shot, and the hunter pumped four more bullets right into its chest before he was slammed to the ground by the enraged animal. The pain-maddened bear literally tore the man apart. It almost severed one arm, inflicted massive wounds all over his body—and tore his head clean off his shoulders. Then the grizzly fell dead, and when the Eskimos later skinned it out they found its heart had been shattered by two bullets. In telling me the story, the Eskimos emphasized that the hunter should never try to kill a grizzly head on, but should get to one side and shoot it in the spine just above the hindquarters, crippling it so that it cannot make that terrible charge. Then it can be finished off with no danger.

Grizzlies and all other animals and birds were a constant challenge in the Arctic to my curiosity. I wanted to learn how they managed to thrive in such bleak country. But to the Eskimos, knowing all about every kind of animal, bird and fish was often a matter of life and death, and with that sort of motivation you really study natural history and ecology, whether you call it that or not.

22

The Honourable Member

Among the first private entrepreneurs in the western Arctic was an old friend of mine, genial, red-bearded Fred Ross. He had taken over an old construction camp in Cambridge Bay and turned it into a sort of transient hotel, which wasn't a bad place to stay if you brought your own sleeping bag. I had come up from Bathurst Inlet with my dogs and was staying with Fred. Several other people dropped in during the course of the evening, and eventually the subject got around to politics, a subject which frankly bored me.

Fred said that the Northwest Territorial Council had just extended the franchise into the Arctic regions. He explained that the Arctic regions were being divided into three constituencies—eastern, central and western Arctic. Then he popped a surprising question. Would I run for the western Arctic for a position on the Territorial Council?

I just laughed. My impression of a politician was a fellow in a top hat and striped pants with only the remotest connection with anything human. I had no interest whatever in politics at the federal, territorial or any other level, and this I told Fred. But he and the others in the room said they had talked the matter over very carefully and they needed me.

We sat there in Fred's room, half a dozen of us, drinking rum and getting pleasantly tight, and before I knew it I had agreed to run. I said, 'Okay, put my name down.' I filled out the nomination papers and entered my name on the list and back I went with my dogs to Bathurst Inlet.

I have to admit I didn't give the matter another thought. I never campaigned for a second. On election day I had been out with a pilot and another man trying to find a good fishing spot, and our plane had got stuck on a shallow stretch of the river and we had a devil of a time getting it off.

When we finally had the plane airborne and the pilot contacted Cambridge Bay, we learned that I had been elected that day. I hadn't even voted and neither had anyone else at Bathurst Inlet. That's how I was elected to the governing body of the Northwest Territories in the fall of 1966.

I didn't know anything about the Council of the Northwest Territories. When I went to Resolute Bay to attend the first session in November, I didn't even know that the Council met twice a year, once each year in Ottawa, then still the capital of the NWT, and once in one of the settlements in the territories. I discovered that there were seven elected and five appointed members in those days.

Membership on the Council certainly opened my eyes to problems in other parts of the NWT as well as problems throughout the Arctic. I was particularly concerned about the game laws, having lived and hunted and trapped in the North since I was eighteen years old. My first action was to propose a number of changes in the game laws, particularly concerning polar bears and caribou.

At that first session of Council, being a total greenhorn as far as parliamentary procedure went, I fell back on what I did know. I knew the Eskimo way of life, and I was representing a constituency where ninety-five percent of the people were Eskimo. I had lived in many of the settlements, and I felt I knew what would be good for my constituents, because I had lived with Eskimos for so long, lived the kind of life they lived, and I spoke their language fluently. I knew which changes would affect them. After I had been elected, there was only a period of a few weeks before the first session at Resolute. I hadn't had a chance to make the rounds of the settlements at all, to find out specifically what the people needed and wanted. I didn't know what my duties as a Council member would be, or what was expected of me.

It seemed to me that one of the major problems concerning the game laws was that these laws were basically drawn up by men who were unfamiliar with the Arctic regions of the

Northwest Territories. The previously elected members of Council had all been drawn from constituencies within the forest region of the North, men who had little or no knowledge of life above the tree line, and they had to accept the opinions of Canadian Wildlife Service experts when they appeared before the Council members as advisors. I do not mean to imply that the previous members of Council were rubber-stamps. Far from it. Like all northerners, they were highly individualistic men who examined each item of legislation and determined its effect on the people of their constituencies before accepting or altering it. But they were no more expert in producing good game laws for the Arctic than an Eskimo would be who attempted to make good traffic laws for Ottawa or New York.

This was the first Council with true representation from the Arctic. Simonic Michael, an Eskimo from the eastern Arctic, and Bobby Williamson from the central Arctic, were elected with me in 1966. Together with Abe Okpik, an Eskimo appointed to the Council, we felt that the Arctic had good representation for the first time. And we were able to make substantial changes at that very first session, particularly in regard to the game laws.

We all knew that the game laws were the legislation most immediately important to the Eskimos and Indians of the Northwest Territories. For example, prior to that session of Council, an Arctic islands game reserve had been set up which covered almost two-thirds of the entire NWT, and within that region there could be virtually no development of the Territories from a game point of view. So we decided in the best interests of the entire population—not just the Eskimo population, but the entire population of the NWT—to throw out that monstrously large game preserve, and we did so.

We had a major battle with the Canadian Wildlife Service over polar bear. They admitted that the then annual kill of polar bear was not excessive, but expressed concern that the kill could increase yearly to the point where the animal population would decline. They therefore recommended that a closed season be declared, and that cubs up to two years of age and their mothers be protected by law. The members of Council agreed with the basic policy of protection of the species, but we differed radically with the Canadian Wildlife Service on how best to achieve these ends.

Instead of a closed season during the ice-free period of the summer, I proposed that a quota system be established that would allow the polar bear to be taken at any period of the year—provided that the quota wasn't exceeded. Rather than simply introducing an annual overall quota for the NWT—which quite conceivably would allow hunters from one region to decimate the local polar bear population—I suggested that regional quotas be established based on the average annual kill for each region over the last five years. By establishing regional quotas we could better protect the species in those regions where the bear population was small and the hunter population large. In conjunction with the regional quota system we established an individual quota to overcome the danger that several hunters from the same region could go hunting bear independently of each other and collectively exceed the regional quota without being aware of doing so.

The Canadian Wildlife Service's other recommendation also went through the mill. My counter-proposal was that both mother and cub, regardless of the age of the cub, should be protected if they were found to be still together, but that any cub or adult female found wandering on its own be considered free game without restriction. From a practical viewpoint this made more sense to me than the arbitrary age limit of two years which had been recommended as the protected age of the polar bear cubs. I pointed out to Council that a bear cub one year, eleven months and twenty-nine days old would be protected under the CWS recommendation while one which happened to be two years and one day old could legally be shot. But how does a hunter tell the difference? Closing in on a bear with an excited team of dogs is hardly a propitious moment to check out its birth certificate. I also pointed out that when we were talking about a cub nearly two years old we were not debating the fate of a cuddly little bundle of white fluff, but an animal probably six foot in length, weighing 250 to 350 pounds and quite capable of taking a man's head off with one blow. If such an animal were found away from its mother, then it was safe to bet that it was fully capable of fending for itself. So why shouldn't it be counted as free game? We rejected the Service's recommendation and substituted our own.

Their third recommendation concerned a particular part of the Arctic, Banks Island, which up to then had been exempted from rules and restrictions concerning the taking of polar bear, and the Wildlife people felt that all regions should be treated the same. We agreed with that.

Although I and other members of the NWT Council were often highly critical of the Canadian Wildlife Service, I must in all fairness record that such criticism lay more against their game policies for the North than against individuals of the Service. Our fundamental objection was that the CWS—a federal governmental agency—appeared to see the Arctic as one big zoo, protecting all the animals all the time whereas we men who lived in the Arctic strongly supported the Game Branch of the Territorial government who took the view that with proper game management techniques, the Territory's wealth of game could be harvested like any other resource and utilized within safe limits to provide an income for the hunters and trappers who had little opportunity for anything else.

We changed the caribou laws too, basing new regulations on the best obtainable census of the animals, region by region. For the first time the whiteman in certain regions of the North was allowed to kill three caribou annually for food. Under the old regulations a man might stand in his doorway and see thousands of the animals stream past and not be able to touch one. That seemed ridiculous to me, and the Council agreed. The Council had many debates and even battles with the Canadian Wildlife Service over this basic dichotomy until the point was reached where the Wildlife Service no longer bothered to make recommendations or to give advice to the Council, because most of the time we paid no attention to their well-meant but useless advice. They wanted to close the country down and keep it as it was for the benefit of the animals. We thought people came first, and we wanted to open up and develop the country for their benefit. Actually, we sought a compromise that would protect and conserve the natural resources but at the same time provide as beneficial use of them by the people as was deemed possible.

At the same time, I recommended sports hunting of polar bears. I said that I saw three steps in the utilization of the polar bear: one, the quota system to insure that the polar bear be protected as a species; two, a sports hunting program whereby an Eskimo hunter who received an individual quota to kill a bear could sell his individual quota to any big game sports hunter for a fee of approximately $2,000; three, game outfitting camps in the Arctic, run by Eskimos, to assist the white hunters who came to take their northern trophies.

I felt that in this way the Arctic could be opened up to big game hunting to the mutual advantage of the trophy-minded sportsman of the South and the needy native of the North. The Eskimos already knew from experience how to hunt the big white bears, so in opening up hunting camps and guiding services they would be rendering an expert service for which they would be amply paid in addition to receiving a fee for the quota licence. With this in mind, the NWT recently permitted sports hunting of polar bears.

When we established the quota system, we reduced the overall average annual kill by two hundred animals—by more than one third—to make doubly sure that there would be no excessive kill which might endanger the species. And we publicized the fact that under the sports hunting program any bears killed would fall within that quota system. We made certain that even the dullest could understand that not one bear would be killed that wouldn't have been killed by the Eskimos anyhow. The only difference was that another finger pulled the trigger, and any Eskimo who sold his quota permit got better than ten times as much money from the bear as he would have if he went out and killed it himself. In recent years in the North the average price paid to an Eskimo for a polar bear skin has been between $150 and $200, generally much nearer the first figure. Under the new system the choice is up to the Eskimo holder of the permit to hunt the bear himself or to sell his quota to a big game sports hunter. When he does sell, the Eskimo also has the job and money for fitting out the tourist, providing guide service and the dogteam with which to hunt the bear, and skinning and preparing the pelt. Additionally, his community finds a direct new outlet for the sale of handicrafts.

We have recommended that a similar system be set up for the muskox. There has been a total ban on the killing of muskox since 1917. When the Wildlife Service and the Game Branch took a census of muskox recently, they found that the total population of the species now stands at nearly 10,000 in the Canadian Arctic. In some places the muskox have become so numerous they have overgrazed the tundra and hundreds have died of starvation. This was documented quite carefully by the

Game Branch of the NWT. The overprotection afforded the once scarce muskox has resulted in an excess, which should now be utilized.

My election to Council quickly and drastically changed my way of living. After I had been through two sessions of Council I realized I must make a choice: either leave the Council to which I had been elected, or else leave the employ of the Hudson's Bay Company, because I could now see that the time spent on Council work would be quite substantial, and I didn't think it was fair to the Company or to the Eskimos in Bathurst Inlet to be away so much of the time, leaving them, in effect, with no trader in their area. Council met twice a year, and each session lasted approximately one month. On top of that, I could see I would have to travel around to all the other settlements in the western Arctic, and there were eleven of them in the several thousand square miles of my constituency. If I were away from Bathurst in another part of my constituency and someone fell ill, there would be no one to look after him, and in case of serious illness or a medical emergency, no one there to get on the radio and call Cambridge Bay for help.

So, reluctantly, I decided that I would have to leave the Hudson's Bay Company. I had been with the Company for eleven years. I had always been proud to be a Hudson's Bay trader, and I was sorry to leave them for another reason. In my last year at Bathurst I was earning approximately $6,000 a year from the Bay, and now I was getting another $5,000 for being a Council member. When I resigned from the Company, I was left with $5,000 only. But this had to cover all my expenses for travelling around my constituency, my expenses in Ottawa or Yellowknife or wherever we sat, everything but my actual travel to the point where Council met.

My constituency was one of the largest in the world, several thousand square miles even if it did have only eleven towns and at best three thousand people. Some of the settlements were a thousand miles apart, and from Paulatuk in the west to Pelly Bay in the east was a good two thousand miles.

It was obvious that I couldn't live and cover my constituency on $5,000 a year, so I just picked up my dogs and went to live off the land with the Eskimos as a trapper. I decided to visit the settlements in my constituency by dogteam in the winter and canoe in the summer.

When I lived with the Eskimos as a trader, I always had the security of the post to draw upon. If I didn't get that seal or that caribou I needed for food, I could go back to the post and grab a tin of ham off the shelf. Now, everything I needed had to come from the land. If I wanted something from the post, gasoline, tobacco, or any of the luxuries I was used to, I had to come up with white fox pelts now.

Nonetheless, I found that I very quickly and easily fell into this new pattern of life. In fact, once I adjusted to it I found it exhilarating. The problems of survival in the Arctic have been grossly overrated. If a man knows the techniques, if he knows how to hunt, how to trap, to build a snowhouse and travel with dogs, and how to handle the ordinary implements and weapons of the Arctic as the Eskimos have been doing for centuries, it is a reasonably simple matter to get by. Of course, if you were to run into bad luck, if the caribou migration missed your area, then it might also be fairly simple to starve to death. But my own experience proves that a man who really wanted to could go into the North and learn enough from the people, and they are infinitely generous with their help, to exist in the Arctic.

I became a partner with a trapper in Bathurst Inlet with whom I had run a trapline long before I started living off the land. The only real difference from my previous life was that I had moved out from the trading post and now lived in my own snowhouse just like the Eskimos. I knew that one of the Sachs Harbour trappers had made in excess of $30,000 in a single year's trapping, but I had no illusions I could make that much. However, the average take for a really hard-working, professional trapper ran as high as $8–9,000 a year, and I did hope to do that well. I quickly found, however, that even here Council business interfered. That first year, for example, I spent most of my time travelling around the settlements in my constituency. I felt that if I were to represent the people of those settlements I ought to talk to them and find out what they wanted their representative to do for them.

Additionally, by the time I resigned from the Company I was facing a second election. My first vote had been a by-election with a term of just one year. Now I had to run again, and this time I was to have opposition for sure. An Eskimo from Cambridge Bay named Qavrana was running against me. The Company suggested that I should not resign until after I saw how the voting went, but I felt that I might as well make it all or nothing. I had stirred up enough noise in the first year for some government people—among others—to hope to knock me out in this election, and they were responsible for putting Qavrana up against me.

I was worried for a while. I was a whiteman running against an Eskimo in Eskimo country—tough competition. When I made my way around the settlements I told everyone: 'The choice is yours. If you want Qavrana, then that's the man to vote for. You should vote for the man you think will do the most for you, who will work the hardest for you, and if you think Qavrana is that man, then you vote for him. If you think I am that man, then vote for me.' Everywhere I went I made a point of explaining to the Eskimos: 'I'm not here to tell you what to do. I'm not your boss. I'm your servant. I come here so you can tell me what to do, and then when we hold a meeting with the government people, I can explain to them what you want.'

It turned out that I had worried for nothing. I was re-elected by a flatteringly large majority.

23

❄ *A Brush with Death*

1967 was a bad year in the western Arctic. Even the big supply ships were impeded by drifting floes. In mid-August I agreed to take a mining promoter named Joe Fleming down into Bathurst Inlet by canoe to do some prospecting. I told Joe that I planned to continue travelling right along the Arctic coast to the Mackenzie Delta, and then up the Mackenzie River to Yellowknife, in time for an upcoming session of the Territorial Council.

Joe commented, 'That's a hell of a canoe trip,' and he was to prove prophetic. He said he was of half a mind to go with me just for the adventure but that he had to check on his mining prospects in the Inlet first. I would have been happy to take him all the way, but I was anxious to get beyond the Inlet as soon as possible as it might be a race to get into the Delta before freeze-up, especially since the ice had been bad all summer.

After nine days of fighting ice packs, rain and terrible weather between Cambridge Bay and Bathurst Inlet, a trip that normally took three days, Joe lost interest in the 1,300-mile trip that I was proposing along the coast. However, while camping at Joe's claim, I ran into a young Dutchman named Erik van Veenen. He was working the circuit of the mining camps for his bed and board, a sort of unpaid choreboy, just to get a taste of Canada's northland.

When he heard about my trip he immediately started pestering me to take him along. I wasn't at all keen on the idea. Erik was a likeable kid, but he had never made a canoe trip in his life; he had never been in the Arctic before; he had never pitched a tent anywhere; and in short he didn't know a thing about the kind of roughing-it we would have to go through on this trip. I did everything I could to discourage him, but I couldn't. He simply wouldn't be put off, and in the end I acquiesced.

We had a twenty foot freighter canoe, one of the regular Hudson's Bay trade canoes with a square stern. It carried a twenty horsepower kicker on it with a smaller, five horsepower motor in the bow as a standby in case our main outboard engine broke down. These sturdy canoes have a five foot beam, making them fairly steady and reliable. We didn't have too much to load up, because I expected to live off the land in part. We threw in a dozen or so gas drums, our sleeping bags, a tent, two small stoves and grub boxes, and a supply of dried caribou meat. I expected to shoot a lot of ducks along the way, maybe something bigger.

But we were delayed by trouble with our main outboard engine and didn't get away until September 6, dangerously late for the sort of trip I planned. September is a month of gales and bad weather along the Arctic coast.

Taking off just west of Baychimo Harbour, we ran into bad weather at once, a foretaste of what was to come. Two hours west northwest out of the inlet, we ran into a dense fog bank. I threw out a line to the stern, a common seaman's trick when caught in a fog, and we could tell by its line if we were keeping a straight course. We planned to hit the Kitaagunnaak Islands before dark, but the fog slowed us, and by the time we reached the islands it was well into night. The wind had risen and the canoe was plunging sickeningly. The combination of the darkness and fog was giving us trouble, and the wind didn't help.

The Kitaagunnaaks (the Cheere Islands in English) feature high cliffs along the coast for several miles. We were driving along the coast, very slowly, bobbing like a cork over the building seas, when the cliff face suddenly loomed up out of the fog in front of us. It was close enough to give us a bit of a fright. The wind was pounding the seas up against the sheer rock, and we narrowly missed being caught in the swell. I knew that if we just followed the cliff along, eventually we would get into the shelter of the islands. There is a tiny gap between the mainland there and an island called Stockport Island. By watching carefully we managed to work our way up a beam sea, putting ourselves in the lee of the wind. Now quite well sheltered, we finally found the narrow opening we were looking for, darted through it and then pulled ashore to make our first camp.

Early the next day we headed west again with a brisk wind. Going around Barrow Point, we aimed towards an island called Iglsuugyuk, a well-known landmark in those parts for dogteam travellers. It was there we ran into our first ice. A lot of drifting field ice lay ahead, but fortunately it was fairly open and we were able to steer the canoe in and out of it quite easily until we came to the passage between Iglsuugyuk Island and the mainland. The channel there, we soon found, was solidly blocked. If we couldn't fight our way through it we were faced with running many miles back to get around the long island and to the seaward side. The way the wind was blowing by then, we didn't want any part of that, so we chiselled our way through, pushing the bow of the canoe right up onto the ice, shoving with paddles. Luckily it was floe ice and mostly small stuff, no more than two or three feet thick; as the floes kept easing away, we would push the canoe in under the power of the kicker, just nudging ice cakes out of our path. We barely managed to keep going, and right in the middle we jammed up tight. Erik and I had to jump out and drag the fully-laden canoe over the ice, but once we managed that, we were clear of that narrow blockade and headed on to Coppermine.

Along the way we were protected by numerous islands, but the wind and bad weather combined to delay us nearly three days. Out beyond the fringe of islands we could see a field of pack ice stretching right to the horizon, and we knew that once we left Coppermine we should be in for some really bad going. About seventy miles northwest of Coppermine lie the Union and Dolphin Straits, and we would need some break from the weather to get through the treacherous currents in them.

We were ice-bound in Coppermine for four days, but enjoyed the company of some Eskimo girls while there. Reluctantly, we decided we had better get out of there or risk being frozen in for the winter. We asked a pilot who had stopped in briefly to circle a bit on his way out and radio back to the DOT office if he could see a lead or break in the ice pack. He radioed back that he could see one long lead out to the northeast and if we could get to that open water, we should be able to make eight or ten miles. It looked as if we should chance it. Our next stopping point for supplies would be Paulatuk, a tiny settlement about 700 miles to the west, so we had to load up heavily at Coppermine, primarily taking on more of the ten gallon gas kegs. They were bulky and heavy, and left us with no more than six inches of freeboard when we left.

It soon became apparent that there was no way we could push through the ice to reach that lead the pilot had spotted. Instead we had to push east, back the way we had come, with the idea that with an east wind blowing, there would probably be gaps of ice-free water at the western end of each island we passed. We thought we could work our way from such gaps into open channels of water.

After eight hours of nosing our way through ice packs, we found our way completely jammed again. We could see a lead headed in the direction we wanted to go, but by the time we worked our way into it, the ice was beginning to close in. We knew that if that lead closed in on us, the pressure on our heavily loaded canoe might be more than it could take. Ice like that crushes big ships like matchwood; our little canoe would be as safe as a seal in a stewpot.

Even as we watched, the lead narrowed to less than 100 yards wide, so we made for a pan of ice about 150 or 200 feet long, the biggest single ice floe we could see. We gunned our motor with the notion that we could climb right aboard the pan with our canoe, but we were too heavy and managed to smash into it instead. Erik and I hopped out onto the ice and began to unload the canoe. We just managed to get everything out of our boat and the canoe pulled up on the ice when the lead closed in. There we sat high and dry in the middle of the icefield. Even though we were safe for the moment, we were jittery, fearful that the ice pack closing in on us might grind up and over the floe we had chosen for refuge or smash it with all our supplies.

Night came, and the ice was on the move. We were able to get our bearings on an island and could tell we were moving with the ice pack, slowly but surely. With no sign of any change in the weather we knew we would be stuck on our ice pan another day or two. We decided against pitching the tent because our floe was only a few feet thick, and with thin ice like that pressure from the pack could crack it any time, just break it up. We took turns standing watch, first Erik while I slept fitfully in the canoe, then I stood watch while he slept. All through the night the wind howled almost to gale force, and all around us we could hear the ice grinding and moaning. Our ice floe would turn one way and then the other, and sometimes, just to keep us alert, it would tilt a bit. We could feel the pressure. There are millions of tons of ice in a big field stretching out like that for sixty or seventy miles. The floe might break up, but above all we were concerned that our canoe might be smashed.

For three days the wind blew and kept the ice pounding in, battering at us. We were confined on that floe, and not very comfortably confined either. We erected a sort of shelter with paddles and the boat tarp, but were still afraid to pitch our tent and set up a proper camp. On the fourth day the winds calmed, and when the winds die down, the ice gradually opens out. Taking the first chance we had we loaded up the canoe and began threading our way out of the ice. With a flat calm and a bright sun shining we had no trouble getting through, but that ice pack was so big that it took a good ten hours to get past it. Then we headed into the mouth of Union and Dolphin Straits.

I knew the country well. I had been through often by dog-team, but never travelled it by canoe. Unlike the high, bold shores of Bathurst Inlet, the shoreline of Union and Dolphin Straits is low and desolate, a land of dismal swamps and depressing plains. There are no easily distinguishable land-marks in the area. We were soon made aware that we were entering the treacherous waters of the Straits as we encountered a heavy, choppy swell almost immediately after leaving Cape Krusenteen. The seas burst on us from the northeast, putting them dead abeam to starboard, where they naturally broke over the gunwale of the canoe and constantly smothered us with heavy spray. Our discomfort increased when we found that we had struck a region of shoals and reefs, which extended far out from shore. For several hours we moved on at dead slow speed under absolutely miserable conditions, and if anything the nature of the sea bed grew worse. In several places our hearts were in our mouths as we worked our way through waters so shallow that jagged reefs clearly showed a few inches beneath the bottom of the canoe. In other spots we kept a tense lookout when passing over waters which churned and boiled like a maelstrom at the foot of a large waterfall, though the seas were jet black and appeared to be very deep. The entire Beaufort Sea channels through the Straits, and the current runs seven or eight knots, very strong indeed. Coming into the Straits we had spotted some swans, and hungry for fresh meat we had managed to shoot one for our dinner. Now in the evening calm we wanted nothing more than to get ashore, make camp, and boil up that bird.

Pushing along the shore, we saw many seal and had decided to kill one when we heard shots and turned to find a boat coming up on us from astern. Its occupant was a Coppermine Eskimo named Ataataksaq, who was camped several miles back. We had passed his camp without noticing it, but he had spotted us and followed us. He was out of tea and short of tobacco—a disaster of the first magnitude for an Eskimo. He was voluble in his thanks when we gave him a pound of tea and a can of tobacco, but wouldn't accept them as a gift and insisted on trading a bunch of dried fish in their place. We accepted the trade gratefully, for we wanted to conserve our store of dried caribou for emergency use. We spoke of mutual friends for several minutes before he turned back home. He tried to persuade us to camp overnight with him, but we wanted to keep going as long as the calm weather and daylight held.

Ataataksaq told us there was an island ahead where we might camp, and we took off at top speed through deeper water, anxious to get our tent pitched before dark. Our speed almost proved our undoing. We were scooting along when the canoe gave a tremendous lurch, heeled over steeply, then—fortunately —came back upright again. It all happened so quickly that we had no time to be frightened. My only reaction was a moment of stunned shock as the canoe tilted, then a sick fluttery feeling in the pit of my stomach when I realized what had happened.

Astern of the canoe an ice-floe bobbed to the surface. It was about seven or eight feet long, three or four feet across, and lay almost totally submerged in the water. It was riding so low that we hadn't seen it, and our canoe struck it dead on, rose up on it, and then dropped back into the water on the other side. Our luck had been fantastic. If we had struck it at an angle, the canoe would have either capsized or had the bottom torn off with the force of the blow. In the icy waters of the Arctic Ocean, we should not have lasted more than a minute.

Erik, who did not realize how close a call we had had, looked at me in some surprise when I let my breath out in a long sigh of thankfulness.

By then it was late afternoon and beginning to get dark, and the island Ataataksaq had told us about was still a long way off. We turned toward shore. Everywhere we ran in we found the sea so shallow that our canoe would ground a half mile offshore. Finally we were reduced to cruising along slowly, using a flashlight to search out a camping site. The best we could locate proved to be swamp, but we didn't have much choice. Trudging inland through the muskeg we tried to calculate how high the tide might rise, knowing that even a couple of feet would inundate everything for hundreds of yards.

When we finally found a pool of water that wasn't too brackish for tea, we pitched tent. Hoping to keep reasonably dry we put down the canvas canoe cover as a sort of ground-sheet, then laid another waterproof sheet on top of that and several caribou skins in layers with our sleeping bags on top. We made ourselves a mug of tea, ate the boiled swan, and hit the sack. When we woke up the next day we were lying in six inches of water. We had to stay there an extra day to dry our-selves and all our gear.

The following day found us battling through ice again, big floes on the move, and only careful steering kept us from ramming more ice cakes. It was slow going, but we did locate the island Ataataksaq had described and made camp. Where we beached the boat there was a great mass of slab basalt lying every which way for some distance. Some of the slabs were as massive as houses and almost as square. We chose the surface of one of those slabs as a tentsite and unloaded our gear. The site proved to be almost perfect. The surface of the slab was about four feet above sea level with one side abutting the sea so that we could unload as easily as at a dock. The canoe could be lifted completely out of the water on a convenient rock ramp which lay only a few feet from the tent. This precaution was necessary because a change of wind would blow all the ice around our campsite and could have made short shrift of any canoe left on the shore.

The next morning we awoke to find a strong northwest wind blowing and the ice solidly packed around the shore. Several wide leads opened up during the morning but closed quickly again as the ice was driven rapidly before the wind. The speed of the icefield in that wind had to be seen to be believed.

There was no point in trying to leave as the canoe wouldn't last an instant amidst that heaving mass of ice. We made ourselves comfortable.

The evening was very clear and cold with a full moon. At ten o'clock the moon was due south of our camp. There are few more beautiful sights in the world than a full moon shining down on a little camp on a small island beset by shimmering ice floes. I stayed outside the tent long after Erik had gone to bed, just enjoying the beauty of the setting.

Progress was slow again the next day as we were forced to pick our way carefully over reefs and shoals and around ice packs. One again in that flat, boggy country we had trouble finding a campsite, and in fact we had a fearful time getting the canoe ashore. We had to unload the canoe from about thirty feet offshore, wading to 'dry' land with our gear, lightening the canoe enough to bring it in. Again we were in swampland, but it was so dark we could go no farther.

Gale force winds were blowing from the north in the morning and the seas were mountainous. I shuddered to think of travelling by canoe in heavy weather like that, so we spent the morning snug and resting in our tent. I should dearly like to have given back to me all the days I have spent windbound at some Arctic camp. This would have been one of the longer days. Our camp turned out to be better than we had expected but still extremely miserable. Our sleeping bags and the upper layer of caribou skins were dry but everything below that was a soggy mess.

Bored sitting around doing nothing, we decided to walk to a low hill about a mile to the west of us and see if we could sight Bernard Harbour from its peak. We knew we must be close to the harbour as there was a rather high island visible from our camp, an island we thought must lie just about parallel to the mouth of Bernard Harbour. We walked across grass-covered beaches to the hill and found that we were looking down on Bernard. If we had only had one more hour of daylight the night before, we could have reached the protection of the harbour and camped at a good campsite with deep water approaches and in a cozy cabin, high and dry. However, such is life in the Arctic and I had long since learned to accept it as it turns out. From the hilltop we could see that a great amount of ice was being pushed in against our shoreline by the heavy wind, so we decided to make a run for Bernard Harbour.

We had hoped to find an Eskimo camp at the Harbour but the settlement was deserted. There were several cabins along the shore which showed no signs of having been occupied for years. There was a solitary cabin on one of the northernmost points of land jutting into the harbour, and towards it we worked our canoe. It was a small affair with one room about ten by twelve feet and a smaller one, which had apparently been used as a fuel shed, attached to the rear. The main room was comfortable with three small beds, a set of tables and an oil stove. There were even cooking pots and cutlery neatly laid out by the last occupant. Utter luxury. There was also a large sign reading *RCMP* above the door. I knew that Bernard had been the site of the Canadian Arctic Expedition from 1913 to 1918, a thriving trading post at the time, later an RCMP station, and then a temporary DEW line camp.

The weather was still exceedingly rough, so we made a cache of our gear on the beach and just carried our sleeping bags and grub box up to the cabin. It was not hard to talk ourselves into camping there. All we needed now was some fresh water, so we took the canoe to look for a small creek. On the way we noticed some crosses on the island on the opposite side of the narrow channel, and went over to have a look. They marked four graves.

Three of the graves were set side by side, while the remaining one lay about twenty feet apart and had a rough wooden cross, which looked as if it had been banged together from the slats of a box and had no name or inscription on it. The other three crosses lay in a row and had been meticulously carved so that the names and inscriptions stood out in relief. I copied down the carving on each cross, for the day would come when the wind and rain and the driven snow would obscure them and make them unreadable. Like the fourth cross, they would bear no witness to these people who had lived in the country before us. It may be that the unmarked cross on the fourth grave was that of an Eskimo, but from the names on the first three I would guess that these were the graves of white people. The inscriptions read:

Samuel McIntyre
Died Jan. 8, 1927
Aged 68 years

Frederick William Bezona
Died Sept. 10, 1927
Aged 44 years

Frederick Talik Bezona
Died Oct. 31, 1927
Aged 2 months

As I stood on the barren, wind-swept slope with the ground drift swirling around my feet I felt an empathy with these people that is hard to describe. Forty years before, they too had been alive and living in Bernard Harbour and had probably been well familiar with the region which seemed strange and unknown to Erik and myself. I wondered about them. Samuel McIntyre, who had been the first to die: he was probably a trader for the Hudson's Bay Company, for the Bay had a post there in 1916, one of the earliest built east of the Mackenzie River along the coast. He had lived his life span and had probably died of old age in a land he knew and loved.

The other two graves had to be the record of a tragedy, the record of a man who had died in the prime of life less than two weeks after the birth of his son and shortly before the baby himself had died. I felt sympathy for the woman who so many years ago must have lost both husband and son within a seven week span and wondered if she were still alive somewhere. If she had died here she would have been buried alongside her husband. Surely her grave would have been marked; it wouldn't be that lonely grave set to one side.

It was unlikely that her husband was a trader. The name Bezona was not Scots, but he may have been a white trapper. The guess was supported by the fact that his son had an Eskimo middle name, Talik, a common name in the area. Presumably his wife was an Eskimo woman who gave her little son an Eskimo name in addition to the whiteman's name he had from his father. It seemed likely that Frederick Bezona was neither policeman nor missionary, for it was not the custom of these people to take native wives.

That night I wrote my daily journal in real comfort, recalling the history I knew of this place. The first whiteman to enter Bernard Harbour was Captain Josephy Bernard of the trading schooner *Teddy Bear*. He first sailed east of the Mackenzie in the summer of 1910 and passed his first winter at the mouth of the Kuugaryuaq (Big River) about twenty miles east of Coppermine. The following year he went back to Alaska and returned east again the year after that, but was caught by the freeze-up in Union and Dolphin Straits and wintered at this harbour in 1912–13.

I had met Captain Bernard in Ottawa the previous spring when a friend asked me to help check the translation and orthography of the Eskimo place names which the captain had recorded in his logbook. She was working on a manuscript of the old book, and we spent hours going over the records of his earlier voyages.

It had been hard to reconcile the kindly, frail old gentleman I met with the man who had spent several years trading and trapping in the Arctic half a century earlier. Captain Bernard was a small man who walked with a limp and was quite deaf, but I had greatly enjoyed our encounter. The harbour had been named after him by members of the southern party of the Canadian Arctic Expedition, who stayed at that harbour several years.

Although Erik and I luxuriated in the comfort of the cabin, we didn't dare spend more than one night in the harbour. Time was running out on us.

Next morning the wind was down, and we decided to try the Straits. The Straits have a bad reputation even in the best of summer weather, and it was too much to hope that we would have even barely decent weather for long. We set out to run between the mainland and a string of islands just out a bit in the harbour where there was a narrow channel. Once again we encountered water so shallow that we were in constant danger of scraping bottom, and when we reached the mouth of the channel, we found big heavy rollers coming. The canoe was plunging up and down, but I thought that we should have no real worries as these sharp, heavy rollers were just bad in this spot because the sea was blowing in—and besides in shallow waters waves were always short, sharp and deep. Confident, I told Erik I didn't think we should have too much trouble once we were clear of the mouth, and decided to head out to deeper water, where I expected long, easy swells.

We plunged and bobbed our way through those heavy rollers, some of them running eight to ten feet. On out to sea we headed, but the farther out, the worse the waves seemed to become. We hit some really huge seas, a combination of the fast current coming through the Straits and a strong wind blowing right across them. We were, in fact, battling two swells, the major swell following the high winds and a not much lesser swell with the current. No sooner would we plunge over one swell than we would find the next coming just off our port bow; we would have to turn to meet that one and then turn hard back.

Now apprehensive, I told Erik that this was no place to be fooling around in a twenty foot canoe; we would head for shore. But it wasn't a matter of simply turning and running for safety, because when a canoe is headed to run down seas it cannot be controlled with a kicker. It tends to surf, and the next thing control is lost and the canoe ends up beam-on to the sea and it broaches or turns over. Anything can happen. We tried to ease off the wind a bit and work our way at an angle to the shore, sidling in towards land. Soon we ran into a lot of ice, big polar pack stuff, thirteen or fourteen feet high, perhaps the remains of a pressure ridge, forcing us to turn and head out to sea again to get around this blockage. I was watching the sea carefully, and Erik suddenly blurted out, 'Reefs!' And when we looked down—we would rise up to the top of a crest where we could see for miles, then plunge down into the trough— right below us we could see reefs inches beneath the boat. That terrified us. Reefs like those could have torn the bottom out of the canoe in seconds. We decided to head farther out, hoping to find deep water. The wind was blowing stronger all the time and white caps were beginning to break now on the top of the seas.

I told Erik it was no good, and we once more started to work our way in. Before we got far I saw a ring of white along the shoreline. I asked Erik to put his binoculars on it. Erik looked carefully for a while, and then said that it was ice grounded along the shore. I thought there would be lots of gaps and holes, and so no problem.

We kept dodging reefs and working our way in closer to look for a gap in the ice wall. In nearer the ice we discovered that it was polar pack ice, presumably driven in by the wind, just hammered up against the shore. The wind and water had made a sheer face of the ice, a wall fifteen feet or so high and slightly undercut by the action of the seas and more ice shipping into it constantly. We still weren't worried. But we kept sliding along and not finding a gap through which to pass. There should have been hundreds of breaks in that ice wall, but if there had been any, the heavy seas and winds must have driven ice into them and sealed them up.

By now we had been out several hours in high seas and conditions were growing steadily worse. The wind was picking up. I really began to get worried, but to steady Erik, and perhaps myself, I said, 'It's all right, you know.'

Theoretically, I knew the canoe could handle those seas all right. We had already learned to trust that little canoe to ride even huge seas. However, every time we rode over a swell, the bow of the canoe would dig in and the sea would come swooshing back right down the length of the canoe. Erik had been in the bow for a while, but I brought him back to the stern to try and keep the bow raised up a bit more.

Things were highly uncomfortable. We had spread a rubber tarpaulin over us to keep the icy spray off, tucking one end under our feet and gripping the other with our teeth. We were both wearing parkas and over that waterproof seamen's sou'westers. But the sea was running whitecaps now and every time it broke over the canoe a mass of frothing white water would deluge us. It was like having a great bucket of ice water constantly dashed in our faces. Each time it happened we would open our eyes and quickly wipe the water away so as to watch for the next swell and turn the canoe to meet it. Then would come the next pail of ice cold water.

Erik finally stuck his head under the tarp. He said his face was clean enough, that he didn't need it washed any more, and he didn't really enjoy looking at those big seas, anyhow. I don't know precisely what the vertical height of the seas would have been, but I would estimate them at ten feet. Scary enough for a veteran, let alone a greenhorn in a canoe.

I had to handle the kicker all the way. Erik had no experience with canoes and in seas like this I couldn't take a chance on him. He kept down under the tarp and bailed until he was pooped. When he couldn't lift another scoop of water over the gunwales, I got busy. Keeping one hand on the kicker, I would bend down and bail and at the same time try to watch the oncoming seas. Naturally I couldn't hold on to that tarp with my teeth and bail at the same time, so I had to let loose. The seas did just what they wanted with me.

Another hour of this passed with both of us fighting exhaustion. Once more we made a run in at the shore, and once again we found ourselves confronted by a continuous, unbroken face of ice. By this time I was profoundly concerned. The seas were becoming higher and stronger and more dangerous. There was no more than two hours before darkness. To make it worse, we were running short of gas. I had never gassed a canoe in my life while underway, let alone in the middle of what seemed like a typhoon. Normally when an outboard has to be gassed the engine is shut off for the operation. There was no way we could stop in the middle of the seas pounding in at us. We should have been out of control and swamped in seconds. And if we got water in the gas, the engine would conk out and we should have had it. I gave Erik the bad news straight.

I had to hand it to him. He just shrugged: 'So?'

It was no use waiting; we had to try it and soon. With a deep breath we pulled the tarp up as tight as we could. I was steering the canoe with one hand and holding the tarp up with the other to try to protect the gas from the salt water spray breaking over us. Erik took the funnel and the felt hats we used for strainers, and standing up in that plunging, rearing little boat, he started pouring the gas from one of the ten gallon kegs. The poor lad was weaving back and forth and trying to kneel so that he wouldn't be popped overboard, and all the time those waves were smashing over us, rocking and pitching like a carny ride. By the grace of God no salt water got in, and we never once lost pressure. That little motor kept chugging merrily away. When we had it filled and the caps back on again, we gave a great sigh of relief. Did we feel pleased with ourselves!

We almost relaxed too soon. Just then a huge wave caught us, breaking the moment we sat down. The canoe slewed halfway around. We ended up on the next swell all skewed around and barely managed to swing into it in time. We took a tremendous smash of water. The bow was half awash and

Erik was bailing so fast he seemed to have at least four arms. He blurted out, 'I just wish I'd been born a squaw duck instead of a human being.' (A squaw duck is a common water duck that bobs up and down in the midst of Arctic seas completely unperturbed.) That tickled me, but for some reason at that moment I chose to remember that a man could last only sixty seconds in water like that we were fighting. It wasn't drowning as much as the terrible shock of the icy water that was so deadly.

There we were, bobbing around like a big cork. Suddenly I announced that I needed to take a leak. Erik proposed to join me. We both laughed. There we were in the middle of no-where, plunging around like mad, in imminent danger of being drowned, half frozen and almost helpless, futilely looking around for a place to go. It wasn't easy. Normally a man just stands up and lets it go over the side, but in those seas there was no way we could stand up. Finally we just knelt down and added to the sea in the bottom of the canoe and then bailed it out.

The light was fading and then it began to snow—we certainly weren't missing anything that day—and that cut visibility even more. We tried again with the binoculars to find a break in the ice wall. Nothing doing, no spit of land, no islands, no gap in the ice.

'Okay,' I said, making a final sweep with the glasses. 'In three quarters of an hour it will be dark and we won't be able to control this canoe then. We are going to have to take desperate measures.'

Erik, bless his heart, a man who had never been in a canoe in his life before and to whom it must have looked as though he would die in one, didn't show a sign of fear. He had turned into a good seaman and a first rate hand on the trip. He just quietly waited for me to tell him what to do.

'First,' I said, 'get out those plastic bags we brought along and stow our gear in them. Wrap the rifles tightly, and tie the bundles carefully to the empty gas kegs.' We had lots of bags and line, and we knew the kegs would float. Erik got started on it. My idea was to head into the ice face and just chuck every-thing overboard. We hoped it would stay afloat and near the ice wall where we could salvage it later. It was a risk, but if we just sat out there until dark we were going to drown anyhow.

As Erik tied the gear to the kegs, I explained my plan. In the bow of the canoe we were carrying a seal grapnel, a three-pronged hook about a foot long, the three gaff-type hooks in the end and about a hundred feet of line attached to it. Once our gear was unloaded, the next step was to ease in as close to the face of ice as possible, backing carefully right up to it, then toss the seal grapnel up over the lip of the ice and try to snag a hummock or something on top. As soon as Erik had the gear ready I had him knot the line on the grapnel at one-foot intervals. If we were able to catch a good snag on the ice wall, then Erik would try to climb up over the ice face. Once on top he could help to pull me up, leaving the canoe and kicker to smash against the ice. Then we would use the grapnel to snag the kegs with our gear lashed to them and pull them up. Thus equipped with what we needed for survival, we would simply give up the trip and walk back to Coppermine, a hundred miles or so.

Erik got everything in readiness, and we began to ease in to shore, when we saw a shadow ahead of us on the ice. Erik saw it first. I took a hard look and my heart jumped. 'I think it's an opening!'

And unbelievably, an oblique passage through the wall showed itself. We worked our way along, and beam sea or not, we were so overjoyed that every time we rode over a sea, we turned and zipped towards the passage a bit and then cheerfully turned round to face into the next swell. But just when it appeared we were going to be able to head in, we found a reef in our path, the seas boiling over it.

There was nothing for it but to turn stern to the seas and run the waves into shore over that reef. I swung the canoe, and we zoomed. We perched on top of a wave like a surf board, with no control at all. The canoe rode high and slid us right down at a steep angle with the curl of the wave. As we headed for the reef I shouted, 'If we hit anything, jump out and hold onto the canoe, one on each side, and we'll walk it in, even if it is smashed. We won't give a damn as long as we can get ashore.'

The canoe shot right over that reef, and we could see it inches beneath the canoe. We slid into a safe harbour behind a gravel bar. The water was calm and full of slushy ice which had been chewed up and spat in over the reef. Only the fact that the opening we had found was angled away from the wind had kept it from being filled up with ice.

We were so cold and tired we could hardly get out of the canoe when it hit land. When we stood up we could feel our legs and backs creaking and we were soaked to the skin from head to foot. We had been sitting or standing in about six inches of icy water for most of the day, and were chilled badly. I have never in my life been so relieved; that was the closest to dying I had ever come in all my years in the North.

We flopped around like soggy scarecrows. The ground was covered with four or five inches of snow, and it was still coming down. Night was falling. We ran up and down the beach to warm up. We must have been a sight trying to do it, but we were so glad to be ashore, we hugged each other. I vowed that I would never leave land again, and never go anywhere in a canoe again.

We stomped up and down until we were warm, then hauled the canoe up, unloaded our gear and pitched the tent. We had a perfect campsite right beside a little fresh water lake, a nice pebbly gravelled beach on a spit of land protected from the wind by the polar pack ice grounded up along the gravel bar.

We stopped there for three or four days waiting for the wind to let up, then we headed west again. On September 27 we were travelling along and spotted a light flashing in the distance. With binoculars we could see it was a DEW line station. We hadn't known there was a station anywhere along there but figured it was a place called Clinton Point. It was towards evening, a beautiful evening, the sea flat and calm. The sun was down, and we ran into a fog bank, but we wanted to get to that DEW line station, so we kept pushing ahead, throttled down so that we wouldn't smash into anything.

We found ourselves drifting along a line of cliffs, the fog blotting out the light of the station. The day died into darkness and the fog wrapped itself around us, thick and clammy. We slowed down and barely made headway, dangerously near the cliff, which we could scarcely see, and with a bit of a swell starting up. I told Erik that we would have to camp at the first bit of beach we could find. I couldn't see where the DEW line station was, and saw the danger of slipping miles past it.

We had been following that cliff over an hour, nosing along without finding anywhere to get ashore; it was just sheer face all the way and no sign of a beach. I had Erik crawl up to the bow with instructions to keep his eyes peeled, and if he saw a reef or a floe, to give me a shout at once.

By this time we were so fogged in that the cliff, only fifteen feet away from us, was no more than a shadowy, indistinct wall. We crept along for what seemed hours until suddenly we heard the sound of surf breaking into something, and I hoped it was a beach rather than a reef or rock outcrop. I handed Erik a paddle so that he could fend us off if necessary and slowed the kicker virtually to drift speed. We couldn't pierce the blackness, so we lit the lantern and Erik held it out in front of him. The light revealed a small beach, about twenty feet deep before the cliff reared up behind it.

Happily we ran ashore and checked to see how high the tide might rise. From beach marks it looked as if the tide was already at maximum, so we unloaded and pitched the tent with just enough room to pull the canoe ashore. We dined on tea and a bit of seal shot earlier in the day. We still had a lot of meat with us in the canoe and quite a bit of seal blood in the bottom, but I was too tired to mess around with it that night.

The next morning we explored our beach. It was about a hundred yards long and twenty feet deep. At the west end the sheer cliff gave way to a steep incline that looked as though it could be climbed. There were all sorts of wolf tracks along the beach but the seal meat in the canoe hadn't been touched. The sun was gallantly trying to break through high in the sky, but the fog held sway at water level. I told Erik that there was no point in moving off yet, as we could easily miss the DEW station entirely.

But he was restless, and said he would take a walk up the incline just to see if he could spot the station from up above where the fog was thinner. He took his rifle, just in case a wolf was hanging around. He said he would be back in a few hours, and I suggested he made it before noon since it looked as if the sun might burn the fog off by then. I should have preferred him not to go at all, because I thought the fog might clear earlier and we could get on our way, but Erik had the jitters, so off he went.

I flopped out in the tent to wait for his return and after some time was awakened by a noise from the canoe, which had been pulled up almost to the tent flap. I thought it was Erik back, and I called out, 'Erik, any sign of the DEW line?'

No answer.

'Okay,' I thought, 'he's browned off because of our dis-agreement about his walk.' So I shouted again, 'Erik, do you hear me?'

No answer.

I cried: 'Erik, what the hell are you up to?' and poked my head out of the tent to see what he was doing. I found myself talking to a polar bear, a giant of a brute, about six feet away, its head down in the canoe, tongue lapping up the seal blood. The bear turned its head and looked at me. I stayed where I was and looked back. Only my head and one shoulder were outside the tent, sticking through the flap. I began reaching down behind me with one arm, feeling around for my rifle. I knew it was close, and I knew it was loaded. The bear watched me, swinging its head slowly from side to side, just as the grizzly at Bathurst had done. Its teeth were as long as my fingers. It gave a little bit of a growl, nothing very fierce, just a warning rumble. It turned towards me, more curious than anything as it seemed to me. I didn't know what it might do, but it didn't look as if it was going to charge or attack, at least not at the moment. It pawed at the ground, and I pawed at the inside of the tent trying to locate my rifle. Finally my hand closed over it, and I eased my shoulder back inside the tent so that I could get both hands on the gun. I levered a cartridge into the chamber, and in the silence between me and the bear the click was the loudest sound in the world.

The bear turned towards me then and reared up. I still wasn't sure what it would do, but it was so close that if it decided to come my way, there would be little time for me to do anything. I swung the rifle up and fired. I shot it right through the heart at point-blank range with a 250/3000, and it flopped over against the canoe with a high-pitched scream like a woman's.

'God,' I thought, 'It'll wreck the canoe,' and I started towards it, but suddenly it jumped right up on its feet and made a beeline into the water. It disappeared, and then popped up again. I was there waiting, and just then I heard Erik shouting from the cliff top. The bear was thrashing around in the water about fifteen feet out, and must have been dying, but I gave it a shot in the head to finish it off. Erik came down that cliff like a mountain goat. This was the first polar bear he had ever seen.

We got a line on the bear and tried to haul it ashore, but it was such a big animal we couldn't muscle it in. I wasn't going to stand in three feet of water and try to skin out a polar bear.

Erik reported that he had seen the DEW line site from the top of the cliff, still ten miles or so ahead of us. It took us a couple of hours to reach the site. We unloaded our gear on the beach and set out to hike up the hill to the station.

No one saw us coming. There we were, burned almost black by the sun and the reflection off the water, dressed entirely in big heavy caribou parkas, pants and mukluks. We must have looked like ghosts out of some Arctic legend. There were four men at that sub-station, and we walked in and shook them rigid.

When they recovered from their surprise they gave us a tremendous time. We didn't even have to put our tent up. They gave us a comfortable room. They stuffed us with fresh milk and ice cream and steaks and they ran off three movies in a row for us.

Much as we were enjoying ourselves, we wanted to keep moving. We were worried about being caught by freeze-up before we reached the Delta, and every day counted. I told Erik we couldn't afford to get hooked on the soft life the DEW liners led.

The DEW liners came down and helped us load up and get away. We made pretty steady time and around October 1, about eighty miles from Paulatuk, we ran across three big bowhead whales, about as big as anything I ever saw alive, around fifty to sixty feet each. For some reason we had a notion that it would be a good idea to shoot one. We thought that if we could kill one of them, perhaps it would float, and we could tow it on to Paulatuk and provide the settlement with dogfood for the entire year. That would make us heroes for certain.

Zipping around in a canoe that looked like a matchbox alongside the whales, we picked out one and slipped in close to its head. We must have shot a box of shells each into the monster and as far as we could see without any effect at all. I was shooting at the same spot I try to hit when shooting the much smaller belugas (white whales), near the blowhole, but it didn't faze these big fellows. We played around with those whales for several hours, but were careful not to get too close; when they dived, they slapped the water with their tails, and one flip too close would have smashed us.

Winter was winning the race. By this time the sea was freezing up along the shores, and the land had turned white with early snow. We were headed almost due south now and close to Paulatuk.

There was a bit of wind next morning but we headed on and before long were in sight of the mission house at Paulatuk. After some difficulty with shallow water on our approach, we made it in and landed at the settlement.

The Eskimos had seen us out in the bay trying to work our way in, so they were all down to meet us. They wanted to know where we were from and when we told them we had started out from Iqaluktuutiaq (Cambridge Bay) this really impressed them.

The Eskimos said we were lucky to get in at all; about ten days earlier the bay had been completely frozen over, then a blow came from the south and washed all the ice out to sea. Then three or four days earlier it had frozen over again, and once more a blow from the south had opened it up. We had just sailed in as easy as punch, not a sign of ice except a bit around the shore.

We had a pleasant visit there. The priest was a fine, friendly man and gave us a mug-up. We stayed on for a while, making ourselves at home. Then, as the south wind continued to blow we decided to pop over to Cape Parry, an easy day's trip. We camped there, but we stayed with the four or five Eskimo families living down by the shore and didn't go up to the DEW line site. We knew that if we went up there they would hold us up with questions and hospitality; and anyhow, there were a couple of really good-looking girls down in the Eskimo settlement, and we knew there were none at the DEW line station. So we spent an enjoyable night with the Eskimos, and then carried on; we had to keep moving.

Cape Parry is a point of land almost dividing one enormous complex bay. Darnley Bay is on the east, about sixty miles wide, and Franklin Bay, about the same size, is to the west. Should a storm come up, the open bay was too dangerous for our small canoe, so we had to creep along the coast. By the time we passed Baillie Island we were finding a lot of ice again. There was fresh, paper-thin ice over much of the sea, extending out several miles, but around Baillie Island there was open water due to the tremendous currents and consequently treacherous seas. Then we headed down the next bay and turned north on the other shore to run up the Tuktoyaktuk Peninsula. The land there is almost desert-like, it is so flat, and the wind comes sweeping over the land and across the shallow sea. We rounded the point of land and turned west again, and even though we were well offshore we found the water was only six or seven feet deep. There were no reefs, just sandy bottom from the silt and sand that is carried down the main channel of the Mackenzie River opening out there into a huge delta. We also found that when we tried to turn in toward shore, the fresh water coming from the river was all frozen over, since fresh water freezes earlier than sea water. We kept testing the edge of the ice; by standing up in the canoe we could actually see the settlement of Tuktoyaktuk, but we couldn't get closer than ten or twelve miles. We could have gone ashore across the bay from Tuktoyaktuk and walked in, but we should have had to cache all our supplies and gear, and we thought it better to head back to Paulatuk, where we could leave all our stuff with friends.

We had started from Cambridge Bay on August 11, and we pulled into Paulatuk on October 25. Altogether we had travelled 1,400 miles, some of this because of our doubling back, of course. It had taken us seventy-five days; we had been wind bound or storm bound several times and delayed when we were caught in the ice. I had spent ten days at that prospecting camp where we started. I had hoped to be able to get into the Mackenzie River system before it froze up so that I could go up river to Yellowknife for the opening of the Territorial Council session, but one of my main objectives had been Paulatuk, the westernmost settlement in my constituency and one I had never seen before, so I was satisfied. The cost to me of that trip was $300, and if I had tried to cover the same ground by plane, from Bathurst Inlet to Cambridge Bay, then to Inuvik and Yellowknife, across to Paulatuk and back, the total cost would have been about $1,500.

We stayed at Paulatuk three or four weeks until freeze-up, and then a Game Branch plane came along and gave us a free lift into Yellowknife just in time for the Council session. And so ended a trip on which death had brushed us very closely, almost closely enough to make us change our names.

24
❄ *Wings*
of the
North

Because there are no roads in the Arctic, we rely heavily on aircraft—and bush pilots. Like most people in the North, the bush pilots are an eccentric bunch, only more so. But they are probably the most competent pilots in the world.

They constantly fly over country which is very difficult to map-read in winter time, even for an experienced man, and the terrain is so bleak and the population so sparse that a single mistake or mishap is apt to be fatal. There is a saying in the North that there are old pilots, and there are bold pilots; but there are no old, bold pilots.

Even the most experienced and competent men can be caught in a sudden blow and forced down or may suffer an engine failure; and the North is full of stories, almost legends, about bush pilots who have miraculously survived days and even weeks in that frozen country after a crash and then made their way back to civilization to fly again. There are as many tales of daring search and rescue missions. Sadly, though, the North must also record the loss of many fine men, and there is a monument in Yellowknife to these heroes of the Arctic.

To mention just one of many, Chuck McAvoy, a top-notch flier, was killed in the Bathurst Inlet region about the time I moved there. No one knows for sure what happened. Chuck was flying for a prospecting outfit, and left on a flight loaded with drums of gas, as well as some dynamite and caps, not an unusual cargo in that part of the world. He had some prospectors with him; the plane and the men simply disappeared.

No one knows for sure whether the plane crashed or blew up in mid-air, or what. No trace of the aircraft or the men aboard it has ever been found.

One of the great pilots in the Arctic is a man named Paul Hagedorn, a German who was a fighter pilot in the Luftwaffe during the war. Somehow he wound up in the Arctic and was flying out of Cambridge Bay when I was at Perry Island.

Paul usually flew a single-engine Otter, a work-horse of a plane. Once I was flying with him, and dozed off in the back of the plane. The next thing I knew, Paul was shaking me and saying, 'Hey, wake up.'

I came out of my dreams slowly, but when I realized it was Paul who was shaking me, I simultaneously realized that no one was flying the plane. I was suddenly very much awake.

Paul calmly said, 'Listen, I'm tired too, and I'm going to have a bit of a snooze, so I guess you'd better go forward and fly this machine.' There was no telling how long it would fly like that by itself, but I dashed forward and grabbed the controls. And Paul went to sleep.

He knew that even though I had never taken off or landed a plane, there would be no problem flying. It was just a matter of keeping on a straight course at the proper elevation and in level flight. I had in fact flown planes in the North many times. It was typical of Paul to be so confident as to walk away from the controls. The son of a gun slept for an hour.

On another occasion, he had to fly a nurse to Spence Bay to look after an injured Eskimo there, and he stopped off at Perry Island and picked me up for company. While the nurse went about her task at Spence Bay, Paul said to me, 'Keep your eyes open. We'll give this nurse a little bit of a surprise on the way home.'

About forty-five minutes out of Spence Bay, we were flying along about a thousand feet above low cloud cover. Paul had the nurse sitting up in the co-pilot's seat with him. I was back in the small cabin in the seat nearest the cockpit. The pretty young nurse was gazing out the window at the dense cloud formation below us, and the old Otter was droning along. Paul turned and gave me a wink. While the nurse looked away, Paul reached forward and made an adjustment to the gas feed. The next thing we knew, the engine had started to sputter. The nurse looked around, her face a question mark, and Paul reached out, fiddled with his dials and knobs, and said, 'Oh, just a little trouble here, nothing much.'

The incident had given our nurse a bit of a start, but after Paul assured her that he had it all under control, she relaxed again. We flew on a few more minutes, and when the nurse looked out of the window again, Paul pulled another gadget which made the plane shudder and shake, and jump all over the sky—it was so realistic I thought for a moment that perhaps something had gone wrong! Our victim's face had gone completely white.

Paul was the only pilot I ever knew in the Arctic to carry a parachute with him; he said that when he was a fighter pilot in the war he had been forced to use one, and it made him feel better to have one around. He was sitting on the parachute, and now he stood up and yanked it out from under him. He told the nurse to sit on it and strap herself in.

Naturally this worried her, because she knew that normally parachutes were not used in this country, but Paul told her it was just a precaution, that he didn't expect any real trouble. He said, reassuringly, 'If the worst comes to the worst, I could dive down through the clouds. Even if the engine cut out completely, these Otters have such big wings, they can glide for miles and miles. I'd have plenty of time to pick a spot of land.'

This settled the nurse a bit, but then Paul added, 'The only problem is that if the engine does cut out suddenly, with all this cloud cover we can't see where we're going, then we'd have to crash land and hope for the best.'

With that cheering message, the nurse became more scared than ever. Paul showed her how to strap herself into the parachute, shoulder harness and all. The engine began to choke badly, coughing and sputtering, and Paul looped the plane over on its side for a moment. That poor nurse was looking more and more upset, and her face was now a ghastly green. She hadn't opened her mouth, only nodded now and then to show she understood Paul's instructions.

Paul pretended to be having more trouble and he told our companion, 'This is worse than I thought. Things are really fouling up. I might have to tell you to jump.' He explained how to pull the rip cord, how many seconds to count before pulling it, but then patted her shoulder and said heartily, 'Don't worry now, the chances of having to jump are one in a hundred.'

We kept going, and he kept fooling with the instruments; the engine would cough and catch, while we flew lower and lower into the clouds. Paul poured on the gas and pulled it back up again and then cut the engine, putting on quite a show for the young lady. In my most concerned voice I would tell her not to worry: 'Paul will get us down—somehow,' but my assurances didn't seem to help much.

Then suddenly the engine just quit. Paul turned to the nurse with a grave expression. 'This is going to be bad. Pryde and I can ride it down and hope for the best in a crash landing, but I think you'll have to bail out. You'll be a lot safer if you jump, so get ready.'

That poor nurse was completely convinced. Utterly terrified by now, she moved quickly, taking us both by surprise. She turned around and grabbed the door handle on the co-pilot's side door, pushing to open it so she could jump.

Paul himself got such a fright that he just leaped across and grabbed her by the arm. It was his face that was now white as a sheet. Had he been a few seconds slower, that girl would have been out of the plane and on her way to earth. Paul earnestly set about explaining to the nurse that he had only been fooling, that he had caused the engine to miss and heave, that he had deliberately been putting on all those manoeuvres. We had a hard time convincing the girl that it was all a joke. She thought we were just trying to calm her down. It was only after we flew another half hour without interruption that she realized it was in fact a prank. She didn't think it funny, and went so far as to swear she would never fly with two such madmen again.

One day some Eskimos came into the Perry Island post with a woman who had been badly injured. I took one look at her and knew she would die unless we could get her medical attention as soon as possible. I got on the radio and made an emergency call to Cambridge Bay. They radioed back that Hagedorn would fly down right away. I called on some of the Eskimos, and we went out to mark a strip for Paul. There was no landing strip at Perry Island, of course, but as is usually done in those Arctic settlements, we simply picked out the smoothest bit of sea ice in front of the post, and set out a series of gas drums in two parallel lines to mark a runway. We expected Paul at any moment.

Unbeknown to us, the weather in Cambridge Bay had prevented him from taking off, and we wondered what had happened to him. Towards nightfall we had a bad white-out at Perry.

A white-out occurs when the colour of the sky, either from cloud or snow, matches the colour of the ground, so there is no contrast, no shadow, no reference point for a pilot. It's a spooky condition and extremely dangerous. The pilot can't see how far off the ground he is and has to rely entirely upon his instruments to tell him whether he is flying right side up or not.

I had almost given up on Hagedorn, and we had been unable to reach Cambridge Bay because of the atmospheric conditions, so I gave the woman some codeine to relieve the pain. All of a sudden a plane zoomed low and flew just over the post. It had to be Paul. He came swinging in to land, but the white-out confused him, and he didn't touch down until he was about three quarters of the way along our makeshift runway and headed straight at Angulaalik's house. He hit the ice very hard and went bouncing and racing along the ice. I was sure he was going to end up in Angulaalik's bedroom, but he made a violent turn to one side at the last moment and shot up the side of a hill, coming to rest at a thirty-five degree angle about half way to the top.

I couldn't help having a laugh at this, and ran out shouting, 'What kind of landing was that?'

He turned towards me, his face white as a ghost, and gave me a tongue-lashing right there and then. Landing in that white-out did not put him in a joking mood. He was so mad at me that it was a good two hours before he would accept a mug of rum.

The next morning we had to hitch up almost every dog in the settlement to pull Paul's plane back down to the runway. We had seventy-five dogs hitched to the plane. It made quite a sight, and did my heart good to see Paul out there swearing and shouting, screaming at the dogs and the Eskimos to get his plane down without wrecking it.

He took the injured woman back with him to Yellowknife where an emergency operation saved her life.

One fall at Perry Island, after the sea had frozen over but while we still had a small patch of open water in the bay, a little girl tripped and smashed her head against a rock. It knocked her unconscious; her eyes turned black, her face puffed up and she was bleeding from the nose and ears. It looked like a skull fracture, and I was in no way equipped to cope with anything like that. I called Cambridge Bay for a plane.

I didn't think it was possible for a pontoon-equipped plane to land in the small patch of open water in front of the post, so suggested that they send a ski-equipped plane. Unfortunately most of the planes in the area were still on pontoons; a ski-equipped craft was not available.

Finally a bush pilot from Yellowknife, Duncan Mathieson, said he would give it a try on pontoons. He came up and circled the open water several times. The girl's condition was critical, and the pilot knew that his performance could make all the difference. He landed without trouble, but after we loaded the child aboard he told me that it would be touch and go whether he could take off or not.

He lined the plane up with the wind and with the longest stretch of water possible and gunned the engines. He revved up and raced across the water, rocking the plane back and forth, trying to get some lift, trying to raise those pontoons. At the last moment he pulled back on the stick and lifted off less than ten feet from the ice. The rear of the pontoons hit the ice edge, and for a moment the plane seemed to hesitate, dipped slightly, then worked its way up, literally climbing the air. That takeoff alone would have put Duncan Mathieson in a class with the best in the North.

Flying conditions are much better in the North now, with more facilities and better planes, but I have never met a bush pilot in the Arctic who wouldn't make every possible attempt to get in when there was a real emergency, no matter what the conditions.

25
❄ Gina

One day in 1967 I flew to Yellowknife from Bathurst Inlet to attend a session of the Northwest Territories Council. I hadn't been settled in my hotel more than thirty minutes when I received a phone call from an old friend, Jim Whelly, who was handling the Canadian Centennial celebrations for the Council. He wasted little time on preliminaries.

'I've got Georgina Blondin here and she'd like to meet you. Why don't you come on over?'

I agreed with alacrity. Georgina Blondin was rated one of the prettiest girls in the North. I had never met her, but knew she had won the territorial beauty contest to be named the Centennial Indian Princess of the Northwest Territories and had been a runner-up in the national contest. Her pictures had appeared in many newspapers and I had studied them avidly. Now we were about to meet—and a fateful meeting it was.

The first thing I did upon being introduced to Miss Blondin was to tell her that Georgina was too long and cumbersome to handle, and that she would be 'Gina' to me.

My first impression of her was that she was very shy. I tried desperately to make conversation, but we didn't seem to make much headway. Then Jim suggested that we go back to the hotel and have a drink. We went to my room and had a couple, and Jim explained that he and Gina had flown in from Fort Simpson where the Centennial barge was tied up. They had both been on a tour, travelling by barge to each of the settlements on the Mackenzie River as part of the Centennial events.

'We're just overnighting here, then we have to get back to work,' he explained. 'We wanted a break from the routine.'

Gina's parents lived in Yellowknife, where her father worked as a gold miner, and she hadn't seen them for some time. Jim and I decided to accompany her there and meet them. We spent several hours with them drinking tea and talking.

We then returned to the hotel, and I really had my eyes on Gina. I suggested that we all have another drink in my room, pointing out that it was still early, only about three in the morning.

Gina said she wanted to go back to her room to freshen up, promising she would be right back. Jim and I enjoyed a drink or two while we waited for her, but that girl didn't show up. I knew then she was a smart one. Jim couldn't remember her room number, and when the desk clerk heard our slurred voices, he suddenly forgot it too.

The next morning Jim and Gina woke me up to say goodbye. That was the first time I met Gina, and it was the last time I saw her for a long while after.

But a year and a half later I was in Yellowknife again for a Council session. I was sitting in a restaurant when in walked Gina. She said she had been attending university in British Columbia, but had come back to Yellowknife before moving with her family to Fort Franklin. Her father had been working in the mine now twelve years or so, and had tired of it. He had decided to take his family back to the bush and start trapping again. Fort Franklin was about four hundred miles down the Mackenzie River from Yellowknife. I knew that if Gina went there, I might never see her a third time. She said they were leaving in a day or two.

'You're not going with them to Fort Franklin,' I told her.

'Who's going to stop me?'

'I am,' I said, and I did.

We got married in June 1969, just before a Council meeting. Stu Hodgson, Commissioner of the Northwest Territories, was of immense help to us in the days before the wedding. He contributed much time and effort to ironing out numerous problems, and even stood in as my father during the ceremony. On the morning of the wedding, he arranged for my best man, Jim Whelly naturally, and myself to be placed under 'house arrest' to ensure that we both arrived at the church in a complete state of sobriety. Some blasphemous souls suggested that Stu's solicitude was due to his desire to see me return to the Council as a stable, married man instead of a rambunctious bachelor.

Friends came from all over the Territories and from several provinces for the wedding. Reverend R. Ferrie and Bishop H. Cook performed the ceremony. When we walked out of the church, we passed under an archway of six ivory narwhal tusks brought from the Arctic coast—a distinctive northern touch. Three hundred and fifty people attended the reception, and a former Minister of Northern Affairs, the Hon. Arthur Laing, toasted the bride.

26
❄ *The Changing Arctic*

The Eskimos of today, young and old alike, are turning more and more to the whiteman's culture. The image of the cheerful little hunter in heavy fur clothing, so long promulgated in print and film, is perhaps no longer valid for most parts of the Arctic. The way of life I met just over a decade ago when I came to the Eskimo country has largely vanished and will never reappear. The people I have known and have attempted to depict lived a way of life that was disappearing even as I was getting to know it.

Already the changes are apparent in numerous small ways, such as Eskimo children at Cambridge Bay eating cornflakes for breakfast and chattering excitedly about the movie they have seen the previous evening, the Eskimo engineer I saw on the Great Slave Railway preparing for bed by putting the cat out and setting his alarm for six o'clock in the morning. The spectacle of an Eskimo setting an alarm clock strikingly points up the cultural revolution that has swept Canada's twelve thousand Eskimos in a single lifetime.

The time concept is the most important concept the Eskimo has been forced to accept, and represents the biggest change in his life style. The Eskimo hunter of old ate when he was hungry, slept when he was sleepy, lived a life attuned to his physical needs rather than to an artificial concept of time. He was concerned with the larger aspects of his environment, with days and seasons, the arrival of sandhill cranes and the departure of caribou, not with hours and minutes. He thought the whiteman a strange being indeed, a man who had to look at a clock to find out when he was hungry, when he was sleepy and should go to bed. It seemed strange that a whiteman would jump up in the morning when the alarm sounded, whether he felt rested or not.

Today that old Eskimo's children live by the clock. Before the school bell rings, they have risen by the clock to have breakfast. When the school bell sounds again at noon it tells them, just as it tells their white peers, that they are hungry and should eat lunch. At night a late radio program reminds them that it is time to be sleepy; far to the south, in Hay River, a young nephew of the old trapper checks his alarm clock to make certain he will be at the railroad yards in time to take the throttle on the next ore train south in the morning. The old Eskimo realizes that his people are living just like the whiteman, whose ways once seemed beyond understanding.

All through the Arctic, change is the only constant. There are still trappers and hunters on the trail, but few—other than the people of Bathurst Inlet—are as dependent on living on the land as were my friends at Baker Lake, Spence Bay, Perry Island and numerous other parts of the Canadian Arctic over the last ten years. Few indeed are the Eskimos who now live in snowhouses as permanent winter dwellings—perhaps no more than the fifty people who still live in the old ways at Bathurst Inlet. Their friends and relatives in the other settlements live in government-financed prefab houses with two and three bedrooms, electricity, oil furnaces and inside toilets. These friends and relatives were born in hunting camps and on the sea ice or by the inland lakes, not one of them with a doctor in attendance; and yet today the children of these people are dressed in stretch pants, the girls perhaps with their hair in curlers, the women shop at the local Hudson's Bay Store, now as modern as any small supermarket in Hamilton or Burnaby, pausing to gossip as they check the frozen food bin for TV dinners—frozen dinners the men, who grew up eating raw frozen food, would complain about if not properly warmed.

The youngest children go to school down the block and the older ones are finishing high school now, the first trickle preparing to go south to university, and there is talk of their own university in the NWT soon.

The change has been unbelievably fast. Eskimo values have changed overnight; shamanism is dying out; wife exchange would be extinct already if it were not for the few isolated places where the practice continues. More and more of the whiteman's values are being tried on with his language. Many of the children and young Eskimos nowadays speak English all the time. In the Mackenzie Delta I have found numerous Eskimos who can't speak a word of Eskimo. I have met Eskimos in Inuvik who, when I addressed them in their own language, stopped me with 'You'll have to speak English. I don't speak that language.'

Yet less than a man's lifespan ago, the Eskimo was a Stone Age man, a nomadic hunter pursuing caribou with crude bow and arrows, taking seals from the sea with a remarkable but primitive harpoon, a people eking out an existence in as cruel an environment as one could find in the world. Only the Eskimo's remarkable ability to adapt to new conditions, new techniques and new tools has enabled him to survive for so long. And he continues to adapt.

Within a decade of the coming of the whiteman, according to the old people who lived through those changes and are still alive, the Eskimos abandoned a style of life that had been their tradition for centuries and adapted to a new life made possible by a better weapon, a new tool which they were quick to recognize and to adopt.

To acquire a rifle and ammunition, the Eskimo had to offer the white trader the only currency in which he showed any interest—fur. So the Eskimo abandoned a life of hunting for a life of trapping, and the difference is greater than might appear on the surface. To trap, a man needed more and more dogs to haul his traps, his furs and his family to the trapping grounds. The average team came to be thirteen animals instead of three. More food was required to fuel the dogs, and so more furs, and the circle spiralled ever upwards. Yet within thirty years the era of the big dogteam has risen and fallen, giving way to the snowmobile, now nearly as ubiquitous in the North as the automobile in the South.

People in the South—and whites in the Arctic—who decry the passing of the old ways and customs in the North forget one vital factor—Eskimos are human beings. They don't want, any more than Joe or Mary in Ottawa or Calgary does, to live in a crummy snowhouse, to be bitterly cold and half frozen and hungry most of the time. If they can make a living in a settlement, by casual employment, by carving, perhaps by running a few traps on the side, not too far out from the settlement, or even by living on welfare, then most Eskimos will accept this chance and even seek it. Most Eskimos vastly prefer to live in a settlement, to live where they have the excitement of community life, where they have daily contact with friends and relatives, where they have movies and a dance hall and a big, well-stocked store. They like gaiety, fun, a busy social life. They are as gregarious, as social as any white group. None wants to return to a life where he must live out on the land, isolated from neighbours and kin, squatting miserably in a snowhouse or shabby shack of driftwood, packing cases and snow, getting into a settlement only two or three times a year. Eskimos are quick to point out that they seldom meet a whiteman who wants this way of life either.

The changes in the brief period that I lived as an Arctic man have amounted to nothing less than the rapid urbanization of the Eskimo. The Bathurst Inlet people are the last to live as a tribe in the old Eskimo way, making their living off the land, existing in snowhouses in winter and tents in summer. Only four frame dwellings for the old people sit alongside the trading post to form the settlement. All other families live scattered throughout the length and breadth of the Inlet. The staple food is still the caribou; the winter economy is still the white fox. But drastic change is in the offing.

In 1970, the Hudson's Bay Company was forced to close down the trading post that served the needs of the people of the region. They did so not on economic grounds alone (the post has not made a profit for many, many years) but because they could find no trader willing to live in total isolation for any length of time. The earlier fur traders accepted isolation as part and parcel of the job; the modern storekeepers do not. And so the post, the last in the Arctic where a whiteman lived entirely alone with the Eskimos, was closed. The repercussions were felt.

More recently, the trading post there has been re-opened by the Territorial government in response to a motion I placed before the Council of the Northwest Territories. It is now operated and serviced by the Eskimo Co-operative from Cambridge Bay. Once a month, the plane flies to Bathurst from Cambridge and the post is re-opened for trade, but the lack of a resident trader within the region makes it, sadly, almost inevitable that the people will sooner or later totally abandon their ancient hunting territory and move to a welfare existence at Cambridge Bay.

There are many dedicated men in the Arctic today who feel as I do that the ancient values of Eskimo culture must not be sacrificed, men who are not sure of the way but who do not want to see their generation charged with destroying the Eskimo, as earlier generations have been blamed for the degradation of the Indian. People in government, missionaries, teachers and business leaders are demanding that the Eskimo be given fair opportunity for employment and for leadership in the North.

Whites and Eskimos alike have put tremendous, and I hope justified, faith in the power of education to accomplish this. When the whiteman arrived in the Arctic to stay, even the older and most traditional Eskimos realized that their children must get a new kind of education, a whiteman's education to make their way in the changing world. Prior to 1955 the only formal education available to Eskimo children was from a handful of tiny mission schools, where they primarily learned to read and write and speak a few words of English, and the emphasis was on whatever brand of Christianity was professed at the mission. In 1955 the Canadian government belatedly accepted its responsibility for the education of the Eskimos. The government program was built around a few centrally located schools and residences or dormitories in the Arctic, or sub-Arctic, transporting children from settlements all over the North to live there in complete isolation from their own culture ten months of each year.

Bathurst Inlet provides a convenient microcosm of what happened. All school-age children, from six to sixteen, were and still are airlifted nearly a thousand miles to a residential school at Fort Simpson because the program didn't require a residential school nearer Bathurst. The old people, barely understanding what was happening but concerned that their children should receive the best education available, swallowed their tears and kept their grief to themselves, and urged the children to go, then returned to their snowhouses and openly cried, men and women, fathers and mothers. Losing their children was like a death to them, but they were concerned with the same things that concern parents anywhere—what would become of the children? How would they turn out? Would they grow up to become good people or bums?

Those children were away from home for ten months in the year, during which time wonderful but frightening things happened to them. They lived in warm, comfortable residences with lots of room and even cupboards and furniture of their own. They became accustomed to three solid meals a day, and they soon learned to prefer the whiteman's food. They had grown accustomed to sleeping on soft beds between clean sheets. They learned to like that way of life.

Then during summer recess they were flown home to spend two months with their parents. When they came back to Bathurst Inlet they spoke English, not Eskimo. Now there was little or nothing about the way of life of their parents that the children liked.

The old people at home, many of whom spoke no English, felt at a loss. They couldn't communicate with their own beloved children, who had become strangers. There was now a real generation gap to worry about, much more difficult to solve than the normal age difference between parents and children, because it included a language barrier. It involved a completely foreign way of life, conflicting with every facet of the old way. The children no longer knew how to hunt or trap, but that could easily have been mended. The real problem was that they saw no point in learning, had no interest in the way their parents lived.

Well-meaning, professional educationalists working for the government had a field day, but they never got around to assessing the damage such a system was causing in completely disorienting Eskimo youth from all its cultural background.

Federal educational policy was needlessly disrupting the entire Eskimo society. Those of us on Council who saw the federal policy develop appreciated that it was both economical and efficient from an administrative point of view to establish only a few educational centres, but we were not happy with a school system that seemed designed for the sake of its administrators and teachers rather than for its pupils and their parents. We daily observed the frightening consequences of this policy and fought to change it. I feel that the changes we were able to effect in federal educational programming number among the most important tasks the Territorial Council has accomplished to date.

I remember one council session in Ottawa, when it appeared that we were going to be overridden once more by the 'experts'. I stood up and in my opening speech announced that unless the government policy of taking children away from their homes for ten months of the year was changed, I intended to return to the western Arctic and personally go to every settlement in my constituency and speak to every parent and advise them to hold their children at home, in short to strike against the school system. I said, 'If the government wants a fight on this issue, we'll take them on.'

Before the end of the week, the federal government announced they were changing their policy and would build schools in every Arctic settlement where the school age population exceeded twenty-five. Because of that fight by the Territorial Council, which I had the honour to help lead, many settlements got their first schools, and the system of hauling little kids hundreds of miles from home, enforcing a ten-months' separation from their home environment, was dropped. Being able to go to school in their own villages, Eskimo children were able to avoid the culture shock, were able to partake of the whiteman's world without losing their own.

It is a strange paradox that the formal school education of the Eskimo children is directly responsible for the massive unemployment of the native people in the Arctic today. Prior to the introduction of the whiteman's system of education, the Eskimo child received a less formal but no less rigorous education administered by the parents, mastering the hunting and trapping skills until he was able to take his place as a fully-fledged contributing member of his family and his community. Now that the young people have lost many of these ancient techniques and have learned instead the ways of the whiteman, they exist in a vacuum between the two ways of life. On graduation from school most of them are unwilling to return to life on the land and unable to find permanent employment in the whiteman's labour force. Less than ten percent of the young graduates find permanent employment. Therein lies the tragedy and the failure of the school system and the major problem facing the government in the Arctic today.

I find it only natural that as the years go by these young

people are looking very critically at their new society. It isn't surprising that they resent the fact that they find whitemen holding down the good jobs in the North. Whites, usually southern whites, but often northern whites, in some cases the very people with whom they went to school, are becoming the managers of the local stores, running the local radio stations, getting the best civil service jobs in town. Unless the territorial government—and the federal government—moves carefully to provide meaningful employment opportunities for Eskimos on a par with those available to whites in the Arctic, the Eskimos are going to walk down the path taken by the Indians in many parts of Canada, defeated, resentful, sullen, and eventually, almost certainly, rebellious. And who can say without justification?

Many Eskimos, of course, have come to realize that there are more employment opportunities in the South, and some have gone south to take jobs there and live like a whiteman. But the vast majority of Eskimos want to stay in the Arctic. It is, after all, their home.

Significant changes are taking place on the land, too, changes which will affect the future of the people of the North. Hundreds of millions of dollars are being spent in a gigantic search for oil and gas and minerals in the Arctic, with oil rigs drilling within 700 miles of the North Pole itself. Little of this enormous wealth is rubbing off on the local people, the Eskimos especially. It is the fear of many veteran Arctic men, white or otherwise, that the development which seems so imminent may be purely one of extractive resources exploitation and never really benefit the people to whom the lands and riches belong. Eskimos in the Arctic have never given up rights to their lands and the resources of their lands, but these aboriginal claims and rights have been disavowed by the federal government and are largely ignored in the interests of southern pressure groups with much stronger claims on the political machinery of the country.

The natives are learning, and political organizations are being formed to protect their rights. Future control of the North may lie with the ability of such groups to obtain a fair hearing before the highest courts of the land, hopefully disassociated for once from the political and executive branches of government.

If future opening of the North and development of the

Arctic could include processing industries, manufacturing and distributing arms of industry, then the natives and true northerners might be able to find employment for which they have been educated and the opportunity to which they are entitled in their own backyard.

Other changes will affect the future value of the North to the whole of Canada. Ecology has become a byword of modern civilization, and not a moment too soon. So far comparatively little damage has been done to the land in the North by those who would extract its wealth and leave their refuse behind as they have in the rest of Canada, and much of the world. Pollution exists in the North, but on a negligible scale in comparison to what has happened elsewhere on the continent. The North can but benefit by public awareness.

Today there are no real fur trading posts in the Arctic. True, the Hudson's Bay Company still does conduct a fur business with the Eskimos, but it is a rather minor part of the concern of its northern division now. The Hudson's Bay posts in the North today are small supermarkets, not fur posts, and the men who run these modern stores are merchandisers and clerks, not fur traders. The stores are even heated.

There will never again be a job such as the one which enticed me as a dreamy-eyed young man all the way from Scotland with romantic notions in my otherwise empty head. There will never be another fur trader in the old tradition, just as there will never again be an Eskimo in the old image.

But I cannot quarrel with this. I found the dream I sought. I found the romance I travelled thousands of miles for, and I have come through those times and like the Eskimos, my friends, I must look forward to new days, new opportunities, and like them. new responsibilities in Canada's Arctic.

Previously published by

ELAND BOOKS

MEMOIRS OF A
BENGAL CIVILIAN

JOHN BEAMES
The lively narrative of a Victorian district-officer

With an introduction by Philip Mason

They are as entertaining as Hickey . . . accounts like
these illuminate the dark corners of history.
Times Literary Supplement

John Beames writes a spendidly virile English and
he is incapable of being dull; also he never hesitates
to speak his mind. It is extraordinary that these
memoirs should have remained so long unpublished
. . . the discovery is a real find.
John Morris, The Listener

A gem of the first water. Beames, in addition to being
a first-class descriptive writer in the plain Defoesque
manner, was that thing most necessary of all in an
autobiographer – an original. His book is of the
highest value.
The Times

This edition is not for sale in the USA

*If you wish to receive details of forthcoming publications,
please send your address to
Eland Books, 53 Eland Road, London SW11 5JX*

Previously published by

ELAND BOOKS

A VISIT TO DON OTAVIO

SYBILLE BEDFORD
A Mexican Journey

I am convinced that, once this wonderful book becomes better known, it will seem incredible that it could ever have gone out of print.
Bruce Chatwin, Vogue

This book can be recommended as vastly enjoyable. Here is a book radiant with comedy and colour.
Raymond Mortimer, Sunday Times

Perceptive, lively, aware of the significance of trifles, and a fine writer. Applied to a beautiful, various, and still inscrutable country, these talents yield a singularly delightful result.
The Times

This book has that ageless quality which is what most people mean when they describe a book as classical. From the moment that the train leaves New York...it is certain that this journey will be rewarding. When one finally leaves Mrs Bedford on the point of departure, it is with the double regret of leaving Mexico and her company, and one cannot say more than that.
Elizabeth Jane Howard

Malicious, friendly, entertaining and witty.
Evening Standard

If you wish to receive details of forthcoming publications, please send your address to Eland Books, 53 Eland Road, London SW11 5JX

VIVA MEXICO!
CHARLES MACOMB FLANDRAU
A traveller's account of life in Mexico

With a new preface by Nicholas Shakespeare

His lightness of touch is deceiving, for one reads *Viva Mexico!* under the impression that one is only being amused, but comes to realise in the end that Mr Flandrau has presented a truer, more graphic and comprehensive picture of the Mexican character than could be obtained from a shelful of more serious and scientific tomes.
New York Times

The best book I have come upon which attempts the alluring but difficult task of introducing the tricks and manners of one country to the people of another.
Alexander Woollcott

Probably the best travel book I have ever read.
Miles Kington Times

His impressions are deep, sympathetic and judicious. In addition, he is a marvellous writer, with something of Mark Twain's high spirits and Henry James's suavity...as witty as he is observant.
Geoffrey Smith, Country Life

*If you wish to receive details of forthcoming publications,
please send your address to
Eland Books, 53 Eland Road, London SW11 5JX*

Previously published by

ELAND BOOKS

THE
WEATHER
IN
AFRICA

MARTHA GELLHORN

This is a stunningly good book.
Victoria Glendinning, New York Times

She's a marvellous story-teller, and I think anyone
who picks up this book is certainly not going to put
it down again. One just wants to go on reading.
Francis King, Kaleidoscope, BBC Radio 4

An authentic sense of the divorce between Africa
and what Europeans carry in their heads is
powerfully conveyed by a prose that selects its
details with care, yet remains cool in their
expression.
Robert Nye, The Guardian

This is a pungent and witty book.
Jeremy Brooks, Sunday Times

This edition is not for sale in the USA

If you wish to receive details of forthcoming publications,
please send your address to
Eland Books, 53 Eland Road, London SW11 5JX

Previously published by

ELAND BOOKS

TRAVELS WITH MYSELF AND ANOTHER

MARTHA GELLHORN

Must surely be ranked as one of the funniest travel books of our time — second only to *A Short Walk in the Hindu Kush* . . . It doesn't matter whether this author is experiencing marrow-freezing misadventures in war-ravaged China, or driving a Landrover through East African game-parks, or conversing with hippies in Israel, or spending a week in a Moscow Intourist Hotel. Martha Gellhorn's reactions are what count and one enjoys equally her blistering scorn of humbug, her hilarious eccentricities, her unsentimental compassion.
Dervla Murphy, Irish Times

Spun with a fine blend of irony and epigram. She is incapable of writing a dull sentence.
The Times

Miss Gellhorn has a novelist's eye, a flair for black comedy and a short fuse...there is not a boring word in her humane and often funny book.
The New York Times

Among the funniest and best written books I have ever read.
Byron Rogers, Evening Standard

If you wish to receive details of forthcoming publications,
please send your address to
Eland Books, 53 Eland Road, London SW11 5JX

Previously published by

ELAND BOOKS

MOROCCO
THAT WAS

WALTER HARRIS

With a new preface by Patrick Thursfield

Both moving and hilariously satirical.
Gavin Maxwell, Lords of the Atlas

Many interesting sidelights on the customs and characters of the Moors...intimate knowledge of the courts, its language and customs...thorough understanding of the Moorish character.
New York Times

No Englishman knows Morocco better than Mr W. B. Harris and his new book...is most entertaining.
Spectator (1921)

The author's great love of Morocco and of the Moors is only matched by his infectious zest for life... thanks to his observant eye and a gift for felicitously turned phrases, the books of Walter Harris can claim to rank as literature.
Rom Landau, Moroccan Journal (1957)

His pages bring back the vanished days of the unfettered Sultanate in all their dark splendour; a mingling of magnificence with squalor, culture with barbarism, refined cruelty with naive humour that reads like a dream of the Arabian Nights.
The Times

*If you wish to receive details of forthcoming publications,
please send your address to
Eland Books, 53 Eland Road, London SW11 5JX*

Previously published by

ELAND BOOKS

FAR AWAY
AND LONG AGO

W. H. HUDSON
A Childhood in Argentina

With a new preface by Nicholas Shakespeare

One cannot tell how this fellow gets his effects; he writes as the grass grows.
It is as if some very fine and gentle spirit were whispering to him the sentences he puts down on the paper. A privileged being
Joseph Conrad

Hudson's work is a vision of natural beauty and of human life as it might be, quickened and sweetened by the sun and the wind and the rain, and by fellowship with all other forms of life...a very great writer... the most valuable our age has possessed.
John Galsworthy

And there was no one – no writer – who did not acknowledge without question that this composed giant was the greatest living writer of English.
Far Away and Long Ago is the most self-revelatory of all his books.
Ford Madox Ford

Completely riveting and should be read by everyone.
Auberon Waugh

*If you wish to receive details of forthcoming publications,
please send your address to
Eland Books, 53 Eland Road, London SW11 5JX*

THREE CAME HOME

AGNES KEITH
A woman's ordeal in a Japanese prison camp

Three Came Home should rank with the great imprisonment stories of all times.
New York Herald Tribune

No one who reads her unforgettable narrative of the years she passed in Borneo during the war years can fail to share her emotions with something very like the intensity of a personal experience.
Times Literary Supplement

This book sets a standard which will be difficult to surpass.
The Listener

If you wish to receive details of forthcoming publications,
please send your address to
Eland Books, 53 Eland Road, London SW11 5JX

A DRAGON APPARENT
NORMAN LEWIS
Travels in Cambodia, Laos and Vietnam

A book which should take its place in the permanent
literature of the Far East.
Economist

One of the most absorbing travel books I have read
for a very long time...the great charm of the work is
its literary vividness. Nothing he describes is dull.
Peter Quennell, Daily Mail

One of the best post-war travel books and, in retro-
spect, the most heartrending.
The Observer

Apart from the *Quiet American,* which is of course a
novel, the best book on Vietnam remains *A Dragon
Apparent.*
Richard West, Spectator (1978)

One of the most elegant, witty, immensely readable,
touching and tragic books I've ever read.
Edward Blishen, Radio 4

If you wish to receive details of forthcoming publications,
please send your address to
Eland Books, 53 Eland Road, London SW11 5JX

Previously published by

ELAND BOOKS

GOLDEN EARTH

NORMAN LEWIS

Travels in Burma

Mr Lewis can make even a lorry interesting.
Cyril Connolly, Sunday Times

Very funny . . . a really delightful book.
Maurice Collis, Observer

Norman Lewis remains the best travel writer alive.
Auberon Waugh, Business Traveller

The reader may find enormous pleasure here without knowing the country.
Honor Tracy, New Statesman

The brilliance of the Burmese scene is paralleled by the brilliance of the prose.
Guy Ramsey, Daily Telegraph

If you wish to receive details of forthcoming publications, please send your address to
Eland Books, 53 Eland Road, London SW11 5JX

Previously published by

ELAND BOOKS

THE CHANGING SKY

NORMAN LEWIS

Travels of a Novelist

He really goes in deep like a sharp polished knife. I have never travelled in my armchair so fast, variously and well.
V.S. Pritchett, New Statesman

He has compressed into these always entertaining and sophisticated sketches material that a duller man would have hoarded for half a dozen books.
The Times

A delightful, instructive, serious and funny book. Norman Lewis has the oblique poetry of a Firbank, the eye of a lynx.
Anthony Carson, The Observer

If you wish to receive details of forthcoming publications, please send your address to Eland Books, 53 Eland Road, London SW11 5JX

Previously published by

ELAND BOOKS

JOURNEYS OF A GERMAN IN ENGLAND

CARL PHILIP MORITZ

A walking-tour of England in 1782

With a new preface by Reginald Nettel

The extraordinary thing about the book is that the writing is so fresh that you are startled when a stage-coach appears. A young man is addressing himself to you across two centuries. And there is a lovely comedy underlying it.
Byron Rogers, Evening Standard

This account of his travels has a clarity and freshness quite unsurpassed by any contemporary descriptions.
Iain Hamilton, Illustrated London News

A most amusing book...a variety of small scenes which might come out of Hogarth...Moritz in London, dodging the rotten oranges flung about the pit of the Haymarket Theatre, Moritz in the pleasure gardens of Vauxhall and Ranelagh, Moritz in Parliament or roving the London streets is an excellent companion. We note, with sorrow, that nearly two centuries ago, British coffee was already appalling.
Alan Pryce-Jones, New York Herald Tribune

If you wish to receive details of forthcoming publications,
please send your address to
Eland Books, 53 Eland Road, London SW11 5JX

TRAVELS INTO THE INTERIOR OF AFRICA

MUNGO PARK

With a new preface by Jeremy Swift

Famous triumphs of exploration have rarely engendered outstanding books. *Travels into the Interior of Africa*, which has remained a classic since its first publication in 1799, is a remarkable exception.

It was a wonder that he survived so long, and a still greater one that his diaries could have been preserved . . . what amazing reading they make today!
Roy Kerridge, Tatler

The enthusiasm and understanding which informs Park's writing is irresistible.
Frances Dickenson, Time Out

One of the greatest and most respected explorers the world has known, a man of infinite courage and lofty principles, and one who dearly loved the black African.
E. W. Bovill, the Niger Explored

Told with a charm and naivety in themselves sufficient to captivate the most fastidious reader...modesty and truthfulness peep from every sentence...for actual hardships undergone, for dangers faced, and difficulties overcome, together with an exhibition of virtues which make a man great in the rude battle of life, Mungo Park stands without a rival.
Joseph Thomson, author of Through Masailand

If you wish to receive details of forthcoming publications, please send your address to Eland Books, 53 Eland Road, London SW11 5JX

Previously published by
ELAND BOOKS

A CURE FOR SERPENTS

THE DUKE OF PIRAJNO

An Italian doctor in North Africa

The Duke of Pirajno arrived in North Africa in 1924.
For the next eighteen years, his experiences as a doctor in
Libya, Eritrea, Ethiopia, and Somaliland provided him with
opportunities and insights rarely given to a European.
He brings us stories of noble chieftains and celebrated
prostitutes, of Berber princes and Tuareg entertainers, of giant
elephants and a lioness who fell in love with the author.

He tells us story after story with all the charm and resource of
Scheherazade herself.
Harold Nicolson, Observer

A delightful personality, warm, observant, cynical and
astringent... Doctors who are good raconteurs make wonderful
reading.
Cyril Connolly, Sunday Times

A very good book indeed... He writes a rapid darting natural
prose, like the jaunty scutter of a lizard on a rock.
Maurice Richardson, New Statesman

Pirajno's book is a cure for a great deal more than serpents.
The Guardian

In the class of book one wants to keep on a special shelf.
Doris Lessing, Good Book Guide

*If you wish to receive details of forthcoming publications,
please send your address to
Eland Books, 53 Eland Road, London SW11 5JX*

Previously published by
ELAND BOOKS

THE LAW

A novel by
ROGER VAILLAND
With a new preface by Jonathan Keates

The Law is a cruel game that was played in the taverns of
Southern Italy. It reflects the game of life in which the whole
population of Manacore is engaged. Everyone from the feudal
landowner, Don Cesare, to the landless day-labourers are
participants in the never-ending contest.

Every paragraph and every section of this novel has been
carefully cast and seems to be locked into position, creating a
structure which is solid and formal, yet always lively...while
we are reading the novel its world has an absolute validity ...
The Law is an experience I will not easily forget.
V.S. Naipaul, New Statesman

The Law deserves every reading it will have. It is and does all
that a novel should – amuses, absorbs, excites and illuminates
not only its chosen patch of ground but much more of life
and character as well.
New York Times

One feels one knows everyone in the district...every page has
the texture of living flesh.
New York Herald Tribune

A full rich book teeming with ambition, effort and desire as
well as with ideas.
Times Literary Supplement

*If you wish to receive details of forthcoming publications,
please send your address to
Eland Books, 53 Eland Road, London SW11 5JX*